Barcelona

0   500 m

0   500 yds

D0486227

※ INSIGHT GUIDE
Barcelona

Editors
Dorothy Stannard *and* **Pam Barrett**
Art Director
Klaus Geisler
Picture Editor
Hilary Genin
Production
Kenneth Chan
Cartography Editor
Zoë Goodwin
Editorial Director
Brian Bell

Distribution

UK & Ireland
GeoCenter International Ltd
The Viables Centre, Harrow Way
Basingstoke, Hants RG22 4BJ
Fax: (44) 1256-817988

United States
Langenscheidt Publishers, Inc.
36–36 33rd Street 4th Floor
Long Island City, New York 11106
Fax: (1) 718 784-0640

Canada
Thomas Allen & Son Ltd
390 Steelcase Road East
Markham, Ontario L3R 1G2
Fax: (1) 905 475 6747

Australia
Universal Publishers
1 Waterloo Road
Macquarie Park, NSW 2113
Fax: (61) 2 9888 9074

New Zealand
Hema Maps New Zealand Ltd (HNZ)
Unit D, 24 Ra ORA Drive
East Tamaki, Auckland
Fax: (64) 9 273 6479

Worldwide
Apa Publications GmbH & Co.
Verlag KG (Singapore branch)
38 Joo Koon Road, Singapore 628990
Tel: (65) 6865-1600. Fax: (65) 6861-6438

Printing

Insight Print Services (Pte) Ltd
38 Joo Koon Road, Singapore 628990
Tel: (65) 6865-1600. Fax: (65) 6861-6438

©2005 Apa Publications GmbH & Co.
Verlag KG (Singapore branch)
All Rights Reserved

First Edition 1990
Fourth Edition 2005
Reprinted 2005

ABOUT THIS BOOK

This guidebook combines the interests and enthusiasms of two of the world's best-known information providers: Insight Guides, whose titles have set the standard for visual travel guides since 1970, and Discovery Channel, the world's premier source of nonfiction television programming.

The editors of Insight Guides provide both practical advice and general understanding about a destination. Discovery Channel and its website, www.discovery.com, help millions of viewers explore their world from the comfort of their own home.

How to use this book

The book is carefully structured both to convey an understanding of Barcelona and its culture and to guide readers through its attractions.

♦ The Best of Barcelona at the front of the guide helps you to prioritise what you want to see. Top family attractions, the best buildings, museums, views and buys are listed, along with money-saving tips.

♦ To understand Barcelona today, you need to know something of its past. The city's history and culture are covered in lively, authoritative essays written by specialists.

♦ The Places section provides a full run-down of all the attractions worth seeing. The main places of interest are coordinated by number with full-colour maps.

♦ A list of recommended restaurants and cafés is printed at the end of each chapter. The best of these are also described and plotted on the pull-out restaurants map that accompanies the guide.

Chief among the contributors is **Judy Thomson**, who, drawing on earlier material from **Marcelo Aparicio**, **Xavier Martí** and **George Semler**, revised and updated the Places section. A writer and translator who has lived and worked in Barcelona for many years, Thomson also wrote the Insight picture story on Festivals, the chapters on Catalan food and wine and the feature Designer City.

Contributors to the history and features section include the eminent historian **Dr Felipe Fernández-Armesto**, who has written his own book on the city: *Barcelona: A Thousand Years of the City's Past.*

The Barcelonans is by **Valerie Collins**, a Barcelona-based writer who also contributed the Language feature, building on foundations laid by the Catalan novelist Carme Riera.

Ann Michie, another Barcelona resident, wrote Art and Inspiration. Architect **Jane Opher**, who has an insider's knowledge of recent developments in the city, wrote the chapter on Architecture.

Roger Williams, a London-based writer and editor, contributed the picture stories on *modernisme* and the Sagrada Família and also advised on the restructuring of the guide.

Most of the pictures were taken by **Gregory Wrona**, who paid a special visit to the city for this edition. Other images are the work of **Annabel Elston** and **Bill Wassman**.

Neil Titman proofread the guide, and **Elizabeth Cook** compiled the index.

CONTACTING THE EDITORS

We would appreciate it if readers would alert us to errors or outdated information by writing to:

Insight Guides, P.O. Box 7910, London SE1 1WE, England.
Fax: (44) 20 7403-0290.
insight@apaguide.co.uk

www.insightguides.com

◆ The Travel Tips section provides all the information you will need for your stay, divided into five key sections: transport, accommodation, activities (such as nightlife, shopping and sport), an A–Z of practical information, and a language guide. For quick and easy reference there is an index on the back cover flap.

◆ A detailed street atlas is included at the back of the book, complete with a full index.

The contributors

This new edition of *Insight Guide: Barcelona*, based on an earlier version by **Andrew Eames**, has been reshaped by Barcelona-expert **Pam Barrett** and Insight editor **Dorothy Stannard**, with the invaluable help of a number of writers living in Barcelona.

Maps

Map Legend **237**

Travel Tips

THE BEST OF BARCELONA

Setting priorities, saving money, unique attractions...
here, at a glance, are our recommendations, plus some
tips and tricks even Barcelonans won't always know

BARCELONA FOR FAMILIES

The following attractions are popular with children,
though not all will suit every age group.

Barcelona is child-friendly in true Latin tradition: locals, shops and restaurants welcome children, street performers abound and the many traffic-free areas in the Old Town are good for bikes and skateboards.

●**Aquàrium** One of the largest aquariums in Europe. *See page 133.*
●**Beaches** Of the 4 km (2½ miles) of beach within walking distance of the centre, Barceloneta and Nova Icària are sheltered by the Port Olímpic and have climbing frames. *See page 136.*
●**Ciutadella** Park with rowing boats, ducks, picnic areas, play areas and a great zoo. *See page 114.*

●**Club Natació Atlètic Barceloneta** Swimming club with an outdoor pool shallow enough for children. Plaça del Mar, 1. Eixample beach. *See page 135.*
●**Jardins de la Torre de les Aigües** is unique: a small outdoor pool (Jun–early Sept) set in an Eixample block. Best for the very young. Roger de Llúria, 56.
●**Concerts and theatre** The Auditori concert hall, the CaixaForum, Teatre Poliorama, Fundació Miró and even the Liceu opera house have regular family programmes.
●**Granja Viader** A magnificent milk bar. Good for thick hot chocolate and the nutty drink *orxata*. Xuclà, 4.
●**Tibidabo** A 100-year-old funfair overlooking the city. *See page 182.*
●**Papabubble** Creative home-made sweets in exciting flavours and colours. Ample, 28.

BEST MUSEUMS

●**CCCB** Technically a cultural centre, this wonderful space stages intriguing exhibitions as well as diverse festivals – film, music and performance. *See page 123*
●**CosmoCaixa** The born-again science museum has plenty of hands-on interest for all ages, including a visit to the heart of the Amazon. *See page 181.*
●**Fundació Miró** Flooded with Mediterranean light, this purpose-built museum has one of the largest collections of Joan Miró's work. *See page 152.*
●**MNAC** After more than a decade of refurbishments the Museu Nacional d'Art de Catalunya has reopened to include a millennium of Catalan art. *See page 147.*
●**Picasso** Comprehensive display of Picasso's startling early work and some later pieces in five medieval palaces. *See page 110.*

ABOVE: one way to get around at Tibidabo
LEFT: pet shop boy on La Rambla. **BELOW:** the Flooded Forest, a recreation of the Amazon rainforest at CosmoCaixa, the science museum.

BEST BUILDINGS

●**CaixaForum** An award-winning *modernista* textile factory that is now a cultural centre. *See page 146.*

●**Casa Quadras** This Puig i Cadafalch house is open to the public as the Casa Asia. *See page 165.*

●**La Paloma** This "Palace of Dance", dating from 1903, drips with gorgeous red velvet, gilt and chandeliers. Tigre, 27. *See page 216.*

●**La Pedrera** If you see no other Gaudí building don't miss this

1910 apartment block. It gives an insight into the brilliance of the city's most famous architect. *See page 164.*

●**Mirador del Rei Martí** A 16th-century skyscraper in the Plaça del Rei. *See page 101.*

●**Pavelló Mies van der Rohe** Less is more in this seminal building of the Modern Movement, designed as the German Pavilion for the 1929 Exposition. *See page 145.*

●**Torre de les Aigües** This water tower, symbolic of Catalonia's industrial past, has survived the developers' bulldozers in Poble Nou. Ferrers 2. *See page 137.*

●**Santa Maria del Mar** This Catalan-Gothic church will make your spirit soar. *See page 112.*

ABOVE: view from the Torre Collserola. **LEFT:** on top of La Pedrera. **BELOW:** Plaça del Rei.

TOP SQUARES

●**Plaça del Rei** The essence of medieval Barcelona. Best early in the morning or on summer nights when it is sometimes a concert venue. *See page 101.*

●**Plaça Reial** Daytime bustle, petty crime and night-time partying don't detract from the handsome 19th-century square. *See page 85.*

●**Plaça Sant Felip Neri** The very heart of the Gothic Quarter. To

feel its peace wait for the children in the adjacent school to return to class. *See page 97.*

●**Plaça del Sol** One of several fine squares in the district of Gràcia, it is a meeting place for young and old. *See page 183.*

●**Plaça Vicenç Martorell** Just off La Rambla in El Raval and popular for its terrace cafés and playground. *See page 121.*

BEST VIEWS

●**Bus Turístic** Worth every centime to see the city from the open top deck of the Tourist Bus. *See page 204.*

●**Torre de Collserola** The lookout platform on the 10th floor of this communications tower gives you a 360º view of Catalonia, including, on a good day, the Pyrenees. *See page 180.*

●**Transbordador Aeri** Get the city into perspective by gliding over the port in the cable car from

Montjuïc, the Torre de Jaume I or the Torre Sant Sebastià. *See page 131.*

●**Waterfront** From the beach end of Passeig Joan de Borbó at sunset look back at the silhouette of the old town's skyline, especially La Mercè, the Virgin holding her child. *See page 135.*

●**La Pedrera** Thumbnails of the Sagrada Familia and other Eixample monuments from the roof. *See page 164.*

FLAVOURS OF BARCELONA

●**La Boqueria** All the food markets are a trip for the senses, but this one gets first prize for its colours, tropical flavours, Mediterranean aromas and overwhelming vitality. Also includes

several good restaurant-bars. *See page 83.*

●**La Seu** An indulgent range of farmhouse cheeses from all over Spain kept to perfection. Tastings take place on Saturday mornings. Also offers excellent

olive oils. Dagueria, 16. *See page 221.*

●**Herbolari** One of many herbalists who can advise and mix your particular potion from drawers full of aromatic herbs. Also sells wholesome honey and natural cosmetics. Xucla, 23.

●**Múrria** A traditional small grocer's shop in the Eixample with its original painted glass façade and a mouth-watering array of goods from the finest hams and cheeses to the most expensive wines. Roger de Llúria, 85. *See page 221.*

●*Pa amb tomàquet* When the bread is fresh, the tomatoes hand picked and the olive oil cold pressed, this traditional accompaniment is a meal in itself and cannot be bettered.

ABOVE: paella cooked in the open air. **LEFT:** fresh produce in La Boqueria. **BELOW:** dancing the *sardana*.

BEST BARCELONAN TRADITIONS

●**Correfoc** Part of the La Mercè festivities, this is the wildest of celebrations when fire-spitting dragons and their accompanying devils threaten to engulf in flames anyone fool enough to taunt them.

●**Dancing** Barcelonans of all ages love to dance the *sardana,* the Catalan national dance.

●**Fiestas** Whether it's buying red roses on the day of Sant Jordi, the patron saint, or roasting chestnuts in the autumn, the people of Barcelona fulfil their traditions with enthusiasm.

●**Going out for breakfast** Sitting up at a classic steel bar with you favourite daily newspaper, fresh crusty sandwich and piping hot coffee is a cherished part of life.

●**Paella** Meeting up with friends or family for a paella on the beach or in the woods is even possible on sunny winter days, and always a treat. This is a dish often cooked by the man of the house.

●**Sunday lunches** Not a Sunday goes by without Catalan families reuniting for a big family meal, usually in the grandparents' house. Someone will bring a dessert, fresh from the pastry shop and wrapped up with paper and ribbon.

●**Weekend escapes** Catalans work hard all week but weekends are sacrosanct. They escape to the ski slopes in winter and the beaches in summer.

BEST BUYS

The best areas for shopping are Passeig de Gracia for department stores and designer shops, Born and El Raval for more original clothes and goods, and the Barri Gòtic for crafts, galleries and antiques. Best buys include:

●**Leatherwear**. Spain is still a good place to buy shoes, bags and coats. The best areas are Portal de l'Angel, Rambla de Catalunya, Passeig de Gràcia and Diagonal. *See page 220.*

●**Fashion**. Local brands such as Mango and Zara are now known internationally. Other, more upmarket, stores include Groc and Antonio Miró. *See page 221.*

●**Bric-a-brac and antiques** Visit Els Encants flea market held in Plaça de les Glòries; the antiques market in the Cathedral Square and the art market in Plaça Sant Josep Oriol. *See page 220 for days.*

●**Home furnishings** From Vinçon in Passeig de Gracia to Bd Ediciones de Diseño, in Mallorca. *See page 220.*

●**Wine and edibles** From cava to hand-made chocolates. *See page 221.*

ABOVE: the free sound and light show at La Font Màgica.
LEFT: leather shoes and bags are one of the best buys.

FREE BARCELONA

●**Cathedral cloister** To the side of the main cathedral is its cloister with 13 resident geese, a fountain and huge palm tree. *See page 97.*

●**La Font Màgica** Designed for the 1929 exhibition, the fountain offers free *son et lumière* displays. *See page 145.*

●**Open-air museum** The side streets off Passeig de Gràcia and Rambla Catalunya arc like a museum of

modernisme: buildings, balconies, stained-glass windows, door knobs, tiled vestibules, carved doors.

●**Neighbourhood fiestas** Not a month goes by without a fiesta, with giants, parades and *castells*.

●**Street performers** Human statues, musicians, opera singers and tango dancers – the streets of the Old Town are full of free entertainment.

MONEY-SAVING TIPS

Half-price theatre tickets
In the Caixa de Catalunya desk in the tourist office of Plaça de Catalunya, or L'Illa shopping centre in Diagonal, theatre tickets are sold at half-price three hours before the performance.

Menú del dia
Most restaurants offer a set menu at lunch time, with three courses including a drink at a price well below the sum of its parts. It can be a good idea to eat your main meal at lunchtime and just snack in the evening. But beware of how the cost of *tapes* can add up to more than you expect.

Museum entrance
Some museums (Picasso, History of Catalonia, Ceramic, Textile, Zoology) can be visited without charge on the first Sunday of the month. The History of the City is free on the first Saturday afternoon of the month and the MNAC on the first Thursday. Others have a reduced rate on certain days, for example, the MACBA on a Wednesday. The CaixaForum and the Caixa de Catalunya exhibition space in La Pedrera are free.

Travel card
One T-10 travel card can be shared among members of the same party

and allows travel to the outer reaches of the city. If you transfer from metro to bus, tram, funicular to Vallvidrera or inner city stations of the FGC (the Generalitat-run suburban train) within an hour and a quarter of leaving the metro (or vice versa) it is considered part of the same journey, and the ticket is not re-punched when it is passed through the machine.

You can also travel from one bus line to another and to RENFE lines, travelling as far as stations within Zone 1, like Castelldefels beach in the south and Badalona or Montgat on the Maresme coast.

AN INSISTENT CITY

Barcelona is a vibrant city, and proud of the characteristics that make it so different from the rest of Spain

Barcelona is the heart and legs of Catalonia, Spain's leading economic region. Covering 6.3 percent of the nation's land mass, Catalonia supports over 15 percent of the Spanish population and produces 20 percent of the country's GDP. Well over two-thirds of the region's people live in the greater metropolitan area of Barcelona itself (5.1 million in total), jammed between the hills of Tibidabo, Montjuïc and the sea.

Catalonia was once a state in its own right and regained a large measure of freedom under the Statute of Autonomy of 1978, although many Barcelonans still believe that the region deserves more autonomy than it currently has. Certainly, Barcelona is like no other Spanish city. It has its own language and its own culture and customs. The Barcelonans are unlike most other Spaniards; they are more introverted, more work-motivated, more self-conscious, more difficult to get to know.

Perhaps because of the Catalans' own insistence on separateness, their city has had a turbulent past, caught between the various powers of Europe in its allegiances against Madrid. The city's growth reflects the eras of its greatest successes, from the Roman walls, through the Gothic Quarter to the palaces of the 17th century, right up to the 19th-century Eixample. Its latest phase is displayed in the work done for the 1992 Olympic Games. The Games transformed the waterfront, created new districts, and were a catalyst for a series of building works and changes which prepared the city for the 21st century.

The Catalan character has had to go underground so often that it expresses itself in surprising ways. The Eixample is studded with the extrovert work of modernist architects, of whom Gaudí was one; Barcelona Football Club has a vociferous following which sees goals as assertions of the Catalan identity. At times the club has been virtually shut down by central government, or forced to share its best players with Real Madrid.

All in all, Barcelona has a lot to offer, and has repeatedly thrust itself to the forefront of European cities. In *Don Quixote*, Miguel de Cervantes wrote: "Barcelona: innately courteous, offering shelter to the travel-weary, hospitals for the poor, home for the brave, revenge for the offended, reciprocating friendship and unique in situation and beauty." This insistent city is worth getting to know. ❑

PRECEDING PAGES: the latest addition to the city, Diagonal Mar; detail on a bench in Parc Güell. **LEFT:** *castellers*, human tower builders, celebrate the festival of La Mercè.

THE MAKING OF MODERN BARCELONA

The city rose to power under Catalonia's medieval count-kings, then struggled for centuries to free itself from Madrid's centralised control. This bred a fierce Catalan identity, strengthened by civil war and dictatorship

Barcelona has all the amenities of a great metropolis and the self-consciousness of a capital city, but much of its dynamism has come from always having had something to prove. In the Middle Ages it was the centre of the greatest Mediterranean empire since Roman times, but never became a sovereign city in its own right, like Venice or Genoa. Until 1716 it was the capital of the nominally sovereign Catalan state and twice fought bloody wars against the rest of Spain to defend that status, but it never became a seat of government in modern times and, with the absorption of Catalonia into the Spanish monarchy, came to be ruled by its upstart rival, Madrid. In the 19th century, it remained the centre of an increasingly vibrant Catalan national culture, which led to further conflicts over its constitutional relationship with the rest of Spain. In the past century or so, Barcelona has risen in economic stature to become the heart of the biggest conurbation of the Mediterranean coastline, and in recent decades has been acknowledged as one of the liveliest artistic centres in Europe.

Roman beginnings

The Roman colony that preceded the city fed well off its "sea of oysters" and had such civilised amenities as porticoed baths and a forum, but it was a small town, covering only about 12 hectares (30 acres). The walls, some of which are still standing, are dwarfed by those at nearby Tarragona and Empúries. Catalan historians like to imagine antique greatness and "continuity" stretching back to the primeval forebears of modern Catalans, but there is no evidence of continuous settlement of the site of historic Barcelona, on Mont Tàber, earlier than the 1st century AD. Pre-Roman Barkeno, a name found on early coins, may have been on the hill of Montjuïc: finds from here include a Roman magistrate's seat set in the remains of a stone enclosure.

Quiet years

For half a millennium after the end of Roman rule, Barcelona's history remains sparsely

LEFT: Columbus returns from the New World.
RIGHT: Wilfred the Hairy, who established the House of Barcelona in the 9th century.

documented. Of the occupiers of those years – the Visigoths, the Moors, the Franks – only the first seem to have esteemed the city highly. Its modest growth during the Visigothic period can be detected in the excavations under the Palau Reial. Evidence here suggests that between the 4th and 6th centuries the *intervallum* between the Roman building line and the ramparts was filled with new constructions. At the same time, streets were narrowed by building extensions. A building of noble dimensions appeared on the present palace site, which may have housed the royal assassination victims.

The city's potential for greatness only began

to be realised when it was conquered, late in the 9th century, by the nascent Catalan state. This was a principality of regional importance, with its granary in the plain of Urgell and its defences in the mountains. Warrior paladins adopted Barcelona as their favourite place of residence, endowed it with religious foundations which stimulated urban growth, and, as the state developed, concentrated their court and counting-houses in Barcelona.

The House of Counts

Of Wilfred the Hairy, the man acclaimed as the founder of the House of the Counts of Barcelona, little trace survives in the modern

city. The count, in a series of campaigns in the late 870s, united the hinterland of Barcelona with most of the other Frankish counties south of the Pyrenees.

By the early 10th century, Barcelona was already, in a sense, the "capital" of sovereign Catalonia. Around 911, Count Wilfred II chose a house of religion outside the walls for his mausoleum. His neglected grave, marked by an inscription discovered among rubble, deserved better treatment, for it was this sort of patronage, bestowing princely status on Barcelona, that began to turn the former backwater into a medieval metropolis.

For the next 200 years, Barcelona's wealth continued to come mostly from war and the agricultural produce of the plain. The first known boom came in the late 10th century. Historians have assumed that this must have been the result of commercially generated wealth, but there is no evidence to support this conjecture and it is possible that the simple presence of the knights, the court and the clergy was the source of stimulation.

The growth of the cathedral chapter is the first clue to the city's expansion. The canons grew in sophistication as well as in numbers, acquiring a reputation for erudition, and building up libraries, which have since disappeared.

In 985 Barcelona was a target of sufficient prestige to attract a raid by al-Mansur, the predatory vizier of Córdoba, but real losses seem to have been slight and, by encouraging rebuilding, al-Mansur may actually have stimulated the boom. The Moorish threat did not long survive al-Mansur's death in 1002. The empire of Córdoba was enfeebled by political intrigue and eroded by usurpations. In the 1030s it dissolved into small, competing successor-states. Like much of the rest of Spain, Barcelona began to enjoy a bonanza on the proceeds of booty, tribute, ransom and the wages of mercenaries.

A golden age

By the 1070s, 95 percent of transactions in Barcelona were made in gold. Some of this money was invested in the maritime enterprise which for the next 500 years supplied the city's wealth and formed its character. In 1060, although Barcelona was already a "great town", according to a contemporary chronicler, the Barcelonans were still hiring their galleys from Moorish ports. By 1080 the counts possessed a fleet of their own.

Two charters of Ramon Berenguer III (who ruled from 1082–1131) mention what sounds like substantial seaborne trade. In 1104 he granted a tenth of dues paid on "all goods that come in on any ship in all my honour"; in the following year four Jews were granted a monopoly of the shipping home of ransomed Moorish slaves. International commerce continued to develop gradually, and in 1160 Benjamin of Tudela reported the presence of vessels of "Pisa, Genoa, Sicily, Greece, Alexandria and Asia" off the beach of Barcelona.

> ### MONEY AND ART
>
> For a flavour of what Catalonia was like in the 11th and 12th centuries go to the Museu Nacional d'Art de Catalunya (MNAC) *(see page 147)*. Its collection of murals from rural churches shows the high quality of work that Catalan money could buy.

Empire and embellishment

The winds and currents of the western Mediterranean meant that Barcelona had to solve its problem of access to the Balearic Islands, in order to become a centre of long-distance commerce, rivalling Genoa and Pisa. In his extraordinary *Book of Deeds*, Jaume I

Most of the buildings of this period were replaced in later eras of even greater prosperity: only Sant Pau del Camp, Santa Llúcia and the Capella de Marcús remain.

In the streets, the explorer can match the map to documents that record the expansion of the city. In 1160, Ramon Berenguer IV gave permission for a new public bath outside the city wall, where today the Carrer dels Banys Nous (Street of the New Baths) curves in the shadow of lost ramparts.

LEFT: Ramon Berenguer III (1082–1131), who presided over a period of prosperous seaborne trade.
ABOVE: the tomb of the conqueror king, Jaume I.

(who reigned from 1213–76) identified his own motives for launching the conquest of the Balearics as essentially chivalric: there was more honour in conquering a single kingdom "in the midst of the sea, where God has been pleased to put it" than three on dry land. To chivalric and crusading satisfactions, the nobles added substantial territorial rewards. The Barcelonans and other merchant-communities of the Catalan and Provençal worlds, participated for purely commercial motives.

The conquest of Mallorca (1229), Ibiza (1235), Sicily (1282), Menorca (1287) and Sardinia (1324), and territorial extension by a series of treaties, gave Barcelona's count-kings something like a protectorate over a number of ports, the landmarks of an empire of grain and gold, of silver and salt.

Imperial exploits were matched by the city's desire to expand and embellish its territory at home. The cathedral is the dominant monument of the 13th century: the cloister portal, with its obscure carving of harpies and wild men dragging a half-naked, pudge-faced warrior, contrasts with the elegant High Gothic of the west front and the interior. The early 14th century, when the profits of empire were perhaps at their height, was a time of frenzied building. The chapel of Santa Agata, in the count-kings' Palau Reial in the Plaça del

scale the shipyards, where galleys for the Mediterranean war effort had been built since the reign of Pere II (1276–85): the eight great bays of the Drassanes at the foot of the Ramblas now house the Maritime Museum. Private builders were also active. The Carrer de Montcada was driven through the old town in a broad, straight line and promptly colonised by the aristocracy.

Price of conquest

As the empire grew, however, its costs came to exceed its benefits. The ambition to control the western Mediterranean sea lanes caused wasteful wars with Genoa, because Barcelona

Rei, was built by Jaume II (who died in 1327). The first stone of the church of El Pi was laid in 1322 and that of Santa Maria del Mar, which still has its medieval glazing largely intact, in 1329.

Not even the Black Death – which killed half the city council and four of the five chief magistrates – could dent the city's confidence or interrupt the building boom. Never was the city so spectacularly embellished as in the reign of Pere III (1336–87); he built the vaulted halls of the Saló de Cent (in today's town hall) and the Saló del Tinell, with its martial wall-paintings, in the palace of the Plaça del Rei. Pere III also rebuilt on a larger

never had sufficient resources to exploit its victories. Mallorca sustained a turbulent political relationship with the count-kings and used Catalan knowledge to set up competitive shipping, arms and textile industries, and Sardinian resistance lasted, intermittently, for 100 years, and exhausted the conquerors.

The empire that made a metropolis of Barcelona also sucked the rural life-blood out of Catalonia; as the centre of gravity of the realm moved towards the city, the balance of population shifted. On the eve of the Black Death, Barcelona contained 20 percent of the population of Catalonia. The countryside could no longer keep the armies supplied with men or the city with food. In 1330 Barcelona experienced its first serious famine.

Never was a city more obviously the victim of its own success. Barcelona evinced the classic symptoms of the monster: corpulence induced by overfeeding.

The passing of glory

The decline of Catalonia in the 15th century should, however, be treated with caution. Barcelona's 15th century was more an "era of difficulties", redeemed by the extraordinary resilience of an indomitable ruling class.

In the century after 1360, not a decade went by without a recurrence of plague, sometimes accompanied by famine; from 1426, the yield of the customs and wool tax plummeted and did not recover until the next century. This protracted insecurity led to the first uncontrollable outburst – the pogrom of 1391, when the authorities were powerless to protect the Jews from massacre. In 1436 and 1437 popular agitations were suppressed, but by the mid-century the failures of the city's natural rulers had attracted the sympathy of the city governor for a movement to democratise the municipal institutions. The name of the incumbent party, the *Biga*, probably signifies a large beam used in the construction of a building; that of the challengers, the *Busca*, a piece of tinder or bunch of kindling. The names evoke the natures of the parties: the solidity of the establishment, the incendiary menace of its opponents. Their conflict in the 1450s did not unseat the ruling élite, but left it enfeebled and embittered against count-king Joan II. His unpopularity had grown as he tried to exploit Catalonia in his attempts to meddle in Castile.

As a result, no part of the realm entered the civil war of 1462 more wholeheartedly than Barcelona; none suffered so much from the results. The insurgents' cause became desperate as each of the pretenders they put up to challenge the king died or dropped out in turn. The siege that ended resistance in 1473 left Barcelona devastated. "We see our city turning into something no bigger than a village on the road to Vic," the *consellers* wrote.

LEFT: a 15th-century painting depicts grain being shipped to Barcelona.
RIGHT: painting on a 16th-century altar urn.

Royal neglect

Barcelona was allowed no share of the rich booty plundered in Central and South America by Spain's conquistadors. Joan II's son, Fernando II, had married Isabel of Castile in 1469, creating a powerful alliance rich enough to finance Columbus's first voyage in 1492.

When Fernando succeeded to the Aragonese throne in 1479 Catalonia became increasingly regarded as an annexe of Castile. Barcelona's decline in the 16th century coincided with the progressive loss of the courtly status which, before the rise of the city's commercial importance, had been the foundation of its fortune. After the extinction of the ruling House of Barcelona in 1412, it had been governed by a series of kings whose main interests were in Castile or Naples and who spent ever less time in Barcelona. For a while – from Fernando II's succession in 1479 and continuously from 1516 – her counts were also kings of Castile and, as such, were mainly concerned with the affairs of that more productive country.

However, with the confidence that has characterised them in every age, the Barcelona city fathers poured money into the creation of an artificial port in an attempt to recover lost trade: the task would remain incomplete for 300 years, but was never abandoned. In terms of public building, however, there was little happening. No visitor to Barcelona can fail to be struck by the relative dearth of great Renaissance and baroque buildings. There are examples of grandeur, but they are elusive: the Palau de la Generalitat hides its medieval core behind a Renaissance facade. Most of what survives

from this time reflects private effort, rather than public wealth. The Carrer Ample was opened as a gesture to Renaissance town planning but the splendid new palaces of the era were built by private patrons.

Yet the patriciate never lost their sense of ruling the capital of a sovereign principality – or even a quasi-*polis*, a city with the potential, at least, to be a city-state like Genoa or Venice. Barcelona affected the status of a foreign power, and its representatives swaggered like the emissaries of foreign potentates. When, for instance, a new viceroy of Catalonia was appointed in 1622, the congratulations of Barcelona were tendered by an ambassador,

attended by 200 carriages, in what was rumoured to be the most magnificent procession ever seen in Madrid.

The different nuances of Castilian thinking led policy makers in Madrid into misunderstandings about the traditions they had to deal with in relations with Barcelona. In Castile, civic liberties normally rested in a charter granted by the king: they were a negotiable commodity, revered but not written in stone. Barcelona's identity, however, was bound up with the status in law of the principality of Catalonia as an equal partner in the Spanish monarchy. It had liberties (*furs*) not granted by the prince as an act of grace, but governed by the *constitucions* – statutes that were irrevocable except by the representative parliamentary assembly of Catalonia (the *corts*), which limited royal authority.

During the early years of the 17th century, when the Spanish monarchy was tottering under the effects of immoderate greatness, the need for money and manpower made the Catalans fearful for their immunities. The implicit constitutional conflict between the interests of Spain and those of Catalonia was bound to be noticed in Barcelona, where all the institutions of the statehood of Catalonia, inherited from the Middle Ages, were concentrated, and where a substantial body of professional lawyers more or less lived by watching the *constitucions*.

Rebellion and war

The cost of the Thirty Years' War and direct hostilities with France from 1635 brought the demands of the monarchy for money and men to a peak and the differences with the principality to a head. When Catalonia rose in revolt in 1640, and the rebels transferred their allegiance to Louis XIII of France, Barcelona was the head and heart of the rebellion. However, the Catalan juggernaut rolled out of control. The élite of Barcelona were forced to share power with popular elements, and 16 years of war devastated its land, depopulated its towns and despoiled its wealth. The siege of Barcelona in 1652 was one of the most desperate episodes of the war and it ended only when the starving citizens were, literally, "reduced to eating grass". However, the successful army commander, Don Juan José of Austria, was the architect of a remarkable restoration of the broken city and of Catalonia's national pride. Ironically, his very success was to raise the danger of another round of similar conflict.

In the second half of the 17th century, Barcelona had little respite. Civic-minded optimists like Feliu de la Penya had hardly begun to revive all things Catalan before the French wars of the 1680s and 1690s exposed her lands to yet more campaigns and the city to another crippling siege.

The War of the Spanish Succession was to plunge the entire monarchy into crisis. The Bourbon claimant, Felipe V, arrived in 1702, scattering rewards and promises with a lavish hand, but he was suspected of an arbitrary disposition and absolutist plans. His insensitive viceroy, Francisco Fernández de Velasco, blundered into other infringements of the *constitucions*. Despite the naturally peaceful inclinations of a mercantile élite, most leading members of Barcelonan society showed themselves willing to respond to Velasco's tactless rule with violence.

In Barcelona it seems, the appetite for war *vient en mangeant* (grew with eating), and the Barcelonans, after their slow start, became the most committed opponents of Felipe V. They joined the allied cause in a calculating spirit but clung on when all the other allies had withdrawn. They dared beyond hope, endured beyond reason and reaped the usual reward of that sort of heroism: defeat.

The recovery of 1652 had been misleading: it encouraged the Barcelonans to believe that resistance would save them. The final siege lasted from August 1713 until 11 September 1714, when the city eventually capitulated (a date now celebrated as the Diada de Catalunya – Catalonia's national day).

The repression so hotly denounced by Catalan historians after Felipe's victory was actually rather mild: clerics and generals were its only individually targeted victims. But the *constitucions* were abolished; Barcelona was reduced to the rank of a provincial city and suffered the indignity of an occupying army billeted in what is now the Ciutadella Park.

LEFT: shield of Barcelona.
RIGHT: the Bourbon Felipe V, who refused to respect the Catalan statutes.

Prosperity and the guilds

Although the city was prostrate and the revival slow, the 18th century as a whole was an era of forward-looking prosperity in which sustained economic growth began, thanks to new activities such as direct trade with the Americas and the beginnings of industrialisation based on imports of American cotton.

Some of the palaces and villas of the Bourbon collaborators can still be seen: the finest of them, the Palau de Comillas, houses the Generalitat bookshop in the Ramblas; around the corner, the palace of the Comte de Fonallar enhances the commercial bustle of the popular shops in the Carrer de Portaferrissa.

The ensemble that probably said most about 18th-century Barcelona was the Barceloneta district, the first industrial suburb, begun in 1753 to house a population beginning to burst out of the diminished city. The tight, neat grid of its streets, in contrast with the traditional cityscape of Barcelona, made it one of the earliest surviving examples of enlightened town planning in Europe. In recent years, however, Barceloneta has undergone massive changes.

In pre-industrial Barcelona manufacturing was a mainstay of the economy, but it was confined to the intimate society of the workshop and the master's home, and regulated by the powerful guilds. A visitor to the Museu

d'Història de la Ciutat in the Carrer del Veguer can see the images that dominated the
guilds: their art reflected professional pride
and devotion to their patron saints. The book
of privileges of the shoemakers is decorated
with an elegant gilt-bronze slipper; the silversmiths' pattern books record the masters'
copyright to thousands of intricate designs.
The market-gardeners' book of privileges is
flanked by busts of their patron saints, and the
gaudily painted coffer in which their relics
were preserved. The images of saints are
reminders that the guilds doubled as devo-
tional confraternities. Evidence of their prestige and wealth can be found around the city

tacular. By 1825, the cloth-dressers had only
three members left; all were too old to work.

In the last quarter of the 18th century a
number of economic indicators accelerated.
The rate of increase in wages was double that
of Madrid. Manufacturers' profits, which had
already doubled between 1720–75, more than
kept pace. In 1787, English economist and
agrarian reformer Arthur Young could hear
"the noise of business" everywhere.

War and its aftermath

After the defeat of the Spanish fleet at Trafal-
gar in 1805 and the abdication of King Carlos
IV of Spain, Napoleon put his brother Joseph

today: the shoemakers' palatial hall, in the
Plaça de Sant Felip Neri, decorated with the
lion of St Mark, who converted the first shoemaker, and the sumptuous premises of the silk
weavers' guild in Via Laietana.

The beginnings of the transformation of
Barcelona's economy to an industrial basis
can be traced in the decline of the guilds. The
18th-century immigrants – most of them from
communities in southern France, where languages similar to Catalan were spoken – preferred factory life to subjection under the
oligarchy of guild-masters. In the textile
industry, which was directly affected by reor-
ganisation into factories, the decline was spec-

on the Spanish throne. He attempted to win
over the Catalans by offering them a separate
government, with Catalan as its official language, but the Catalans were having none of
it, and supported the Bourbon side throughout the war (1808–14). Napoleonic forces
wreaked a great deal of destruction in the
region, sacked the monastery at Montserrat,
and destroyed a number of churches.

Inevitably, the war and its aftermath,
together with a terrible yellow fever epidemic
in 1821, interrupted economic progress.
Working-class poverty, degradation and unrest
became a feature of life in Barcelona in the
mid-19th century. In 1835, insurgents had

attacked steam-powered factories, representatives of the government and houses of religion; the disturbances of 1840–2 culminated in a political revolution by a coalition of the disaffected; it was suppressed by force. Riots became a regular feature of the summer of 1854. Increasingly, they took on revolutionary proportions. A series of strikes and "Luddite" outrages began in defiance of the rapid automation of the textile industry. The riots were soon deflected into political channels by the fall of a progressive ministry in Madrid; respectable radicals joined the mob in resistance. The barricades of Barcelona were reconquered in the bloodiest scenes the city had witnessed since 1714. A Conservative observer noted with satisfaction: "The rebels were massacred as they were captured … The spectacle was magnificent."

Barcelona expands

Despite the unrest, trade and industry flourished with the spread of steam power and mechanisation. The new bourgeoisie, formed by old families of the urban mercantile aristocracy, cotton and iron industrialists, and makers of fortunes in the Americas, had now come into its own. In 1836, the first steamship rolled off the slipway of Barceloneta; gaslight was introduced in 1842; and in 1848 Spain's first railway linked Barcelona to Mataró, 30 km (19 miles) to the north. Catalonia was now the fourth largest cotton textile producer after England, France and the United States.

Yet Barcelona was the most insanitary and congested city in Europe. Observers blamed the cholera epidemic of 1854, which claimed 6,000 lives, on overcrowding in insanitary conditions. It was still a strategic city, a walled stronghold watched over by two hated military enclaves, Montjuïc and the Ciutadella (the citadel built by Felipe V in 1714 after demolishing 1,262 dwellings for the express purpose). Strict military ordinances banned building outside the walls. Inside, every inch of space was occupied. Not even three major epidemics and violent outbursts of social unrest could stem the population explosion. Barcelona was bursting at the seams.

One obsession united all Barcelonans: the need to demolish the walls and expand the city. The walls were finally demolished by Royal Order in 1854–6, and the idealistic civil engineer, Ildefons Cerdà, was commissioned to draw up "Studies for the Extension and Reform of the City of Barcelona".

Cerdà's plan for the Eixample (Extension) extended to the limits of the hinterland towns with an extensive network of criss-crossing streets, parallel and perpendicular to the sea and broken only by two great diagonal avenues. Cerdà's grand but egalitarian layout

THE WORLD EXHIBITION

Barcelona's growing prosperity and the exuberance of the age were symbolised by the 1888 World Exhibition. With less than a year to prepare, the city entered a period of frenzied building work. As well as the buildings and cascade in the Parc de la Ciutadella, Sants and La Concepció markets, the Columbus Monument, the Palace of Justice and the Hospital Clinic were built during this period. The Gran Hotel on the Passeig de Colom was built in 53 days, only to be knocked down as soon as the Exhibition was over. The exhibition opened 10 days late but was a huge success, drawing exhibitors from 20 countries and attracting over 2 million visitors.

LEFT: Catalan wall tiles depicting the crafts and industries of the town and countryside, displayed in the Museu d'Història de la Ciutat.
RIGHT: fine citizens on La Rambla in the 19th century.

was a utopian socialist dream, but with a scientific basis. The forward-looking plan specified that only two sides of each block were to be built up, leaving ample space for parks and gardens. Most of the criticisms of today's Eixample – the lack of parks and gardens, for example – result from the gradual debasement of Cerdà's plan by the city council.

After the September Revolution of 1868, which swept the Bourbons from the Spanish throne, social peace ensued. In December 1869, the land on which the hated citadel, symbol of repression, had stood was handed over to the city and became a public park – today's Parc de la Ciutadella. The movement for the recognition

of Catalonia's distinctive institutions and the revival of its language and literature – later to become known as the *Renaixença* (Renaissance) – gained much ground, and Barcelona developed a flourishing café society.

A new era

Immigrants began to pour into the city from the poorer and less industrialised parts of Spain. The establishment of democracy and the proclamation of the Republic in 1873 gave an extraordinary impetus to the workers' movement. The building of the Eixample – and the debasement of the Cerdà Plan – continued apace. Barcelona witnessed a display of capitalism at its most euphoric.

The Eixample became the fashionable quarter of the city to which the new merchants and professional classes moved, abandoning the narrow streets of the Gothic quarter. Antoni Gaudí (1852–1926, *see page 172–3*) graduated at a time when the city was hungry for architects with original ideas, as the new Eixample proprietors began to compete with each other for the most opulent and stylish buildings. The *modernista* style reflected an enthusiasm for new forms in art: the intricate, the elaborate and the capricious set against the coldness and rationality of the machine age.

But by now, two separate forces operated in the city of Barcelona, one representing the new Catalan bourgeoisie, who sought modernisation and economic and political autonomy, the other the new class of factory and immigrant workers and artisans, who sought, ultimately, revolution.

BARCELONA AND THE CIVIL WAR

The Spanish Civil War began on 17 July 1936. Barcelona rapidly became a Republican stronghold and it was not until January 1939, after a sustained bombing campaign, that Franco's Nationalist forces captured the city.

Early in the war, anarchists and communist militiamen effectively controlled the city – although the Catalan Nationalist leader Lluís Companys was nominal president of the Generalitat. Companys succeeded in disarming both communists and anarchists in May 1937 when, with the help of police loyal to the Republic, he laid siege to the anarchist-held telephone exchange in Plaça de Catalunya and negotiated a ceasefire between the war-

ring factions. There was much bloodshed in the city, including the executions of more than 1,200 members of the Catholic clergy. Many churches, too, were desecrated, ransacked or destroyed.

After the 1938 Battle of the Ebro in southern Catalonia, the Republicans were unable to defend the city. Many of those who had been loyal to the Republic fled across the border to France, fearing for their lives as the Nationalist forces drew closer. Savage reprisals followed – around 35,000 people were executed for their part in the conflict, including Companys, who was captured in France, returned to Barcelona and shot on Montjuïc hill.

Unrest grew with the loss of Spain's colonies and the American markets in 1898. Anarchism took hold in the workers' movement. There were general strikes in 1901 and 1902, and in 1909 the city would suffer the Setmana Tràgica, a week of rioting and destruction, when 70 religious buildings were systematically burned by the anarchists.

Some of these tensions were reflected in the work of the *modernista* artists, the most representative being Ramon Casas (1866–1932), whose oeuvre includes a number of remarkable political paintings. Many of his works can be seen in the Museu Nacional d'Art de Catalunya *(see page 117).*

Repression of Catalonia

In 1914 the Mancomunitat of Catalonia was formed as a confederation of the four Catalan provinces, whereby Barcelona recovered its administrative powers. With World War I the city saw new opulence generated by supplying the warring countries. But after the war the market shrank, sparking an economic crisis. Barcelona became increasingly chaotic as the social conflict worsened.

Repression by the authorities triggered a period of violence practised by both workers and employers. The bourgeoisie supported the dictatorship of Miguel Primo de Rivera, initiated in 1923, only to be rewarded with increasing repression, and the banning of the Catalan flag and public use of the language.

Meanwhile, work for a second International Exhibition in Barcelona began, with Montjuïc the main setting for the new buildings. The event had a decisive influence on immigration: from 1924–30 Barcelona received around 200,000 immigrants, tipping the population over the million mark, including an enormous 37 percent who had been born outside Catalonia.

When the left-wing coalition won Spain's 1931 general election, Alfonso XIII went into exile, and the Second Republic heralded a major step forward for Catalan aspirations. Socialist leader Francesc Macià returned

from exile to become president of the Generalitat of Catalonia. What Pau Casals would call a "veritable cultural renaissance" began. The years between 1931 and the Civil War were seen by Catalans as another golden age.

But Macià's ambitious plans for the city were cut short by the military insurrection of 1936. The Spanish Civil War ushered in one of Spain's darkest periods, and under Franco's iron hand the Catalan national identity was subjected to brutal repression for nearly 40 years. Local government was in the hands of the collaborationist bourgeoisie, and Catalan culture was once again driven underground.

Legacy of dictatorship

During the dictatorship, the middle classes worked hard, looking after their businesses and making money, firmly establishing Barcelona as the economic capital of the Spanish peninsula. Ironically, it was economic growth that posed the main threat to Barcelona's identity.

Madrid, which held Spain's purse-strings, had neglected and underfunded "Spain's factory", allowing it to degenerate and lose its identity as vast waves of immigrants, mostly from impoverished Andalucía and Murcia poured in during the 1950s and 1960s, looking for work. The population increased to

LEFT: Catalanism and autonomy became heated national issues.

RIGHT: victorious Nationalists in the Plaça de Catalunya at the end of the Civil War in 1939.

around 1.8 million, and cheap and nasty housing was thrown up for the newcomers without a thought to infrastructure, amenities or social consequences. The uncontrolled building boom resulted in a ring of densely populated and poorly serviced outlying neighbourhoods, creating tremendous social problems.

Autonomy and regeneration

In the first democratic general elections of 1977, the socialists and the Conservative Convergència party emerged as the two main forces in Catalonia. Pressure for autonomy continued and in October the president-in-exile of the Generalitat, Josep Tarradellas,

green spaces were to be restored, and public amenities built. In 1986 the council made an agreement with the Generalitat to renovate significant spaces and buildings. In the late 1980s the Caixa de Catalunya savings bank bought Gaudí's Casa Milà (better known as La Pedrera) and set about restoring it to its breathtaking pristine state.

Another key element in Barcelona's regeneration was the hosting of the Olympic Games in 1992. Barcelona's tradition is one of looking forward, so there was nothing new about using a big international event as a catalyst for development, modernisation and beautification of the city. What could beat hosting the

returned to a euphoric Barcelona after negotiating terms in Madrid.

With the new Spanish Constitution and Statute of Autonomy unveiled in 1978, Catalonia regained a measure of self-government. In the elections of 1979, the communists won every working-class suburb of Barcelona, and the socialists took control of the city council; in 1980 the Convergència party was elected to the Generalitat.

The council set about tackling the legacy of dictatorship, and came up with radical solutions. People and their quality of life rather than profit were to be the priorities. Grants and subsidies were offered for cleaning up facades,

Olympic Games and putting the city back on the international map where it belonged?

Post-Olympic city

After the euphoria of the Games, the anti-climax and the economic crisis bit hard. It is a measure of the popularity of the charismatic mayor, Pasqual Maragall, that he retained public loyalty even when the crisis necessitated large tax increases. Building work continued: Barcelona was to have better communications; it was to be greener, more sporting, more cultured, cleaner, and more open to the sea. And it has succeeded. As well as the high-profile undertakings – the restoration of the Parc Güell and the rebuilding of the Liceu opera house (badly damaged in a fire in 1994) – improvements are legion. Between 1992 and 1999, 19 new parks were opened, and the number of trees in the city increased by nearly 27,000.

The metro network has been extended; a vast plan of action implemented in the Old Town, with the opening of the stunning Museu d'Art Contemporani de Barcelona in El Raval, and other cultural centres; Port Vell (the Old Port) has been redeveloped, with the Imax cinema, the Maremàgnum commercial complex, the Aquarium and the Museu d'Història de Catalunya; fountains and squares have been created, monuments and facades cleaned and innumerable buildings restored throughout the city; bicycle lanes have been provided on major thoroughfares.

Maragall resigned as mayor in 1997, and his position was taken by his deputy, Joan Clos, but policies have remained largely unchanged. In October 1999 Maragall challenged the Conservative Jordi Pujol in the Generalitat elections but was narrowly defeated, and the status quo was retained. However, in 2003 Maragall finally defeated the Convergència party, to become president of a left-wing coalition government.

Covering the waterfront

The most obvious and most stunning new development is the waterfront. The Olympic Village has become a smart residential district, the Olympic Port a favourite haunt for eating and drinking. Within 10 years the number of visitors to the beaches nearly tripled. With its return to the sea, Barcelona seems to have distilled the essence of the Mediterranean city.

Late 1998 saw the completion of the Carrer Marina, one of the principal arteries of the new Barcelona, which finally links the Eixample directly with the sea. The new Marina has been transformed into a citizen-friendly boulevard with wider pavements, a bicycle lane, new trees and new urban furniture. Past the Sagrada Família and the Monumental Bullring, Marina skirts Plaça de les Glòries, where the gleaming

new Glòries shopping centre, the neoclassical Teatre Nacional de Catalunya and the Auditori de Barcelona are only a stone's throw from the traditional Els Encants flea market. Marina sweeps over what used to be the railway line and on past the Olympic Village towards the sea, where there are kilometres of promenades and beaches: to your left, the coastline stretches as far as the eye can see; to your right is the backdrop of Montjuïc.

To the north lies Diagonal Mar, a newly created residential district of high-rise apartment blocks, parks, a landscaped waterfront and a large shopping mall. It has a new metro station, El Maresme/Forum, and can be reached

by the brand-new tram, which speeds up and down most of Avinguda Diagonal. It was also the venue for the latest idea to bring international attention and investment to the city, Forum 2004, a universal forum of cultures sponsored by UNESCO.

All these changes are a reflection of the confident spirit that guides the city. Barcelona is not only the capital of Catalonia, but the centre of a much larger Mediterranean region with nearly 15 million inhabitants. The future for the city, says its council, is as the southern gateway of Europe, and its vocation is to be the model for everything that a European city should be. ❑

LEFT: the post-Olympic waterfront with Frank Gehry's copper fish to the fore.
RIGHT: the Rambla de Mar in the redeveloped Port Vell.

Decisive Dates

Early History: c.700 BC–AD 476

c.700 BC The Iberians settle in the fertile area between the Riu Llobregat in the south and the Riu Besòs in the north.

c.600 BC The sails of Greek ships appear off the Catalan coast. Among the Greek settlements is Empòrion on the Costa Brava.

c.300 BC The Carthaginians penetrate as far as Catalonia.

264 BC After the First Punic War between the Romans and Carthaginians, there are far-reaching changes in the Iberian peninsula.

Hannibal crosses the Ebro in 217 BC, and Roman troops capture Barcelona. In the peace treaty of 197 BC the Carthaginians have to relinquish their Spanish conquests.

200 BC–AD 300 Barcelona flourishes, and a magnificent city centre develops around the forum (today Plaça Sant Jaume) on the small hill called Mont Tàber. Around the time of Christ's birth, under the rule of Emperor Augustus, Barcino is renamed Julia Augusta Faventia Paterna Barcino.

AD 476 The Visigoths enter eastern Spain. They call the territory extending south of the Pyrenees Gotalonia. They capture Barcelona and make it their Iberian capital.

Moorish Rule to the Thirty Years' War: 700–1659

c.700 The Moors invade Spain and capture Barcelona in 713. They are forced out by the Franks in 801. Arabic influences are less marked than in other parts of Spain.

8th–9th century The Franks found the *Marca Hispànica* (Spanish Marches). Wilfred the Hairy *(Guifré el Pelós)* unifies the areas south of the Pyrenees and establishes the House of Barcelona, a dynasty that lasts for 500 years.

985 Al-Mansur, Grand Vizier of the Caliph Hisham II, reaches Barcelona and destroys large parts of it. The Franks free the city again.

988 The county of Barcelona is declared autonomous. The foundation is laid for the development of an independent Catalonia. This year is celebrated as the birth of the state.

1137 Berenguer IV, Count of Barcelona, marries Petronilla, heiress to the throne of Aragón. Barcelona becomes capital of the kingdom of Aragón and enjoys a period of great success.

1284–95 The Catalan–Aragón confederation extends its power over the whole Mediterranean area as far as Naples. Several splendid buildings are erected in Barcelona's Barri Gòtic.

14th century Catalonia is one of the Mediterranean's chief maritime nations; its rule book, the Consolat de Mar, governs sea trade.

1359 The Corts Catalanes, a representative body of nobility, citizens and priests which had met since 1289, is officially appointed. A body later given the name Generalitat de Catalunya is set up to regulate financial and political matters.

1395 Annual competitions for poets and troubadors, called the Jocs Florals, are initiated. They are based on a similar event in Toulouse.

1469 Fernando II of Aragón marries Queen Isabel I of Castile, uniting the two kingdoms.

1492 The unification leads to the fall of Granada, the last bastion of the Moors. Under the absolute monarchy of the Catholic Monarchs Catalonia becomes less important. Trade with the new colonies in the Americas goes via the Atlantic ports. Barcelona suffers economic decline.

1635 The Thirty Years' War with France: Catalans rise up against the centralist rule of Felipe IV, and are supported by the French king Louis XIII. Spanish troops are unable to recapture Barcelona until 1652.

1659 In the Treaty of the Pyrenees, all Catalonia north of the Pyrenees is ceded to France.

War of Succession to the Present

1714 Barcelona sides with Habsburgs in the Spanish War of Succession. The Bourbon king Felipe V destroys the whole of the Ribera area, abolishes the Corts Catalanes and has a citadel built. This date *(La Diada de Catalunya)* is the national day of celebration in Catalonia.

1808 The inhabitants of Barcelona rise up against the French. Napoleonic troops destroy large parts of the city.

1814 onwards The city experiences an boom under Fernando VII. The industrial revolution has a positive effect and Barcelona becomes Spain's leading centre for technical developments.

1848 Spain's first rail link, between Barcelona and Mataró, is built.

1854–6 The citadel and the old city walls are razed to the ground.

1860 The building of the new city (Eixample), designed by Ildefons Cerdà, begins.

1888 Barcelona hosts its first Universal Exposition. Numerous *modernista* buildings are erected.

1901–9 Anarchism in the workers' movement results in general strikes by workers in 1901 and 1902, and the Setmana Tràgica (Tragic Week) in 1909, when widespread rioting leads to the destruction of 70 religious institutions.

1914 The Mancomunitat, a Catalan provincial government, is set up and Barcelona recovers administrative power. Industry flourishes during World War I.

1923 The military dictatorship of Primo de Rivera (1923–30) suppresses Catalan freedoms

1929 A second Universal Exposition is held in the grounds of Montjuïc. Numerous buildings, including the Poble Espanyol, are built.

1931 Under the Second Republic Catalonia is granted its first statute of independence. Francesc Macià becomes president of the Generalitat de Catalunya. The statute barely takes effect, however, as the Spanish Civil War breaks out in 1936.

1936–9 After bitter fighting and widespread destruction, Barcelona falls. Franco's troops enter the city. Franco forbids the Catalan language and the expression of Catalan customs. The statute of autonomy is revoked and the president of the Generalitat, Lluís Companys, is exe-cuted in Montjuïc Castle in 1940. Immigrants from southern Spain flock to Barcelona for work, resulting in huge dormitory towns with social problems.

1975 After Franco's death a constitutional monarchy is set up by plebiscite. Juan Carlos is proclaimed king. Catalan is recognised as an official language.

1978 Catalan Statute of Autonomy.

1980 Jordi Pujol, leader of the Conservative Con-vergència party, becomes president of Catalonia.

1986 Barcelona is chosen as host for the 1992 Olympic Games. A massive wave of building activity ensues, presided over by Pasqual Maragall, the socialist mayor.

1992 The Olympic Games are a huge success.

1995 The Port Vell development is completed. The Contemporary Art Museum (MACBA) opens.

1997 Mayor Maragall resigns and is succeeded by Joan Clos.

1999 The National Theatre and Auditori are completed. The Liceu Opera House reopens after being devastated by fire in 1994.

2003 President Jordi Pujol resigns and former city mayor Pasqual Maragall is elected president in a left-wing coalition.

2004 Barcelona's latest brainchild, the Forum, is celebrated on a new site on the waterfront. The city council becomes the first in Spain to declare its opposition to bullfighting. ❑

LEFT: Roman remains in the Plaça de la Vila de Madrid.
RIGHT: Lluís Companys, president of the Catalan Generalitat in 1933, was executed in 1940.

THE BARCELONANS

Life in Barcelona is characterised by dynamic commercial activity and a vibrant social scene – tempered by a dash of Catalan coolness and given a cosmopolitan veneer by the many outsiders who come here to work and play

Catalans in general, and Barcelonans in particular, are famed for their business acumen, their passion for work and their economic ability. In southern Spain they are seen as cold, tight-fisted and work-obsessed. The laid-back, *mañana* attitude of the popular Spanish stereotype scarcely exists in Barcelona. But then, as the Catalans will never tire of telling you, and as the history of their nation clearly shows, Catalonia and its capital are definitely *not* Spain. In Barcelona, 10 o'clock means 10 o'clock, not half past 11. *"Anem per feina"* is a common expression, once pressed into service as a Catalan nationalist election slogan: "Let's get down to work."

Shop 'til you drop

Like England, Catalonia has been dubbed a nation of shopkeepers and, indeed, Barcelona has a staggering number of shops. This is not so surprising when you consider that its background is purely mercantile, right back to the Phoenicians and Romans. This bourgeois city was built up through family enterprise and is now being promoted as one of *the* places to shop. The slogan that once graced the carrier bags of the famous Vinçon design store puts it in a nutshell: "I shop, therefore I am."

Barcelona exudes an air of prosperity and elegance and is no longer a particularly cheap city. The standard of living is high, but it has

to be paid for, and the work ethic is especially noticeable if you come here from elsewhere in Spain. You can see it in the comparatively early closing of bars and restaurants (well, early by Spanish standards) and the long opening hours of shops. Efficiency, punctuality and deeply serious reliability are of the essence. Barcelona works *very* hard. It bustles with immaculately dressed and groomed urban professionals striding in and out of shops, offices and banks with document cases, folders and parcels, all with mobile phones clamped to their ears – this is life on the fast track.

In Andalucía they have a saying: "The Andalucian works to live, the Catalan lives to

---

PRECEDING PAGES: buying a pet on La Rambla.
LEFT: shopkeepers pose for the camera in El Raval.
RIGHT: good humour rules.

work." But it is not as straightforward as this. For how do we square this view of Catalonians with the wild celebrations of La Mercè, for example, the week of festivities around 24 September, the day of Barcelona's patroness, when giants and fantastical creatures parade around the city on stilts, the night sky blazes with fireworks, thousands dance to rock bands in (usually) rather sedate historic squares, and fire-breathing dragons chase reckless citizens through the streets?

On the other hand, in the cool light of day, Barcelonans actually tend to make self-regulating queues in shops, which comes as something of a surprise in Spain.

Prudence versus impulse

The Catalans call these apparently contradictory facets of their character *el seny* and *la rauxa*. The former is a combination of prudence, profound common sense and sensible judgement, the latter a fit, impulse or emotional outburst: a kind of attack of wildness.

You can see both sides of the Catalan character in the way they drive, for example. In contrast with other flamboyant cities, Barcelona traffic is, in fact, extremely disciplined and orderly. Drivers keep in lane and are very good at indicating. They stop on red, and go on green – fast. But if you hesitate for just a split second, or worse still, stall, you'll be

DANCING THE *SARDANA*

The *sardana* is Catalonia's national dance, one which unites old and young, rich and poor, and which, in its present form, grew out of the 19th-century *Renaixença* when Catalans were rediscovering their cultural identity. No festival is complete without it, and every Sunday in every town and village, you will see it performed. In Barcelona the *sardana* is danced in the cathedral square each Sunday at noon and Saturday at 6.30pm, and occasionally in Plaça Sant Jaume. First the band, the *cobla*, starts up: the leader plays a *flabiol*, a three-holed pipe, and has a *tabal*, a small drum strapped to his elbow. The woodwind players are seated, with the brass players standing behind

them; each tune lasts about 10 minutes, and, just as you might think it is dying away, it starts up anew.

As the music gets going, a few people in the growing crowd will start to dance, sometimes just a group of four, forming a small circle, in the centre of which will be placed a bag of some kind. Soon others join in, making their own circles or joining existing ones, until the whole square is filled with dancers, linked hands raised high, solemnly counting the short sedate steps, which suddenly change to longer, bouncy ones. Real *aficionados* wear espadrilles with coloured ribbons, but most people dance in their ordinary shoes, be they Sunday best or trainers.

deafened by furiously honking horns. When the traffic gets really snarled up, as it often can, the *rauxa* takes over. Patience is no longer a virtue; you must get going, be on the mark, have your wits about you.

Passionate energy

Barcelonans may work until they're blue in the face, but they're still a Mediterranean people: wild, creative, fun-loving, noisy and gregarious. As Barcelona's celebrated Olympic Games of 1992 set out to show the world, Mediterranean high spirits and street life do not have to be synonymous with sloth and inefficiency, and Barcelonans are capable of first-class technol-

mountains. They have little time for the wishy-washy: theirs are the strong, bright primary colours of Miró. They are efficient, enthusiastic and resourceful. They are adventurous travellers, visiting the most remote corners of the world. They value and cultivate initiative and pioneering enterprise. Barcelona is intensely involved internationally in science, education, ecology and other fields.

But they certainly come over as reserved and serious beside the large number of citizens originally from southern Spain, the immigrants who flooded in during the 1950s and 1960s in search of work, mostly from Andalucía. Coexistence has often been less

ogy and efficiency without relinquishing any of their vibrancy and zest. The key to this unique exuberance is that "passionate energy" noted by George Orwell in 1937 as he watched Barcelonan men, women and children build barricades in the war-torn city. Whatever they do, they give it everything they've got.

A clash of cultures

Barcelonans work hard all week, then sit in traffic jams every Friday afternoon so that they can enjoy weekends by the sea or in the

LEFT: dancing the *sardana*, Catalonia's national dance.
ABOVE: getting a polish on La Rambla.

than easy, with ethnic, class and cultural differences coming into play: the Catalan middle classes tend to take a dim view of the ebullient non-Catalan working class, and vice versa.

Known by the derogatory nickname of *xarnegos* (the original meaning of the word is a child of a Catalan and a non-Catalan), these "other Barcelonans" form a distinct group, living in the outlying neighbourhoods of the city, with their own extrovert, boisterous lifestyle. Barcelona's Feria de Abril (April Fair), held in the city, is no longer a pale, homesick imitation of the Andalucian original but a big event in its own right that in recent years has attracted nearly a million visitors.

Moreover, it is largely thanks to the socialist voting habits of this huge community that Barcelona got its municipal act together under the socialist-led city council. And, of course, the second and third generations of these so-called *xarnegos* are Barcelona born and bred.

Barça fans

Barcelona Football Club is more than the city's football team, it is one of Catalonia's flagship institutions: during the repressive Franco years the dice were always very carefully loaded in favour of Real Madrid, and so Barça – "the army of Catalonia" – was the only possible outlet for the collective expression of Catalan national identity – rage, resistance and pride *(see panel below)*.

Now, Barcelonans and Catalans of all ages, classes, genders, shapes, sizes and persuasions happily unite to dance in the streets in wild celebration when Barça beats Madrid or wins some kind of cup or league. The red and gold of the Catalan flag combine with Barça's blue and maroon *(blau grana)* in a swirling mass down La Rambla. Corks pop and *cava* sprays while fireworks fizz and bang far into the night.

Taking to the streets

Like all good Mediterraneans, the Barcelonans are a street people. All it takes is a few tables and chairs squeezed onto a postage stamp of pavement, and there they'll sit for hours over their drinks and *tapes*, apparently oblivious to the fumes, traffic noise and even the dust and din of building works. When it rains, the milling throngs leap into cars and taxis, causing the traffic to "collapse", as they put it, in a cacophony of honking horns. Fortunately, it doesn't rain too often.

Dynamism rules

One of the highest accolades a Barcelonan can receive is that he or she is *espavilat* or *espavilada*, which may be translated as a dynamic, bright, assertive person who goes out and gets things done. This proactive zooming around encompasses not only work, of course, but a host of other activities – from culture, shopping and social life to voluntary work, chauffering children, sports... you name it, Barcelonans do it with gusto.

FOOTBALL FEVER

Barcelona Football Club – Barça – was founded in 1899 by Hans Gamper, a Swiss living in Barcelona. It is one of the oldest clubs in Europe, and during its long and chequered history it has played a surprising political role, championing Catalan nationalism and liberty. The unusually high number of Barça members – 105,000 – is proof enough of the club's popularity. Memberships pass from father to son and newborn babies are made members only hours after birth. No fewer than 80,000 of the members have permanent seats in the impressive Camp Nou stadium, one of the largest in Europe with a seating capacity of 98,787.

During the last years of the Franco dictatorship Barça came to symbolise freedom. Thousands of members and fans waved the blue-and-garnet flag of Barça as a substitute for the forbidden Catalan flag. A victory over Real Madrid was equivalent to a victory over the oppressive central government. The re-establishment of democracy has done nothing to lessen the support for Barça. Indeed, the enormous social and financial back-up of Catalan society provides the basis for its power.

Football fans from around the world visit Camp Nou. Getting tickets for a match isn't too difficult unless it's for a game against Real Madrid *(see page 224)*.

Tradition with a difference

The Barcelonans adhere fiercely to tradition and convention, as anyone witnessing them dancing the *sardana*, Catalonia's intricate national dance, outside the cathedral on a Saturday evening or Sunday morning will confirm (*see panel, page 36*). Yet at the same time they are open to innovation and creativity. These perceived contradictions are only skin deep.

Barcelona has always thought of itself as a cosmopolitan capital city. Its traditions are inextricably bound up with Catalonia's defence of its identity as an independent nation – an advanced, cultured and tolerant nation which is always open to new ideas and influences, and looking forward to new horizons.

Barcelona has always worked magic on foreigners. In his memoir *Homage to Catalonia*, George Orwell chronicled the ideologically boiling Barcelona of 1936, filled with young foreigners from all over the world who had come to defend democracy. In the 1960s, as the Spanish-language publishing capital, the city was home to writers and intellectuals such as Gabriel García Márquez and Mario Vargas Llosa. The 1970s saw a huge influx of South Americans fleeing the vicious dictatorships in Argentina and Chile.

Since the break-up of the former eastern bloc and the formation of the EU, the foreign community has continued to grow. Irish pubs, Greek restaurants and Pakistani grocery shops abound. Barcelona's popularity as a venue for trade fairs and international meetings of all kinds makes for an exciting cosmopolitan buzz. As modern technology and telecommunications make physical location increasingly irrelevant, more foreigners are choosing Barcelona for their *pied-à-terre*, attracted by its mild climate and laid-back lifestyle.

Catalan independence

This tradition places a high value on independence, both collective and personal. The mild climate allows Barcelonans to live life outside. They are masters of sociability when out in the streets and squares, bars and restaurants; and they engage fully in the community life of offices and shops, parks and sports fields.

LEFT: Barça crazy at Camp Nou.
RIGHT: a handicrafts demonstration on La Rambla.

However, they are fiercely protective of the privacy that they enjoy in their homes, which they view as a safe haven.

This translates into a great respect for individual privacy. The Infanta Cristina of Spain has lived in the Sarrià neighbourhood of Barcelona for years, living, working and hav-

ing babies in the same way as anyone else, with no intrusive interest from the media or the proud but protective Sarrià locals.

Open-minded outlook

Barcelona is one of the most tolerant places in Spain. Gay and feminist movements were largely pioneered here, and alternative medicine, self-help and New Age culture thrive. There is little obsession with petty titles and nobility: Barcelona is more of a meritocracy than anything else. And look at Gaudí: far from being the archetypal misunderstood artist, he was positively sought out and encouraged in his fabulous creative flights.

Above all, good humour rules. Walk through any of Barcelona's markets. The stall holders have been up since dawn, buying goods at Mercabarna, loading and unloading their provisions, as well as cooking lentils, chick peas and the like. Yet they're filled with good cheer, cracking jokes and gossiping, their talk peppered with endearments like *rei, reina, maco, maca*. They are shopkeepers to the core, but they are enjoying themselves.

Putting on a show

This good humour and flair for combining work, fun and creative imagination is the essence of life in Barcelona. On (pre-Lent)

Carnival Thursday, for example, it's business as usual at the big market on La Rambla – but in fancy dress. A cardinal in full regalia blesses the shoppers trundling their carts in and out. Ballet dancers, black chest hair bristling from their pink tutus, cart crates of potatoes around. Plumed cavaliers slice ham and chorizo, while Roman emperors weigh out oranges and Moorish princesses gut fish.

In the old districts of Gràcia and Sants the locals work hard all year round preparing for their *festa major* (annual fête) in mid-August. Entire streets are turned into theme parks, with prizes for the best. Each street or square organises its own programme of events. The kids get puppet shows and hot chocolate parties; live salsa and rock bands play through the night. But during the day it's still business as usual: except you'll go shopping in Jurassic Park, a space station, a medieval village, or something out of the *Arabian Nights*.

A day of roses and dragons

The crowning achievement, the epitome of the Barcelonan personality, is exemplified by the celebrations for Sant Jordi (St George), the patron saint of Catalonia, on 23 April. This is also the anniversary of both Shakespeare's and Cervantes's death, and is celebrated by giving gifts of books and roses. What makes Sant Jordi such an inspired blend of culture, money-making and fun is that it's not actually a public holiday, so everyone is sucked into the festivities as they go about their usual business.

All the bookshops set up stalls in the streets and squares and give a 10 percent discount. It's a field day, too, for journalists and chat-show hosts, with round-the-clock live TV coverage from La Rambla, including celebrity signings and interviews. Massive public collections of books for hospitals are organised. The city's hawkers make a killing too, selling roses in the metro stations and at traffic lights instead of cleaning windscreens or peddling strings of garlic. Kids in national dress, miniature hairnets, red caps and espadrilles, greet their care givers at the school gates with paper roses and paintings of expiring dragons.

In the evening, as men hurry home from work, each one, regardless of age or status, bears a single red rose beautifully wrapped in cellophane and tied with red-and-yellow ribbon. At night there are discos and shows, parties and dances. And not to let the partying get in the way of business, record sales figures appear on the late-night news, of course.

Peaceful co-existence, solidarity, integration, caring, citizen participation, a pluralist society – these are just a few of the buzzwords bandied about by Barcelona's planners, policy makers and copywriters these days. Even Barcelona's animals and trees, they tell us, are citizens. And you can't get more integrated, pluralist and caring than that. ❑

LEFT: father and daugter during festivities on the Plaça Sant Jaume.

The Catalan Language

Catalan is a Romance language, a sister to Castilian (Spanish), French, Italian and Portuguese. It is spoken by at least 6 million people in Catalonia, Valencia, the Roussillon region of France, Andorra, some border areas of Aragón, and in the Balearic Islands and the city of Alghero in Sardinia, which were ruled by Catalonia in the 13th–14th centuries. Spoken Catalan has a sharp, staccato quality that makes it sound very different from Spanish.

Catalan literature had its own Golden Age in the 15th century. *Tirant lo Blanc*, a novel of chivalry written by Joanot Martorell, preceded Cervantes's *Don Quixote*. Regarded by some critics as the best European novel of the 15th century, *Tirant* has been translated into many languages.

After the War of Succession (1705–15), Catalonia was punished for defending the Archduke Charles. Castilian became the official language and Catalan was relegated to religious and popular use. But with the industrial revolution and the emergence of a dynamic middle class in the 19th century, an economic and cultural revival known as the *Renaixença* (Renaissance) took place, and Catalan was recovered as a vehicle of culture. In 1907 the Institut d'Estudis Catalans was formed for "the re-establishment and organisation of all things relating to Catalan culture". With the establishment of the Generalitat in 1931, Catalan once again enjoyed the status of official language.

However, Franco's victory in the Spanish Civil War (1936–9) put a tragic end to all that. Catalan was banned entirely from public use. Books, newspapers and films were subjected to draconian censorship. The enforced implementation of an all-Castilian education system meant that a generation of Catalan speakers were unable to read or write their mother tongue.

With the recovery of democracy, Catalan was established alongside Castilian as the official language of Catalonia. The government set about implementing a policy of "linguistic normalisation" whereby Catalan was reinstated in all aspects of public life, government, education and the media. In 1990 the European Parliament passed a resolution recognising Catalan and its use in the European Union. Now, once again, Catalan thrives in the arts and sciences, the media and advertising.

Barcelona is a bilingual city, although different degrees of proficiency in different languages are evident. Some older people

educated before the Civil War may have an imperfect knowledge of Castilian. While Catalan is almost universally understood, older immigrants from elsewhere in Spain may not speak it. People schooled during the past two decades are generally proficient in both languages.

The rationale behind the linguistic policy is that if Catalan is not actively defended it will decay into a local patois. Its detractors, meanwhile, allege narrow-minded nationalism. For the most part the two languages happily coexist, with most people slipping from one to the other, depending on the person they are talking to. ❑

RIGHT: Catalan is the official language.

FURIOUS FIESTAS

The Barcelonans' reputation as sober workaholics is seriously undermined when one of the city's many annual festivals brings the streets to life

Hardly a month passes in Barcelona without at least one excuse to party, or a *festa major* (celebration of local patron saint), which calls for a public holiday, enormous family meals, flowing *cava* and noisy antics in the streets.

Depending on the *festa*'s status it will probably entail dancing *gegants* (giants), *dracs* (dragons), *dimonis* (devils) and legendary beasts, plus processions of dignitaries and mounted guards *(guardia urbana), castells* (human towers), as well as *sardanes* (the traditional Catalan dance) in public squares which are taken over by rock or jazz bands at night. Nearly always there is an air-raid of fireworks.

There are also more demure festivals, such as the Fira de Sant Ponç (11 May), when medicinal herbs, honey and crystallised fruits are sold. At the other extreme are the wild festivals like La Mercè, the *festa major* in September, which consists of a whole week of uproarious fun culminating in the *correfoc*, a pyromaniac's dream. It is also worth looking out for the numerous cultural festivals, including Grec, a five-week-long summer festival of music and the arts.

LEFT: the five-year-old *anxeneta* crowning a five-storey or more *castell* is the most breathtaking and unmissable moment of a *festa*.

ABOVE: Carnival *(Carnestoltes)* in February or March is an excuse to dress up and party before bidding farewell to indulgence during Lent. Everyone gets into the spirit, including shop-keepers and market traders.

ABOVE: La Mercè is the festival to beat all festivals when the city celebrates its patron, Mercè, for a whole week around 24 September. With fireworks, devils and concerts by night, *castells* (human pyramids, *see left*), *gegants* (giants) and dragons by day, there's something for everyone.

OTHER FESTIVAL HIGHLIGHTS

BAM
Barcelona Acció Musical is now an established part of the Mercè fiesta *(see left)* providing free concerts of independent music in locations around the city, from the Cathedral esplanade to the Rambla del Raval.

Castanyada
An autumnal festival held around All Saints' Day (1 November), in homes, schools and public squares. Roast chestnuts and sweet potatoes are eaten, followed by *panellets* (small almond-based cakes) with muscatel sweet wine.

Grec
For over 25 years the city has held this five-week summer festival of music and the arts, attracting leading talent and using locations all over the city

L'Ou com Balla
Often missed, this low key celebration of Corpus Christi is one of the most delightful: an egg dances in the beautifully decorated fountains of the medieval courtyards of the Gothic quarter.

Sant Joan
Bonfires, fireworks and flowing *cava* last all-night long on the eve of Sant Joan (23 June). The festival marks the exciting start to summer. Inevitably the next day is a very quiet public holiday.

BELOW brilliant firework displays accompany many festivals, including La Mercè in September and Sant Joan in June.

RIGHT Sant Jordi (St George), the patron saint of Catalonia, is celebrated on 23 April. According to legend, the blood of the slain dragon transmutes into a rose. Men and women exchange gifts of books and roses, as this date is also the anniversary of Cervantes' death. Streets are filled with bookstalls and huge vats of red roses.

ARCHITECTURE

Barcelona has a rich architectural heritage, from soaring Gothic arches to flamboyant *modernista* mansions. And a spate of exciting new building projects has rejuvenated the city's image in the past two decades

In 1999, the Royal Institute of British Architects awarded their annual gold medal, widely perceived to be the most prestigious award for architecture in the world, not to an individual but, for the first time, to a city: Barcelona. The award stated: "Inspired city leadership, pursuing an ambitious yet pragmatic urban strategy and the highest design standards, has transformed the city's public realm, immensely expanded its amenities and regenerated its economy, providing pride in its inhabitants and delight in its visitors."

Since the 1980s Barcelona has attracted the attention of architects from all over the world for its bold contemporary architecture, urban design and successful programme of renewal. The effect has been to catapult the city from a dusty European backwater to a shining example of how cities should be managed.

Catalans have long considered architecture the most durable way of representing their culture. They use it to express their independence of thought and liberalism compared to the rest of Spain, as well as to create a strong connection with the rest of Europe.

Architecture has always been on any visitor's agenda due to the works of Antoni Gaudí and his *modernista* contemporaries, but their work, extraordinary though it is, comprises only a part of the rich architectural heritage of present-day Barcelona.

LEFT: the ceiling of the nave of Santa Maria del Mar, a prime example of Catalan Gothic.
RIGHT: 15th-century architecture in the Barri Gòtic.

Understanding the city

Set between the sea and the Collserola mountains, and contained by Montjuïc to the south and the River Besòs to the north, Barcelona is the most densely populated area in Europe. At its heart lies the Casc Antic, the medieval area which, up until the middle of the 19th century, contained the entire city within its walls – the oldest of which date back to the Romans. For complicated political reasons the city was not permitted to expand until the 1850s, by which time the density of population was comparable to 10 times that of contemporary London. Most of Barcelona's pre-19th-century buildings are in the narrow streets of this area.

Catalan Gothic has a distinctive character: dignified but somewhat dour. The interiors of the buildings are often strikingly large. Some are very fine, embodying the secular and religious splendour of the time. Not to be missed are the Saló del Tinell, with its enormous arches, in the Palau Reial Major, the Museu Marítim/Drassanes, where the galleons of the Armada were made and, of course, the Església de Santa Maria del Mar, for its elegance and serenity. The area's dwellings are mixed; dingy flats opening onto interior lightwells rub shoulders with splendid merchants' palaces in Montcada, which now houses the Museu Picasso and other notable institutions.

A radical solution

In the 1850s, with the liberation of the city from Madrid's control, it was necessary to build an expansion, or "Eixample", to relieve overcrowding. Engineer Ildefons Cerdà proposed the laying out of an enormous grid that would spread out over the surrounding plain, intersected by avenues lined with trees. The project was radical at the time, proposing a vision of the city that would be full of sunlight, air and open spaces, well ordered, with integrated public facilities and transport networks.

The existing Eixample, however, is very different. Almost as soon as the grid was laid out, the council allowed plots of land to be

Inventive restoration

Restoration of such palaces has been carried out as part of the city's regeneration programme. Contemporary insertions and details now sit proudly and comfortably beside medieval structures in a style that does not seek to create exact replicas. The purpose has been to complement the existing buildings rather than trying to imitate past architectural styles.

This attitude is prevalent in all restoration work done in the city. A notable example is the 18th-century Casa de la Caritat, in El Raval, which has been transformed into the stunning Centre de Cultura Contemporània by architects Vilaplana and Piñón.

bought up, and families made their fortunes building speculative housing. The quality of housing was graded depending on location; the fashionable streets became the sites for some extremely grand *modernista* blocks, with glazed balconies and tiled and carved facades. In the more obscure locations are poorer imitations – badly built, narrow, dark flats, usually with similar but smaller layouts and sometimes with a touch of *modernista* detailing on the ground floor entrance and facade. All sides of the blocks were developed, and the internal spaces, originally intended as communal parks, became factories, workshops and, later on, car parks.

The Eixample development has been a continuous process from the early *modernista* housing, through 1960s architecture, to contemporary blocks of flats. The height restrictions and building lines of the strict grid layout have generally been maintained, resulting in a lively but homogeneous urban design.

The population of the Eixample is great enough to sustain the small shops and bars that give the place its pulse, and the area has adapted well to changes in transport and lifestyle. Recent measures to reduce the traffic have improved conditions, and industry has been discouraged, allowing new parks and open spaces to be reclaimed.

FASHION VICTIM

In the years immediately following its heyday, *modernisme* was considered to be the epitome of bad taste, but today the pendulum has swung back again, and *modernista* buildings have become symbols of a vibrant city.

of immigrant workers from the rest of Spain. These are variable in quality and some estates have severe social problems.

Architectural regeneration

After the stagnation of Franco's rule (ending with his death in 1975), the new Ajuntament

Village life

The city has a number of outlying "villages", such as Gràcia, Sants and Sarrià. Although enveloped by the Eixample, these areas still manage to keep a strong and vibrant identity, with their own local history, fiestas and culture. The buildings are generally smaller in scale, with narrower streets, small squares and parks, four- to five-storey blocks of flats and even a small amount of single occupancy housing. The whole city is ringed by blocks of flats built in the 1960s to house the thousands

LEFT: the sinuous window of Gaudí's Casa Batlló.
ABOVE: the Mies van der Rohe Pavilion, Montjuïc.

THE MIES VAN DER ROHE PAVILION

Built by Ludwig Mies van der Rohe (1886–1969) for the 1929 International Exhibition on Montjuïc, this pavilion challenged contemporary notions of space. It had no windows, doors or walls in the conventional sense; steel columns supported the roof, and the space flowed seamlessly from interior to exterior rooms. Frameless glass blurred the concept of thresholds, with panels and screens used to create particular spatial effects.

Probably one of the most influential buildings of the 20th century, it still appears very modern. Controversially, a replica of the original was built in 1986 to mark the centenary of the architect's birth.

(City Council) of Barcelona was quick to implement plans for the city's regeneration. By the time the Olympic bid was won in 1986, the city was already receiving international attention for its architecture programme. Design was clearly the highest consideration, with dramatic architectural solutions retaining existing positive elements in the city.

Each of the city areas was subject to a plan based on a detailed study of all aspects of the urban fabric, from the provision of schools and parks to the organisation of traffic and major infrastructure projects. The plans proposed ways in which each area could be improved, from the the creation of parks and

squares – "urban spaces" – to the construction of a motorway interchange at Plaça de les Glòries. The improvements were carried out either within the public works department or as commissions by talented local architects.

International profile

For the high-profile public buildings, and to lend international status to the programme, "star" architects were invited to contribute: Japanese architect Arata Isozaki built the Palau Sant Jordi *(see page 151)*, a huge steel-and-glass indoor arena with a levitating roof, on Montjuïc hill; English architect Norman Foster built the Torre de Collserola *(see page 181)*,

ARCHITECTURE OF THE VALL D'HEBRON

The Vall d'Hebron Olympic site, located at the end of metro line 3 at Montbau, is home to some of the most interesting, if lesser known, Olympic buildings.

The most impressive is the Velodrome, built by Esteve Bonnell. It is a beautifully simple, modern interpretation of an ancient, essentially Mediterranean, building type, set in a landscape surrounded by cypress trees. It was built in 1984, at a time when postmodernism was prevalent, incorporating a characteristically classical pastiche and superficial decoration, using high-quality materials such as stone, marble, steel and glass. The site also contains the now dilapidated archery range by Enric Miralles

and Carme Piñon, and a replica of the 1937 Pavilion to the Spanish Republic, designed by Josep Lluís Sert for the Paris Exhibition, and used to exhibit Picasso's *Guernica*. Sert established modern architecture in Barcelona in the 1920s and 1930s after coming into contact with other European modernist architects, most notably Le Corbusier, but was later exiled to the United States.

The pavilion was rebuilt using the original cheap materials of thin steel sections and asbestos panels, but is nevertheless very sophisticated. It creates a sense of enclosure while capturing the flavour of a traditional Spanish courtyard house.

now an icon of the skyline and sometimes known as the Torre Foster; US architect Frank Gehry constructed the huge copper fish glittering on the sea front *(see page 137)*, while another American, Richard Meier, designed and built the city's contemporary art museum (MACBA). Unlike Meier's previous buildings, which are on open sites, the MACBA is an urban building, forming one side of a square and framing vistas from the surrounding streets with the sculptural elements on its facade.

Home-grown talent

Also extraordinary is the confidence of the work undertaken by many virtually unknown

City of interiors

Catalan architects have always designed more than just buildings. The structure of the profession, with technical architects dealing with the day-to-day construction, allows more time to be spent on design and innovation. Street furniture, kiosks, paving slabs, tree grills and shopfronts are architect-designed. Such work still tends to be craft-based, and the continued existence of small metalworking shops, marble masons and stained-glass ateliers, combined with a lack of prefabricated building products, allows buildings to be more creatively detailed.

Although in the post-Olympic period there

Catalan architects. The trust invested in them by the planning authorities and the support of the city's inhabitants, as well as a close appreciation of their cultural and architectural heritage, have enabled them to flourish.

On Montjuïc and the Vall d'Hebron are many buildings constructed for the 1992 Olympics, notably the Institut Nacional d'Educació Fisica de Catalunya (INEFC), a kind of sports university designed by Ricardo Bofill (who also designed the Teatre Nacional).

LEFT: Centre de Cultura Contemporània de Barcelona (CCCB) in El Raval.
ABOVE: the Forum, Diagonal Mar.

has been a slowing down of building work, the regeneration programme continues. Newer projects are now coming to fruition, such as the area around Plaça de les Glòries, now the site of Rafael Moneo's Auditori de Barcelona and Ricardo Bofill's Teatre Nacional, built like a neoclassical temple. French architect Jean Nouvel's Torre Agbar is also here where Avinguda Diagonal continues to the sea.

The port area of Barcelona has also been opened up as a major shopping and leisure area, alongside the new World Trade Centre at the end of La Rambla. Several large new shopping centres have been built, such as L'Illa, also by Moneo, and in Diagonal Mar, the new seaside neighbourhood. Leading national and international architects like Herzog and De Meuron were brought in for some of the Forum 2004 building work *(see page 139)*. These projects have nearly all been commercially led and tend to lack the freshness of earlier work carried out in the city.

Current projects

Barcelona's city council, however, is still building. There has been renovation of the city's food markets, remarkable when the rest of Europe is becoming more oriented towards a supermarket culture. Bernadetta Tagliabue, widow of Enric Miralles (architect of the new

tural forms to be read more clearly. The lack of weathering also makes flat facades and the use of rendering and tiling appropriate.

The population of Barcelona has a high degree of design consciousness. The city has always nurtured her architects, indulged their idiosyncrasies and encouraged them to be forward-thinking and individualistic in their approach. Catalan architects understand the history of Barcelona's architecture, they love Gaudí, Domènech i Montaner and the Saló del Tinell, but they are not intimidated by them, building alongside this legacy in a confident and contemporary style. Their achievements are as good as or better than their predecessors',

Scottish Parliament), is completing his avant-garde projects. Their Mercat de Santa Caterina in La Ribera with its brightly coloured wooden mosaic roof is a wonderfully daring public building.

The extensive *Posat Guapa* (Make it Beautiful) campaign in the Casc Antic, placed an emphasis on restoring facades and houses; EU grants were obtained for the purpose. Parks are still being constructed in peripheral areas, the Sagrera area is being regenerated to accommodate a high-speed rail link to France, and new hotels appear regularly.

Barcelona has an ideal climate for fine architecture, the strong light allowing sculp-

and have their roots in the same traditions of attention to detail and local craftsmanship.

The best way to see the city's architecture is simply to walk around the streets. To help you on your way there are some excellent architectural guidebooks, obtainable from the basement shop in the Col·legi d'Arquitectes opposite the Cathedral in Plaça Nova, many of which have been translated into English. Recommended books are the *Guide to Architecture in Barcelona* and the *Barcelona Design Guide*. Both are published by Editorial Gustavo Gili.   ❏

ABOVE: sculpture in the Parc de l'Espanya Industrial.

Urban Spaces

In 1981, architect Oriol Bohigas was asked to establish a new department of urban design for Barcelona city council. Previously, he had been the head of the city's School of Architecture, so he took with him his most able students, who become known as the Golden Pencils. Each architect was allocated an area of Barcelona and asked to develop a plan for its regeneration. Throughout the city there was a desperate shortage of public space and, since buildings were expensive, parks and squares became the focus of the regeneration. The proposals ranged from small areas of paving to large parks on derelict land, and from the opening up of the Eixample blocks to the renovation of traffic interchanges. Bohigas's young architects and others commissioned by the council were allowed to keep authorship of the projects, the design and originality of which were regarded as crucial in order to achieve high-quality results.

Plaça Fossar de les Moreres (Grave of the Mulberry Trees) by Carme Fiol, was created next to the Gothic Església de Santa Maria del Mar, and commemorates the Catalan Martyrs of 1714. The paving design reflects the existing geometry of the site and surrounding streets, while the red granite wall is reminiscent of a gravestone and has a commemorative inscription.

The Parc Creueta del Coll by Martorell Bohigas Mackay is in the site of an old quarry in an outlying area of the city (at Vallcarca, metro line 3). Its somewhat rugged quality is in marked contrast with its urban context, but good use is made of the site. An enormous sculpture by Eduardo Chillida is suspended above a pool .

The Parc de l'Escorxador on the site of the old abattoir near Plaça d'Espanya is now fully mature and, like most of the spaces, well used, What was once a dry and dusty space has been transformed into a series of rectilinear terraces and walkways, highlighted by an enormous Miró sculpture. The park is dif-ficult to categorise, but has been described as falling somewhere between a formal garden and a wild Mediterranean landscape.

In Gràcia, architects Bach and Mora have redesigned each of the eight existing but neglected squares. Plaça del Sol now has lampshades resembling the setting sun, while the design of Plaça del Diamante contains references to the book of the same name, including a rather nondescript figure of the book's heroine.

A more recent work is the Plaça Islàndia by architects Arriola and Fiol, built in the not-so-glamorous Sant Andreu district just steps away from the arterial route into Barcelona.

It is set along Carrer Bofarull which, although almost obliterated by the superimposed Cerdà grid, was the original route of the aqueduct from the river Besòs into the Casc Antic in Roman times.

The aim of the redesign was to acknowledge the historical context within the more recent Cartesian grid. Water was introduced as a symbolic element, while trees, paving and furniture were laid out so as to reflect the Roman waterway. The name of the square derives from the fact that the central pool contains an artificial geyser, sponsored by the Icelandic government and opened by its president. ❏

RIGHT: the Parc de l'Espanya Industrial, built in 1985, was one of the first urban spaces.

ART AND INSPIRATION

With a legacy left by Picasso and Miró, with Tàpies still
making his mark, and a lively contemporary aesthetic, art in
the city has never been more alive and exciting

To visit Barcelona is to breathe in a complex and exciting visual art history. The streets map the impressions that have inspired three of Spain's prime movers in the story of modern art: Pablo Picasso, Joan Miró and Antoni Tàpies. Ironically, Picasso only spent a few years here before moving on to Paris; Miró also came and went. Only the still-living Tàpies made his permanent base here, but the legacy left by these three great artists is clearly appreciable through the work of young contemporary Catalan artists.

Pablo Picasso

Pablo Ruiz Picasso (1881–1973) was born in Málaga, Andalucía, in southern Spain. His family soon moved on to La Coruña in Galicia before arriving in Barcelona in 1895, where Don José Ruiz, Picasso's father, took up the post of Painting Professor at the city's La Llotja School of Art. One department of this school can still be found in Carrer Avinyó, and the story goes that a brothel located in this street inspired the title (and content) of Picasso's landmark painting *Les Demoiselles d'Avignon* (1906–7). The painting caused shock and outrage among art critics.

Picasso's precocious genius is legendary: at the age of 14 he entered his father's school, completing the month-long entrance exams in a single day. He was to repeat this feat two years later at the Royal Academy in Madrid

LEFT: *Donna amb mantellina* from Picasso's pointillist period, in the Picasso Museum.
RIGHT: the young Picasso, drawn by Ramón Casas.

before abandoning his studies and setting out as a painter in Paris. Meanwhile, he was to encounter Barcelona's artistic circle that met at the now famous Els Quatre Gats (The Four Cats) café. It was here, on 1 February 1900, that Picasso exhibited for the first time.

The 150 drawings of friends included portraits of Jaume Sabartés, Picasso's lifelong friend and secretary. The Museu Picasso in Barcelona was initially founded largely thanks to Sabartés who donated his personal collection of the artist's work. Picasso also designed the menu cover for Els Quatre Gats, which was influenced by Henri de Toulouse-Lautrec (1864–1901). This influence was just one stage of many during Picasso's phenomenal development. Picasso entered his melancholy Blue Period (1901–4) after the death of his Catalan friend, Casagemas, before emerging into the warmth of the Rose Period (1904–6).

Then came the pioneering breakthrough into cubism, which he was to develop over the next 20 years. He returned to Catalonia on several occasions, and donated a considerable number of paintings (almost all his youthful works and the *Las Meninas* series from the 1950s) to the Museu Picasso in Barcelona.

The Picasso Museum *(see page 110)* occupies a series of 15th-century palaces. In the same medieval street, Montcada, several more

with texts in English, and shows on a par with those in most capital cities. Start at the Palau de la Virreina in La Rambla for information about current shows, or go to the Santa Mònica Centre at the end of La Rambla. Both venues put on good exhibitions .

At the end of Montcada is the Passeig del Born, where the vast Metrònom space in Fussina promotes experimental art and video.

Joan Miró

Walk out of Barcelona airport and you will find one of Miró's ceramic murals, made in collaboration with his friend Llorens Artigas. Barcelona born and bred, Miró (1893–1983)

palaces serve as art venues, including the Galeria Maeght. The Maeght family opened the Barcelona branch of their empire in 1973. Opposite is the Sala Montcada, a contemporary-art space funded by La Caixa bank. This large cultural foundation is worth noting for its many and varied exhibitions, particularly in its new cultural centre, CaixaForum, located in a magnificent *modernista* building on Montjuïc.

City of art

Barcelona is exceptional for the quantity and quality of exhibition venues and is a sheer delight for any visitor interested in art. You will find well-produced catalogues, usually

returned here throughout his life, during periods spent in Paris and Mallorca, where he eventually moved permanently. While studying at La Llotja School in Barcelona he passed through the Cercle Artístic de Sant Lluc, which still exists. Here he met Joan Prats, who became an art dealer and a friend for life.

Miró was already aware of Dada at this time, though fauvism, cubism and Paul Cézanne (1839–1906), in particular, were the major influences on his work. Catalan landscapes featured strongly. *The Farm* (bought by Ernest Hemingway and now in Washington), a major painting of his *detalliste* period, portrays the family farm, Mont-Roig, near Tarragona. It features many of his subsequent motifs: stars, insects and animals, as well as showing a characteristic respect for manual labour. Gradually, realism gave way to suggestion and poetry, a progression aided by his contact with French surrealism.

Like Picasso, Miró suffered greatly during the Civil War, and he produced (among other things) the *"Aidez L'Espagne"* poster to raise funds for the Republic. Picasso and Miró were friends in Paris, although Picasso at times viewed his friend's curious "constellations" of signs, symbols, women and birds, and simple palette, with amusement. In fact, Miró's works, showing limited use of certain colours, were precisely composed. He also had wide-ranging skills, turning his hand to theatre design, print-making, tapestry, ceramics and bronze sculptures as well as painting and drawing. The permanent collection at the Fundació Miró *(see page 152)* on Montjuïc covers all of these areas. This building is testimony to the understanding Miró had with his friend Josep Lluís Sert, who designed both this and Miró's studio in Mallorca. It is a celebration of Miró's work, and showcases a varied programme of exhibitions, as well as important works such as Alexander Calder's *Mercury Fountain*, the Joan Prats room and the Homage to Miró section.

You will find evidence of Miró all over the city, whether walking over his ceramic pavement in La Rambla, admiring the monumental *Woman and Bird* sculpture in the Parc de Joan Miró, or simply noticing the La Caixa bank logo he designed.

Antoni Tàpies

Antoni Tàpies (born 1923) is probably Spain's best-known living artist. His work forms an artistic link between Miró's generation and the new work being produced in the Catalan art world. Tàpies knew Miró and revered his work; the latter's influence is seen in Tàpies's early work, on view at the Fundació Tàpies *(see page 162)*. The museum, which redeploys an important Domènech i Montaner building, has a

permanent collection of work by Tàpies as well as high-quality contemporary exhibitions.

Tàpies is "deeply committed to pluralism and diversity" in art, a fact that is reflected by the exhibitions and the library – accessible to scholars by appointment only. The first thing to strike you when you arrive at the building is the mass of metal wires on the roof. This work, entitled "Cloud and Chair", is Tàpies's emblem for the building.

A dirty aesthetic

During the repression under Franco, when all Catalan culture was effectively illegal, methods of expression were forced to become

MIRÓ AND THE SURREALISTS

An apocryphal story about Miró tells of how, in his desperation to be considered a member of the Surrealist group, he went about trying to get himself arrested – the surest way to attain credibility among his peers. Although he was peaceful by nature, Miró summoned up the courage to walk around the streets of Paris shouting: "Down with the Mediterranean!".

Miró was invoking the Mediterranean in its symbolic role as the cradle of Western civilisation, but his choice of words was ironic given the importance of Mediterranean light and colour in his work. Of course, no one arrested him and the rest of the group scorned his efforts.

FAR LEFT: detail of a Nativity frieze designed by Picasso but executed by Norwegian Carl Nesjar, on the exterior of the Col·legi d'Arquitectes, Plaça Nova. **LEFT:** a Miró sculpture in one of the Fundació's patios. **RIGHT:** *Núvol i Cadira* (Cloud and Chair) by Tàpies.

highly creative. In 1948 the Dau al Set (Dice on Seven) group was set up, with members Tàpies, Tharrats, Cuixart, Ponç, Puig and Brossa. The "visual poems" of Joan Brossa, a long-neglected, now deceased Catalan artist-poet, have been at the forefront of recent Catalan art – in his seventies Brossa represented Spain at the Venice Biennale (with Valencian Carmen Calvo). Given the political climate it made sense for these artists, fascinated by magic, alchemy, the writings of medieval Catalan mystic Ramon Llull and surrealism, to resort to codes to veil their messages.

Catalan artists also employed street graffiti to voice dissent. The use of signs and symbols,

already seen in Miró's painting, emerged in Tàpies's work. In keeping with the international Arte Povera and Art Autre (Informal Art) movements, Catalan Informalism combines existentialist ideas with simple materials to produce the so-called "dirty aesthetic". This aesthetic still reigns in Barcelona, and materials such as wax, marble dust and varnish are prevalent. If you visit the Joan Prats Gallery in Rambla de Catalunya you will find representative work from contemporary and older-generation artists. Or try Consell de Cent, the commercial-gallery street round the corner from the Fundació Tàpies.

The art scene today

The Informalist legacy is tempered by Catalan Conceptualism nowadays, as represented in the Museu d'Art Contemporani's (MACBA) permanent collection. There is also work from the Dau al Set group, and the bed-piece hanging at the entrance is, of course, by Tàpies.

There have been changes in the directorship of the museum since its opening in 1995 – the collection was deemed to be outdated and the shows too esoteric, although there have been some huge successes, such as Miguel Barceló's retrospective. This youngish Mallorcan painter now carries the torch for art in Barcelona. His stays in Mali, West Africa, have produced some epic "relief" paintings. If you visit the theatre at the Mercat de les Flors and look up at the ceiling you will be able to get some idea of Barceló's vision.

Pere Jaume's panoramic exhibition brought in the crowds, as well. His work is great fun,

THE PHENOMENON OF STREET ART

Street art is prevalent in all areas of the city, thanks to the initiatives in the 1990s to create new parks and urban spaces. Eduardo Chillida's heavyweight sculpture, *Elogi de l'Aigua*, in the Parc Creueta de Coll is a fine example. Artist-poet Joan Brossa is ever-present in the city: his giant-sized letters are scattered about the Passeig Vall - d'Hebron, and his bronze tribute to "Barcino" (the Roman name for Barcelona) is set in front of the cathedral.

In the Passeig Picasso, Tàpies pays homage to his idol with a large glass cube containing planks, a piano and painted blankets. The cube itself was designed by the great-grandson of Lluís Domènech i Montaner.

On the beach at Barceloneta is Rebecca Horn's reminder of the original beach huts and restaurants which were torn down to make way for the new waterfront development. Models of the huts, cast in bronze and lit like beacons from within, lie piled one on top of the other.

Also down by the port is Lichtenstein's *Head*, just in front of the main post office. This massive piece uses Gaudí's technique of setting broken pieces of ceramic into cement to impressive effect, but was originally intended to be placed in the Parc de Collserola so that it could be viewed from a distance. In its present location it rather towers above onlookers on the street below.

neatly fusing questions of representational art and how to frame it. This theme is on permanent display in the new ceiling of the Gran Teatre del Liceu, rebuilt and reopened in October 1999, after a fire five years earlier .

Susana Solano, another internationally known Catalan artist, finally gained an ample retrospective of her enigmatic metal constructions here in the late 1990s. Other artists representative of established trends include painters Xavier Grau, Ràfols-Casamada, Hernàndez-Pijuan and Grau Garriga. Artists producing work in multi-disciplinary techniques include Carlos Pazos, José Manuel Broto, José María Sevilla and Sergi Aguilar.

restored building offers a fabulous opportunity to marvel at Catalonia's wealth of Gothic and Romanesque painting and sculpture. Many of these items, which include sections of medieval wall-paintings and carved beams, were removed from the region's churches and monasteries amid much protest and cries of desecration, but, had they been left *in situ*, they may have crumbled away completely.

In a bid to collect all Catalan art under one roof, the pieces in the former Museu d'Art Modern were transferred here in 2004, including important works by Ramón Casas, Santiago Rusiñol and other major *modernista* artists from the late 19th and early 20th centuries.

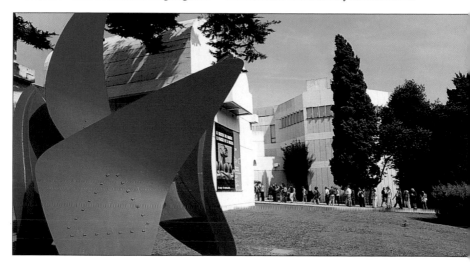

The Museu d'Art Contemporani is right next door to the Centre de Cultura Contemporània de Barcelona (CCCB). This labyrinthine building was set up as a force for social, urban and cultural development, promoting shows on themes as diverse as Pessoa's Lisbon, Kafka's Prague, and the Cosmos.

Preserving the past

On Montjuïc hill, not far from the Miró Foundation, the Museu Nacional d'Art de Catalunya (MNAC) is unmissable. The recently

LEFT: interior of the CaixaForum exhibition space.
ABOVE: the Fundació Miró

Another delight is the Thyssen-Bornemisza collection. The majority of the collection is housed in Madrid, but a substantial part is exhibited in the Museu Nacional d'Art de Catalunya *(see page 147)*. It contains some wonderful pieces of medieval sculpture, and paintings by Florentine Renaissance artists, among which are the exquisite tempera panels of St Claire and St Catherine. The 16th century is best represented by the works of Titian and Tintoretto, and the northern Europeans by Lucas Cranach. Outstanding among the European baroque works in this collection is the enormous *Christ on the Cross*, by the Spanish artist Zurburán (1598–1664). ❑

DESIGNER CITY

In Barcelona your whole day is likely to be a designer experience, from breakfast in your designer-hotel to dinner in a designer-restaurant via shops and museums that have had the designer treatment

Buying the greens in your local market in Barcelona can be a designer-experience, going to pay your dues in the Town Hall as well, and, if you have the misfortune to need attention in the Hospital del Mar, console yourself with the fact you are walking into a carefully planned architectural space where designer-seats in the waiting room offer views over the designer-promenade that looks onto landscaped beaches where even the showers have the stamp of a well-known designer. Exaggeration? Well, no, because this is the city which brought the world the most striking Olympic Games in modern times. This is the city where design forms part of daily life.

The great boom in design that swept through Barcelona in the 1980s following Franco's death and the ensuing liberation of ideas is legendary. Fuelled by the challenge of preparing for the Olympics it forms the basis of contemporary Barcelona. But innovative design has never been an alien concept in Catalonia, a society that has always striven to represent its own individualism to the world. Catalan Gothic stood out from other Gothic architecture in Europe in the 14th century. As Robert Hughes comments: "Catalan architects did not want to imitate the organic profusion of detail in northern Gothic. They liked a wall." Similarly, with *modernisme*, Catalonia had its own particular take on the art nouveau movement in Europe. The extraordinary creativity of Gaudí was an extreme case for any society to accept, yet it was the bourgeois industrialists who became his patrons and had their homes built by him. They had their designer-hospital

too, thanks to Domènech i Montaner who designed the revolutionary Hospital de la Santa Creu i Sant Pau, still in use today.

Since "designer-bars" like Nick Havanna and Torres de Avila made their impact in the 1980s and architectural magazines began to talk of Barcelona's urban spaces, the design movement filtered down to street level. It is particularly noticeable in the public sector, where the authorities have been keen to support local talent, to say nothing of its enhancement of Barcelona's image abroad. Street furniture is designed by the likes of Oscar Tusquets, and drinking fountains by the Santa & Coles design group. The city markets are being given multimillion euro facelifts: the most famous, La Boqueria in La Rambla, has been renovated to improve its structure, but not without the due designer-elements in its facade, its stalls and administrative offices. Meanwhile, the Mercat Santa Caterina has been overhauled to form part of a whole urban scheme, including housing. Designed by the late Enric Miralles, of Scottish Parliament fame, and Benedetta Tagliabue his widow, it provides a backdrop to the bustle of daily gossip and shopping trolleys.

The same is true of the Hospital del Mar, a public-health hospital whose catchment area is one of the most needy in Barcelona. Amidst scenes of hardship and suffering one is struck

while restaurants with starched tablecloths and serious waiters were patronised by day. Nowadays visitors swarm in for a sophisticated blend of culture and commerce. The hand luggage on return flights is a walking advertisement for Zara, Mango and Camper. Impersonal chain hotels are snubbed for new boutique hotels like Omm, Neri and Banys Orientals.

Neighbourhoods in the Old Town are being transformed. Where once the Born was visited for the Picasso Museum and the church of Santa Maria del Mar, it is now visited for its exclusive fashion boutiques, stylish wine bars and world-class restaurants. El Raval, once known for its Barri Xino, is next in line for the

by the Mediterranean light filtering through skylights, the spaces, the outlook on the sea and the healthy breezes sweeping through the forecourt where patients stroll.

A change of image

There was a time when visitors used to be attracted to Barcelona for its fascinating mix of Mediterranean culture and the kind of decadence that comes from being a major port. Bars selling absinthe and seedy cabarets plying porn in the Barri Xino were sought out by night,

designer treatment. Already home to the Contemporary Art Museum and CCCB (Centre for Contemporary Culture) to say nothing of the FAD (El Foment de les Arts Decoratives), an organisation promoting architecture, design and image located in a Gothic convent, it is sprouting new galleries, boutiques, restaurants and hotels. It remains to be seen whether the balance will be kept between these and local groceries and cobblers. The designer- city has its attractions and its pursuit is undeniably in the Catalan genes, but may the characteristics of this Mediterranean city that give it its colour and charm never be totally extinguished. ❑

LEFT: Vinçon, high temple of interior design.
ABOVE: the street, *c'est chic*, in the Born.

A PASSION FOR FOOD

In Barcelona you will find some of the best food in Spain. An abundance of fresh fish, superb meat and cheese, a cornucopia of great vegetables, plus Catalan inventiveness have produced a distinctive and delicious cuisine

No one should visit Barcelona without making some attempt to get to know Catalan food. The experience would be incomplete otherwise, and any assessment of its people merely superficial. Eating is an important part of Catalan culture, something to be valued, taken seriously and enjoyed to the full, in true Catalan style.

The acerbic political commentator, eminent writer and novelist Manuel Vázquez Montalbán was passionate about food; he bestowed a certain grace on any restaurant where he chose to eat. In his opinion, "Catalan cooking is one of the most distinguishing signs of the national identity." It is also a composite of the nation's past, embodying the many influences of the different peoples and cultures that have swept through, settled in or bordered Catalonia, to say nothing of the lands dominated by Catalonia over its millennial history. The original fusion food, perhaps.

Nature's bounty

Catalan cooking is also a reflection of the geographical and physical characteristics of the country. Many dishes are based on the nuts, garlic, olive oil, tomatoes, herbs and dried fruits indigenous to these lands. Catalans are justifiably proud that their country can offer miles of rugged coastline and sheltered beaches, as well as awesome mountain ranges and rich valleys, and all within easy reach of each other.

LEFT: great seafood restaurants abound.
RIGHT: locals love to eat outside in summer.

Similarly, the cooking combines the natural products of the sea, the fertile plains and the mountains in a style known as *mar i muntanya* (sea and mountains). It makes for strange-sounding, though delicious, marriages on the menu, such as *mandonguilles amb sèpia* (meatballs with cuttlefish), or *gambes amb pollastre* (prawns with chicken).

The Mediterranean diet is almost a cliché these days, and a selling point in many an advertising campaign, but here it still exists in its pure unadulterated form. One of the most famous Catalan dishes is perhaps the most simple, yet one of the best: the ubiquitous *pa amb tomàquet*. This fresh peasant bread rubbed with tomato, a trickle of virgin olive oil and a pinch of salt is the Mediterranean answer to northern Europe's thinly sliced bread and butter, and not surprisingly provokes a certain amount of southern pride. A delicious accompaniment to meals, it can be eaten as a snack served with anchovies, cured meats or cheese.

Getting to know Catalan food is hardly a chore. Along with Basque cooking, its reputation ranks highest in Spain. And with nearly 3,000 restaurants in Barcelona, choice is not a problem. Sightseeing and museum visiting both can and should be interrupted to recharge the batteries and experience the culinary offerings of the city.

Do as the locals do

Try and adapt to local timing to get the best results: have breakfast when Barcelonans do, lunch with them, even have "tea" with the old ladies and children, and then you will easily be able to wait until after 9pm for dinner.

Breakfast veers wildly from being a dull, cursory affair of milky coffee and biscuits, to a full-blooded *esmorzar de forquilla* (fork breakfast), which is a mid-morning meal of hearty dishes like pigs' trotters and bean stews. This is more of a rural market-town tradition, not meant for an efficient morning in the office. It is common, though, to have a large ham sandwich or wedge of traditional Spanish

PASTRY HEAVEN

In Barcelona the number of pastry shops per square metre must rank among the world's highest. For each feast day and festival there is a corresponding traditional sweetmeat: *bunyols* (a small doughnut) during Lent, *la mona* (a sort of brioche, often with fancy decorations) for Easter, *panellets* (little marzipan cakes decorated with pine nuts) for All Saints and for *castanyades* (autumnal parties centred on roasting chestnuts). Throughout the long summer months the different neighbourhood and village feast days are celebrated with an abundance of fireworks, *cava* and *cocas* (pastries covered in sugar, crystallised fruits and pine nuts).

omelette (*truita* in Catalan, *tortilla* in Spanish) with a glass of wine around 10am, and to chase the morning coffee with a *conyac*. For the faint-hearted, bars and cafés serve good *cafè amb llet* (large coffee with milk), *tallat* (a shorter version) or *cafè sol* (small, black and intense) with a range of pastries or croissants.

Visitors can indulge in what is more of a weekend treat for residents: an aperitif around 1pm. This consists of a drink such as red vermouth, often with soda, served with olives and other *tapes* (snacks) like *boquerones* (pickled anchovies) or tinned *berberechos* (cockles). The temptation to turn this into a light lunch is where visitors often lose the local rhythm.

The advantages of conforming and having a lunch (*dinar*) are manifold: the food has just arrived from the market and is at its best; it can be slept or walked off; the whole city is tuned in to lunch – a sacred quiet descends, especially on Sunday; and most offices, shops and museums are closed until 4 or 5pm.

Peak lunchtime is 2pm, lingering on to 4pm or even later at weekends – although there is a danger of not being served after 3.30pm. Lunch is also the most economical meal, when nearly every restaurant has a *menú del dia* (set menu). Even the most basic of these offers a choice of starters (soup, salad, or vegetables), a main course of meat or fish, a dessert and

Local specialities

Look out for *menús* that include any of the following: as starters, *arròs negre*, black rice, a more interesting version of paella made with squid and its ink; *escalivada*, grilled peppers and aubergines dressed with oil; *esqueixada*, salad of raw salt cod, onions and peppers; *Xató*, a salad from Sitges of frisée lettuce with tuna, salt cod, anchovies and a *romesco* sauce; *espinacs a la Catalana,* spinach sautéed with raisins and pine nuts; *faves a la Catalana*, small broad beans stewed with herbs and pork and sausage meats (best in spring); *canalons*, a Catalan tradition brought from Italy, always eaten on 26 December; *fideuà,* an excellent

wine, beer or a soft drink. Obviously the standard and the price vary, but for around €7 or €8 (£5–5.50 or US$8.50–10) you can expect an excellent, balanced meal.

Sauces may be rich but can be outweighed by a crisp fresh salad and fruit to follow. The option of simple grilled fish or meat, garnished with a *picada* of garlic and parsley is hard to equal, especially when accompanied by *allioli* (a strong garlic mayonnaise which is also served with rice dishes).

LEFT: tempting choices in Mauri, on the corner of Provença and Rambla de Catalunya, the Eixample.
ABOVE: Bar del Pi, in the Barri Gòtic.

and lesser known variation on paella, noodles cooked in a fish stock; and a strictly winter dish, *escudella*, the most traditional Catalan soup, usually followed by *carn d'olla*, that is, the meat and vegetables that have been cooked to make the soup. Now a traditional Christmas dish, this used to be part of the staple diet of every Catalan household.

Among the main courses, be sure to try the very Catalan *botifarra amb mongetes*, a tasty sausage served with haricot beans; *fricandó*, braised veal with *moixernons*, a small, delicate wild mushroom; *bacallà*, salt cod served in many ways such as *a la llauna* (garlic, parsley and tomato) or *amb xamfaina* (tomato, pepper and aubergine sauce, also served with meat); s*uquet,* a seafood stew; *calamars farcits,* stuffed squid; *oca amb naps,* goose with turnip; *conill,* rabbit, either grilled and served with *allioli,* or stewed; *xai,* lamb – the cutlets *(costelletes)* are especially good.

Fish *(peix)* and shellfish *(marisc)* should not be missed in Barcelona: the simplest and perhaps the best way is grilled (a mixed grill, *graellada,* is a good option for two) or done in the oven, *al forn.* It is worth going to a good restaurant for a paella; cheap imitations are usually disappointing.

If you have any room for dessert, don't miss

OCTOBER HARVEST

October is a great time to be in Barcelona, because it's mushroom season, when fans of wild fungi will be in their element. The market stalls are rich in autumnal colours and the smell of damp woods is intoxicating. The generic name for the various wild mushrooms is *bolets.* *Rovelló* is one of the best, especially just grilled with garlic and parsley, but also delicious in stewed meat dishes at this time of the year. For the best range of fresh, dried (or, if need be, frozen) mushrooms, and unusual fresh herbs, go to Petras, Fruits del Bosc, at the very back of La Boqueria market. Ignore the arrogant service and enjoy the superior products.

the famous *crema catalana,* a cinnamon-flavoured custard with a burnt caramel top. Other traditional *postres* include *mel i mató,* a curd cheese with honey; *postre de músic,* a mixture of roast nuts and dried fruits, usually served with a glass of sweet *moscatel;* and *macedonia* (fruit salad).

The advantage of the light-lunch option is being able to face a *berenar* (afternoon snack). From around 5 to 7.30pm *granjes* (milk bars) overflow as people manage to drink extremely thick chocolate (the authentic version is made with water and needs to be "drunk" with a spoon) and very creamy cakes. For a classic *berenar* try the cafés around the Plaça del Pi, especially in Petritxol, or sit at a marble table in the Granja M.Viader in Xuclà, the oldest *granja* in Barcelona, where *cacaolat* (a children's favourite) was invented.

Shops and offices are open until 8 or 9pm, so family dinner is around 10pm, and is usually quite light: soup and an omelette, for example. Restaurants serving dinner before 9pm are probably oriented towards tourists and best avoided. Restaurants do not usually have a set menu at night, so eating out can be more expensive than at midday. If you've had a good lunch, this is the ideal time to "do *tapes*" – visit several bars for a glass of wine and a snack in each.

The *tapes* tradition

Although it's not originally a Catalan tradition, there are nevertheless many bars offering *tapes,* including a new wave of Basque bars, and some Catalan ones that specialise in *torrades* (large slices of toast) with which you can make your own *pa amb tomàquet* and request different toppings. Choose with care, especially with mayonnaise-based dishes in the summer. A delicious, safe bet is *pernil salada* or *jamón serrano* (respectively, the Catalan and Spanish words for cured ham cut from the bone – *Jabugo* is the best), *llonganissa, fuet* (spicy sausages) or cheese (try *manchego seco* for a strong flavour, *cabrales,* a potent blue cheese from Asturias wrapped in vine leaves, or *cabra,* goat's cheese).

Other favourites are chunks of *tortilla* or *truita,* Spanish style omelettes, which may be *española* (potatoes and onions); *espinacas* (spinach); *payés* (mixed vegetables); *ajos tier-*

nos (young tender garlic). *Francesa* is the classic French omelette without a filling. Incidentally, you should be careful with the Catalan word *truita*, as it means trout as well as omelette. *Patatas bravas* – fried or oven-baked potatoes with a hot spicy sauce – or garlic mayonnaise; *ensaladilla*, Russian salad, with potatoes, vegetables and mayonnaise; *pescaditos*, small fried fish; *pulpo*, octopus, a speciality from Galicia.

International influences

Apart from these traditional dishes, the creative spectrum is broadening into many variations on the basic Catalan theme, in *tapes*

the market, introducing ingredients from other countries into Catalan dishes, and adding a strong dash of *"amor y arte"*. His artichoke soup with lime-and-black-pepper ice cream and Palamos prawns won a prize among young chefs in Spain. He is not afraid to defy convention in any way: in his restaurant Ot, in Gràcia, customers are given no choice about what they eat, yet they flock to its doors.

As an increasingly cosmopolitan capital, Barcelona has a broad range of restaurants that reflect the tastes and demands of its inhabitants. There are restaurants from other regions of Spain, particularly Galicia, from top-notch,

and main dishes. There is a new generation of chefs, seemingly inspired by internationally renowned Ferran Adrià of the expensive and heavily pre-booked El Bullí restaurant on the Costa Brava. Their rebellious spirit, combined with the essential Catalan love of food and passion for the Mediterranean, is a formula that makes for exciting results.

Chef Felip Planas would look more at home at a heavy metal concert than in a kitchen, yet he waxes lyrical about cooking. He experiments with whatever is available in

top-price Botafumeiro with fine oysters and fish, to the average corner bar. And then there are French, Italian, Greek, Lebanese, Mexican, South American, Indian, Pakistani, Chinese and Japanese, and a growing number of vastly improved vegetarian restaurants – vegetarians used to have a hard time in Spain, but this, too, is changing. There really is no excuse to resort to one of the fast-food outlets insidiously taking root in some of the most historic streets and squares of the city – the latest, inevitable, sign of cultural colonisation. So get out there, make new discoveries, and immerse yourself in local culture in one of the most enjoyable ways possible. ❏

LEFT: autumn bounty in La Boqueria market.
ABOVE: *tapes*, an adopted tradition.

WINE

The reputation of Spanish wine has changed enormously in recent years, and Catalonia is one of the regions that is now attracting attention from international connoisseurs as well as visitors with a taste for the good things in life

There was a time when Spanish wine meant plonk, sangria was associated with packaged holidays on the Costas, and the only Spanish vintage to have any international acclaim was Rioja. Today, these misconceptions are in the past, and anyone who believes in the importance of accompanying good food with a decent glass of wine will be aware that Spain has many different wine-growing regions, producing a range of interesting and increasingly high-quality wines.

One of these is Catalonia, which itself has nine wine regions officially classified as D.O. (*Denominació d'Origen*, similar to the French *appellation contrôlée*): **Empordà-Costa Brava**, near the French border; **Alella**, on the outskirts of Barcelona in the Maresme, a tiny area known for its white wines; the well-known **Penedès**, to the south-west of Barcelona; the most recent, **Pla de Bages**, near Manresa; **Conca de Barberà**, with its *modernista* wine cellars, in the province of Tarragona; **Costers del Segre**, home of Raimat wines, to the west in Lleida; and **Tarragona**, **Terra Alta** and the **Priorat** with terraced vineyards on steep hillsides in the south.

With over 68,000 hectares (178,000 acres) of vineyards, the Catalan wine industry is one of the most important in Spain, yielding twice as much wine annually (350 million litres) as La Rioja. In a bid for stronger identity in the international market, a recent controversial move by the large companies backed by the Generalitat (Catalan autonomous government) to introduce a denomination for the region as a whole, D.O. Catalunya, has been successful. The smaller denominations will continue to exist within this framework.

The Catalan region with the highest profile abroad is the Penedès, mostly due to the giant Torres, a family firm in Vilafranca del Penedès that exports wine to more than 90 countries, has vineyards in Chile and California and is held in high esteem in the wine world. With the sixth generation of the family now in the business, they continue to produce award-winning wines, like Gran Coronas Black Label, Fransola, Gran Viña Sol and Viña Esmeralda. The Penedès is also the largest region (26,400 hectares/65,990 acres) where about 100 companies produce 65 million litres of still wine annually. And that's not including the *cava*.

In the last few years there has been a lot of activity in regions that were previously lesser-known, and among the smaller bodegas across Catalonia, with experimentation, new techniques, introduction of different grape varieties and maximising of the indigenous grapes like *xarel·lo* and *macabeo* (white), and *carinyena, garnatxa* and *monastrell* reds. It is reflected in improved quality, and some notable wines are emerging.

A visit to Barcelona is the perfect opportunity to taste some lesser-known wines from different regions, which are probably not available in the large supermarkets back home, but which are increasingly gaining prestige and respect amongst oenologists. In a restaurant the house wine *(vi de la casa)* may be good. It is often a young wine, or in rural areas a strong, dark-red country wine.

Up-and-coming labels

One of the most fascinating areas is the Priorat, which is experiencing a boom after years of neglect. It was traditionally known for the cheapest, strongest wines bought from barrels in the dark bodegas of Barcelona, but its wines are now demanding the highest prices. Large companies from La Rioja and the Penedès have started working there, and some highly prized wines are emerging from its low-yield, high-alcohol-content grapes. International wine buffs are paying attention, and there has been an influx of visitors to the previously neglected villages. The region feels remote, but it is only a couple of hours from Barcelona and makes a wonderful weekend excursion.

Along with Priorat wines, some recent labels from Conca de Barberà are now found in the highest price range too. **La Ermita**, from Riojan winemaker Alvaro Palacios, who started working in the Priorat in the early 1990s, retails at £100 (US$160). Other wines to look out for, not necessarily so highly priced, are **Cervoles**, a red from Costers del Segre, **Can Rafols dels Caus**, **Can Feixes**, and the ecological wines **Albet i Noia** from the Penedès, and from another up-and-coming

area, the Empordà, where new wines are being developed. Watch out for **Oliver Conti**.

Catalans are proud of their wine but not over-serious about it. They do like to accompany a well-cooked meal with a wine that does it justice, yet it could easily be a simple, home-grown country wine. At family gatherings you may still see the *porró* in use (a glass carafe with a spout, used for communal drinking). Don't be surprised if the red wine is served chilled in summer. Whatever your view on this practice, there is no doubt that the recent burgeoning of the industry is driven by an increasingly discerning home market as well as by international market demands. ❏

THE CORDONIU EMPIRE

Ninety-five percent of Spain's *cava* is produced in Catalonia and the greater part from the Penedès, where it was created by Josep Raventós in 1872. From that celebrated first bottle grew the Codorníu empire, which shares with Freixenet the title of undisputed leader of the *cava* industry. This sparkling wine, made by the *méthode champenoise*, is obligatory at fiestas and a ubiquitous companion to Sunday lunch (it is usually served with dessert). Regarded as one of the world's great sparkling wines, *cava* is warmer, earthier and less acid than Champagne *(see pages 192–193)*.

LEFT: vineyard in the Penedès region, Catalonia's chief wine-producing area.
RIGHT: winebar in the Barri Gòtic.

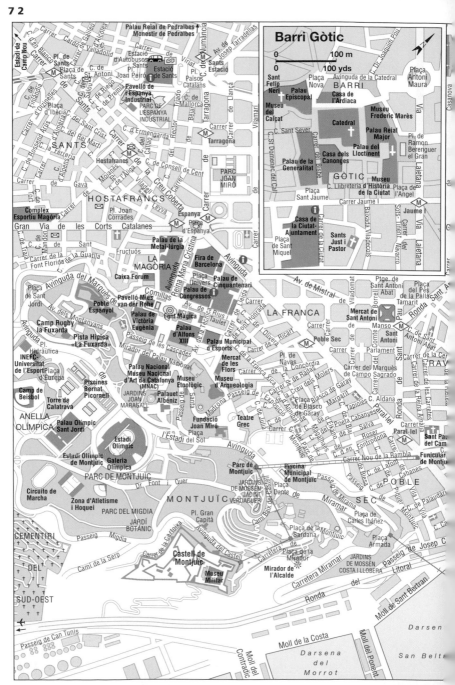

Barri Gòtic

0 — 100 m
0 — 100 yds

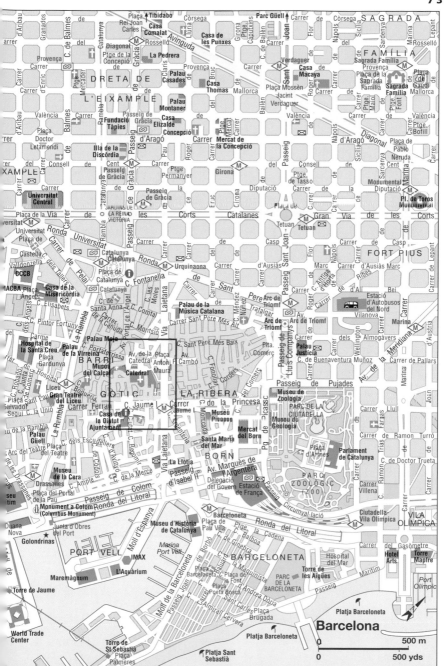

Barcelona

| 0 | | 500 m |
| 0 | | 500 yds |

PLACES

A detailed guide to the entire city, with principal sites
clearly cross-referenced by number to the maps

Barcelona is everything you have ever heard about: Gaudí and the Sagrada Família, *modernisme* and contemporary design, Olympic achievements, nightlife, thrusting Catalans and Mediterranean quality of life. But it is a lot more besides. The Places section will guide you through itineraries that go beyond the main tourist attractions (though by no means overlooking them) in an attempt to get closer to real life on the streets of this dynamic city.

The geography of Barcelona is easily fathomed. If you can get to one of its high points early in your visit – Montjuïc, Tibidabo, the Park Güell, or even Columbus's column – it will put the city into focus. It is not surprising that this is one of the world's densest cities (15,230 inhabitants per square kilometre): packed in between the Collserola range of hills and the Mediterranean, and bordered by Montjuïc and the River Besòs, all the available space has been consumed. Parks tend to be in rocky knolls where no building could have been erected, or created latterly in disused industrial spaces. The latest developments are centred on the sea, with planned extensions to the port and the reclaiming of land by the Diagonal Mar.

Plaça de Catalunya is a good place to get one's bearings. From this crossroads between the old town, the **Ciutat Vella**, and the new town, the 19th-century **Eixample**, it is easy to get a sense of place and history. The old town, containing most of the city's historical landmarks, is divided into the **Barri Gòtic**, **La Ribera** and **El Raval**. The Barri Gòtic (Gothic Quarter) is in the middle, bordered by **La Rambla** and **Via Laietana**; La Ribera is the district of medieval mansions on the other side of Via Laietana, and El Raval lies on the other side of La Rambla, where convents turned cultural centres rub shoulders with the notorious **Barri Xino**.

Plaça de Catalunya, like an all-encompassing terminal, is also a good departure point for most excursions. Airport buses and trains arrive there, buses to most parts of town and beyond can be caught on one of its sides, two metro lines run through it and the FGC trains to the Parc de Collserola leave from here. Even trains to the coast and the mountains depart from beneath this central square. ❏

PREVIOUS PAGES: night view of La Pedrera; corner of Carrer de Mallorca and Passeig de Gràcia. **LEFT:** view towards the Torre Agbar from the top of the Sagrada Família.

PLAÇA DE CATALUNYA AND LA RAMBLA

The life and pulse of the city are perfectly reflected in the spectacle and colour of the celebrated promenade leading from Plaça Catalunya down to the waterfront

At the northern limit of La Rambla, **Plaça de Catalunya ❶** is not the kind of picturesque square that you might make an effort to visit, but it *is* the kind of place you inevitably do visit on any trip to Barcelona. Whether arriving from the airport by bus or train, coming into the city from other parts of Catalonia, visiting the Old Town from uptown or vice versa, Plaça de Catalunya is bound to be part of the trajectory. It is more of a pivotal *plaça,* acting as a logistical centre for the city's transport.

From the top

Here you'll find the metro underground train service; FGC trains (the Ferrocarrils de la Generalitat de Catalunya, which run to uptown areas and the suburbs); RENFE trains; public and privately run buses like the Tombús; and tourist coaches and taxis. A world of underground corridors, confusing and exhausting to start with, leads to the trains, so allow time when travelling. The main Barcelona city tourist office is also here, marked by a tall "i" above ground. Run by the tourist board, it offers an efficient and helpful service, dishing out leaflets, maps and all kinds of information, as well as operating a hotel reservation service, money exchange

and an Internet connection. For many, Plaça de Catalunya also marks the beginning of another inevitability in Barcelona: a walk down the famous avenue of **La Rambla**.

Before embarking on that flow of humanity down to the sea, pause a moment in the welcome shade of Plaça de Catalunya's trees, or in the bright winter sunshine that fills it with a light and warmth which barely reaches the narrowest of the Old Town streets. As well as being the hub of Barcelona in terms of transport

Map on page 78

LEFT: Plaça de Catalunya.
BELOW: *La Deesa* (Goddess) by Josep Llimona on the Plaça de Catalunya.

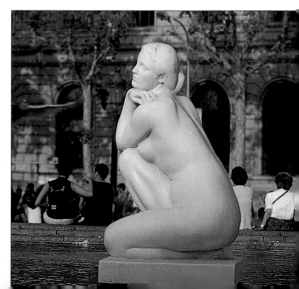

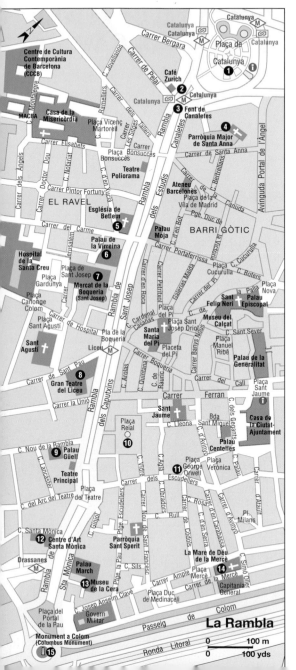

and city communications, this *plaça* is the centre of the city in a wider sense: if you look in the middle of the square itself you'll find paving stones arranged into the shape of a star which, they say, marks the centre of the capital of Catalonia.

Pigeons flock here to be fed by children and old ladies. Tacky stalls sell plastic toys and caramelised nuts. Families wander around aimlessly, lovers meet beneath the gushing fountains and predatory youths lurk, with an eye on swinging handbags and cameras. On the newly paved and urbanised outer rim, men gather to play chess beneath the monument to a much-loved Catalan leader, Macià, designed by contemporary sculptor Subirachs, accompanied by electronic Andean pipes relentlessly churning out the "Sound of Silence", making you yearn for the real silence of the *altiplano*.

But the square is more of a created centre than one with a real Catalan heart. Consider its history. When the medieval wall of Barcelona was demolished in 1854 to extend the city by making a new district, the **Eixample**, the *plaça* was a large field outside the city, traversed by a mountain stream (the stream bed later formed the foundations of La Rambla) and connected to the inner city by means of an entrance called the Portal dels Orbs. The entrance was later renamed the **Portal de l'Angel** because, so the story goes, when Sant Ferrer crossed through this doorway with his followers, he was greeted by an angel. The 19th-century Plan Cerdà, a project for the redevelopment of Barcelona, called for the creation of a square a little further inland, at the junction of **Passeig de Gràcia** and the **Gran Via**.

Another rival project presented by Antoni Rovira i Trías proposed an enormous *plaça*, 800 by 400 metres (2,600 by 1,300 ft) to be called the

"Forum Isabel II". Yet another plan for a *plaça* similar to that which we know today was designed in 1868 by Miquel Garriga.

While the authorities were trying to reach an agreement, the owners of the corresponding plots of land got fed up with waiting and began to build. In 1902, Lord Mayor Ledesma ordered the demolition of all these buildings, but it was another quarter of a century before the *plaça* took on its current appearance. Based on a design by Francesc Nebot, the square was officially opened by King Alfonso XIII in 1927.

Ever since this uneasy birth, the winds of change have swept through the square, taking away any vestiges of nostalgia and tradition. Now it is bordered by banks and giant shopping institutions that seem to have been transplanted from Madrid and elsewhere like some kind of late-20th-century colonisation. On the corner now dominated by the Hard Rock Café and Sfera, part of the El Corte Inglés empire, stood the almost mythical Maison Dorée café. Such was the character of this establishment that, when it closed its doors in 1918, another café of the same name opened at No. 6. "It was never the same," wrote Lluís Permanyer, city historian, who relates that it was here that a tradition of "five o'clock tea" was introduced to Barcelona.

Another meeting point of intellectuals was the old Hotel Colón, which has since become the headquarters of the Banco Español de Crédito (Banesto). Older generations of Republicans remember when the facade of the hotel was covered in portraits during the Civil War. With giant posters of Marx, Lenin and Stalin, there was no mistaking that this was the headquarters of the Unified Socialist Party of Catalonia (PSUC), then the leading socialist group.

Shopping emporia

It's difficult to miss the monumental department store **El Corte Inglés**, which has now taken over the whole of the northern side, and has a new branch in the former Marks & Spencer. The store is so named ("The English Cut") because its distant origins lie in a humble Madrid tailor's shop, a far cry from today's exhausting air-conditioned expanse of goods and madding crowds. On the opposite side, where a broad new pavement makes a tenuous link between La Rambla and **Rambla de Catalunya**, two other favourites, the Cine Vergara and the Café Zurich were subsumed into what is now **El Triangle**, a large commercial centre redeemed, perhaps, by the **FNAC**, several slick floors of books, music and technology and a *quiosc* on the ground floor with a vast range of magazines.

At the point of the "triangle" where **Pelai** meets the top of La Rambla is **Café Zurich ❷**, a new replica of the original café on the same spot. Thanks to its vantage point at a busy crossroads, and with

El Corte Inglés, Spain's favourite department store, has several branches in Barcelona.

Map on page 78

BELOW: sunflowers and sunshine on La Rambla.

The terrace of Café Zurich at the top of La Rambla is a great place to observe the passing scene.

BELOW: La Rambla follows the course of an old river bed that marked the limits of the city under Jaume I.

the same old bad-tempered waiters, it may yet take on the persona of the former landmark.

Whether you are seated on the Café Zurich's terrace, or emerging blinking from the Metro exit at the top of La Rambla, contemplate the panorama ahead. This is La Rambla, one of the most famous boulevards in Europe, and for many one of the distinguishing features of Barcelona. This kaleidoscopic avenue throbs day and night, exerting an undeniable magnetism which attracts both visitors and locals, and which never fails to entertain.

The best advice is to plunge in, go with the flow and enjoy the constant weird and wonderful activity all around you. Let yourself be carried past lottery ticket booths, shoe shiners, cheap *pensions,* human statues, northern Europeans in shorts in December, and locals in sharp suits. Let your senses be assailed by the squawking of caged birds, the perfumed air of the flower stalls, the chatter of the gossips and the shrieks of the lads delivering fruit to the market. Don't miss a thing,

especially the ubiquitous pickpockets who inevitably prey on such a bountiful crowd. Being aware and strapping cameras and bags tightly to your body is usually enough to deter thieves.

River to road

Originally, La Rambla was the river bed (the Latin name *arenno* was replaced by the Arab word *ramla*) that marked the exterior limits of the city fortified by King Jaume I. But when the city expanded during the 15th century, La Rambla became part of the inner city.

In due course, a number of religious houses were built throughout the surrounding areas and the river bed came to be known as the "Convent Thoroughfare". It was not until the beginning of the 18th century that La Rambla became a more clearly defined street, after permission was granted to build on the ancient walls in the Boqueria area. In 1775 a section of the city walls was torn down and a central walkway built, lined with poplar trees and higher than the roadway that ran along either side.

Within the small and densely populated area of the ancient fortified city, La Rambla was the only street of any significance, and it became the city's focal point. Renovations were constantly under way during the 19th century, and the street settled down to become more exclusive and aristocratic; this change of status was aided by the disappearance of some of the surrounding buildings and convents, creating space for new squares and mansions.

La Rambla assumed its present shape between 1849 and 1856 when all the remaining fortifications were torn down. The first plane trees, brought from Devesa in Girona, were planted in 1851, and the street became "the fashionable promenade route, where the cream of Barcelona

Map on page 78

parades on foot, by carriage or on horseback", according to the 19th-century journalist Gaziel. Today's promenaders are more mixed and much more cosmopolitan, though the "cream" can still be spotted wrapped in furs on their way to the opera at the Liceu. Since the prettification of the Old Town in the 1990s, more uptown residents are now venturing down to these "picturesque" parts.

Between the top of La Rambla and the Columbus monument where it ends there are five different parts to the promenade. The first, **Rambla de Canaletes**, is named after the **Font de Canaletes** ❸, one of the symbols of Barcelona. A small brass plaque at the foot of this 19th-century cast-iron fountain confirms the legend that all those who drink its waters will be enamoured of Barcelona and always return. It is a favourite meeting place, and posses of retired men regularly gather here for *tertúlies* (chatting in groups and putting the world to rights – often around a table after a large meal). The font is at its most jubilant when

Barça football fans of all ages gather there to celebrate yet another victory for their heroic team.

Tucked just inside Tallers, the first street on the right, is **Boadas**, the oldest cocktail bar in town and probably the most atmospheric, with its 1930s decor and walls lined with caricatures of the original owner. His daughter, Dolors Boadas, still mixes a mean *mojito*, a skill inherited from her father who learned his art in Cuba, to where, like so many Catalans in the 19th century, his parents had emigrated. At the next junction, with Bonsuccés, is the *modernista* pharmacy of Dr Masó, and across La Rambla are the diverging streets Santa Anna and Canuda, the former a good pedestrian shopping street.

Just down here, through a half-hidden doorway on the left, is the **Parròquia Major de Santa Anna** ❹ (Mon–Sat 9am–1pm and 6.30–8pm; avoid weekends, the time for weddings and Masses), an oasis of peace. The Romanesque church and Gothic cloister are marvellous examples of the architecture of their time. Return to La Rambla via **Plaça**

A drink of water from the Font de Canaletes just south of Plaça de Catalunya is said to ensure your return to the city one day.

BELOW: Dolors Boadas mixes a mean cocktail in Boadas.

La Rambla by Night

As night falls La Rambla takes on a nocturnal persona, losing nothing of its daytime energy and pace: the flow of human traffic at 3am is much the same as at midday. After dark it becomes the main artery for anyone going *de juerga* (out for a wild time) in the Old Town. There are the young ones going out for a dose of *leche de pantera* (a dangerous mix of alcohol and milk), yuppies off to Maremàgnum on the Waterfront, the cocktail set leaving Boadas and moving on to dinner, immaculately coiffed ladies in fur coats on their way to the opera, and after 2am the dance crowd in search of the latest sounds. After important victories Canaletes roars with jubilant Barça fans, climbing lampposts and waving banners.

Witnessing the goings-on through impervious eyes are the newspaper kiosk attendants, who replace yesterday's papers with today's first editions in the small hours. And while the fun continues, out come the municipal cleaners in force, like some kind of eco-angels, sweeping, collecting rubbish and vigorously hosing down the gutters in preparation for a new day on La Rambla. Woe betide any *juergistas* who get in their way.

The old music store next to the Palau de la Virreina is a little modernista *gem.*

BELOW: the Palau de la Virreina, a venue for interesting temporary exhibitions.

de la Vila de Madrid, reached from the narrow street Bertrellans almost opposite the church: it is an attractive, newly landscaped square with some Roman ruins and a wonderful jacaranda tree. On the corner, at Canuda No. 6, is the **Ateneu Barcelonès**, a traditional cultural enclave with walk-in exhibitions in a building dating from 1796. Steal a glimpse of the hushed library and the romantic rear garden.

Rambla dels Estudis

Back on La Rambla, the crowd gets denser and the noise level rises as it passes through a corridor of caged birds, fish and small rodents, against a background of large hotels which were modernised for the 1992 Olympics. This is the **Rambla dels Estudis**, so named because the 16th-century university was here. The Reial Acadèmia de Ciències i Arts on the right also houses the **Teatre Poliorama** with regular performances and good shows for kids on Sunday mornings. On the exterior of the building, which was designed by Josep Domènech i Estapà, is the

clock which has been the official timekeeper of the city since 1891. The decoration at the **Viena** next door is not genuine, but the coffee is. Of all the vast conglomeration of the former university, only the **Església de Betlem ❺** (beyond the former Filipino tobacco company, now a hotel) remains, a long and rather depressing bulk. The baroque facade on **Carme** was built in 1690 but the main structure was not completed until 1729.

Opposite is the **Palau Moja** (also known as the Marquis de Comillas Palace), an important 18th-century neoclassical building converted into offices of the Department of Culture of the Generalitat (the Catalan government). Under the arcades is the official Generalitat bookshop, with a few titles of general interest amid the weighty tomes of statistics on Catalonia.

At the corner, **Portaferrissa** leads into a world of commerce and numerous fashion shops, cafés selling hot chocolate and sticky confectionery, and the central part of the **Barri Gòtic** *(see pages 93–103)*. To

the right of La Rambla is Carme, an interesting street going into the heart of **El Raval**, worth a brief detour for **El Indio**, a textiles shop (at No. 24) founded in 1870 and little changed since. Inside there are long wooden counters for proper display of the cloth, and wooden chairs for stout ladies to rest their legs.

Back on the **Rambla de Sant Josep** (better known as the Rambla de les Flors), the air smells sweet. During the 19th century this was the only place where flowers were sold, and each vendor had his favourite clientele. The Catalan Impressionist artist Ramón Casas (1866–1932) picked out one of the flower-sellers here to be his model, and later his wife.

On the right is the **Palau de la Virreina ⑥**, a magnificent 18th-century rococo building set back from the road for greater effect. In 1771 Manuel Amat, Viceroy of Peru, sent a detailed plan from Lima for the construction of the house that he planned to build in La Rambla. The final building was not completed until 1778, and the Viceroy died only a few years after taking up residence. It was his young widow who was left to enjoy the palace, which became known as the palace of the "Virreina" or vicereine. Today it is an excellent exhibition venue, the official information centre for all cultural events in Barcelona, and a booking office. Wander into its handsome courtyard: around fiesta time there is usually some *gegant* (giant) or *drac* (dragon) lurking, before being brought out on parade. Designer souvenirs of Barcelona and good books are available in the shop. Next to it is a music store with a charming *modernista* front.

Get back on La Rambla to appreciate fully, half a block further down, the entrance to the city's most popular and famous market, the

Mercat de la Boqueria ⑦, or Mercat de Sant Josep. The first stone was laid on 19 March 1840, Saint Joseph's day, to appease the saint whose convent on the same spot had been burned down in the 1835 riots. Again, take plenty of time to enjoy shopping there, or simply to observe. Discerning shoppers – restaurateurs early in the morning, housewives mid-morning and the men in charge of the Sunday paella on Saturdays – queue patiently for the best produce, bark their orders and refuse to be fobbed off with anything below par. The fishwives also shriek, trying to seduce passers-by into the day's best catch. It is a heady experience, and despite the frantic crowds, exceedingly heart-warming: there is something quintessentially Mediterranean about the noise, human warmth and the serious business of buying and eating wonderfully fresh produce.

On the opposite side of La Rambla is the **Palau Nou**. The total antithesis to La Boqueria, it is an ultra-modern building that is supposedly completely automated,

Map on page 78

The sign of the Mercat de la Boqueria, just off La Rambla. Within its 19th-century iron frame some 300 stalls overflow with fish, meat, cheese and fresh produce of every kind.

BELOW: La Boqueria has several good places to eat.

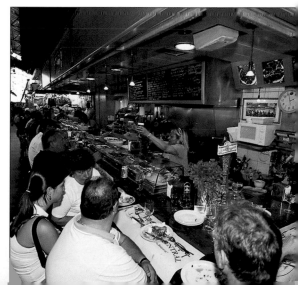

Oriental details on the Casa Bruno Quadras on Pla de la Boqueria.

including "robot parking" on nine levels underground. It also provides a short cut through to the **Plaça del Pi**, and effectively frames the beautiful Gothic tower of the *plaça*'s church, Santa Maria del Pi.

Pla de la Boqueria

Continuing on down, La Rambla enters the **Pla de la Boqueria** (marked only by a widening of La Rambla, and a break in the shady avenue of trees). This was the site of executions in the 14th century, when it was paved with flagstones. The name dates from the previous century when tables selling fresh meat, *mesas de bocatería,* were erected here (*boc* was the Catalan for goat's meat). In the 15th century the tables of gamblers and cardsharps replaced the meat stalls.

Today the flagstones have been replaced by a Joan Miró (1893–1983) pavement created in the 1970s – look out for his signature. On the corner is the **Casa Bruno Quadras**, built by Josep Vilaseca in 1891. The colourful, extravagant decoration includes umbrellas, fans

and a great Chinese dragon, demonstrating the Oriental influence felt by the modernists.

At this point the **Rambla dels Caputxins** begins, so called because, until 1775, the left side was the site of the Capuchin Convent and its adjacent vegetable garden. The mood changes slightly now, as this stretch is dominated by the **Gran Teatre del Liceu** ❽ (to book tel: 902 332211; for information tel: 93 485 9913), cathedral of the *bel canto* in Spain and launch-pad for names such as Carreras and Caballé. The original building, dating from 1861, was badly damaged by fire in 1994, but still peeks out of the enormous new edifice within which it is now enclosed. With its new technology and second stage, the opera house now takes over a whole block.

Alongside the theatre, Sant Pau leads down to Església de Sant Pau del Camp in El Raval *(see page 123).*

Back on La Rambla, **Café de l'Opera**, opposite the theatre, retains all the charms you would expect of one of the few remaining old-fashioned cafés in Barcelona.

Opened in 1929, it is a good place to read the newspapers in the morning – subdued and peaceful – yet builds up to a giddy pitch late at night.

The Gran Teatre del Liceu ends opposite Ferràn, one of the most elegant streets in Barcelona in the first half of the 19th century. Remnants of this time can still be seen despite the invasion of fast-food outlets and souvenir shops. Now pedestrianised, the street leads up to the Plaça Sant Jaume at the heart of the Barri Gòtic. The **Hotel Oriente**, a little further down La Rambla, preserves the structures of the Collegi de Sant Bonaventura, founded by Franciscan monks in 1652. The convent and cloister, built between 1652 and 1670, are there in their entirety. The cloister is now the hotel ballroom, surrounded by the monks' gallery. A wall-plaque reminds readers that this was the first public place in Barcelona to use gas lighting.

The Palau Güell

In the first stretch of **Nou de la Rambla** is the **Palau Güell ⑨**. Currently being renovated, it is closed until 2007, but it is still worth seeing its facade. It was built by Antoni Gaudí between 1885 and 1889 as the home of his patron, Count Güell. With this structure, the architect embarked on a period of fertile creativity. Here, Gothic inspiration alternates with evidence of Arabic influence. The building is structured around an enormous salon, from which a conical roof covered in pieces of tiling emerges to preside over an unusual landscape of capriciously placed battlements, balustrades and strangely shaped chimneys.

Plaça Reial

Back on the other side of La Rambla, an arcaded passageway leads to the infamous **Plaça Reial ⑩**, another Barcelona landmark and one of the most handsome yet decadent of its squares. Attempts to "clean it up" have done little to change its character, so tourists on terrace bars still jostle with junkies, and backpackers share benches with tramps. Restaurants, bars and clubs predominate, like the well-estab-

Map on page 78

Among the ceramic decorated chimneys and balustrades of the Palau Güell.

BELOW: the facade of the Liceu.

The Liceu

Philanthropist Manuel Gibert i Sans, a national militia commander, started the "Liceo Dramático de Aficionados" with the aim of organising soirées to raise funds for his battalion. The theatre staged its first opera in 1838. In 1842, looking for a bigger venue, he bought the land of the former convent of the Trinitarios on La Rambla and the company became a wholly artistic and social foundation. Construction began in 1844 of a project second only to that of La Scala in Milan, with space for 4,000 spectators and every type of performance, from musical galas to operas and ballet. Stravinsky, de Falla, Caruso, Callas, Plácido Domingo and Pavarotti have all performed here, as well as Catalonia's own Pablo Casals, Montserrat Caballé and Josep Carreras.

In 1994 a fire gutted the interior. City authorities announced that the opera house would be rebuilt, and architect Ignasi de Solà Morales doubled its size while conserving its original style. It reopened in 1999 to much public acclaim. In attempts to broaden its appeal, its programme includes late-night cabaret and jazz, sessions in the foyer and opera film cycles. A shop and café are situated below street level.

Clowning around on the Plaça Reial.

lished **Jamboree** jazz club, along with its sister club **Tarantos** for flamenco, both open after the show for dancing. **Sidecar**, considered one of the most fashionable spots, has live music. The buzz never lets up, day or night.

On Sunday, stamp and coin collectors gather around the **Font de Les Tres Gràcies** and the two *fanals* (street lamps) designed by Antoni Gaudí. Inspired by the French urban designs of the Napoleonic period, this is the only one of the many squares planned in Barcelona during the 19th century that was built entirely according to its original plan. Its uniform, arcaded buildings were constructed by Francesc Daniel Molina on the plot where the Capuchin Convent once stood. Return to La Rambla through Passatge de Bacardí (the Cuban rum was created by a Catalan). On the corner with La Rambla is Arpi, a highly regarded photographic shop.

Plaça del Teatre

The terraces that line La Rambla along this stretch are spurned by locals, but as long as you don't expect the ultimate culinary experience it is tempting to sip a cool drink and watch the world go by. Where the promenade opens up again into the **Plaça del Teatre**, or **Plaça de les Comèdies**, another notorious street, **Escudellers**, leads off to the left. A kind of cross between ingrained seediness and 1990s trendiness, it is representative of many parts of Barcelona today. Walk along it to feel the pulse of the harsher elements of the city, and to observe its present evolution.

Escudellers opens up at the far end into a newly created square, **Plaça George Orwell** ⓫, the result of dense housing demolition, where several trendy bars and an excellent pizzeria have opened. The supposedly "surrealist" sculpture here is by Leandre Cristòfol.

Return back down Escudellers, passing small grocers, falafel bars, discos and dives. Narrow streets lead off to the right and left, most hiding late-night bars and one, leading back to the Plaça Reial, an African restaurant. Particularly rec-

ommended are **Zoo**, which has a buzzy atmosphere and is good for light, alternative snacks; the more traditional restaurant **Los Caracoles** (with sizzling chickens on a blazing grill on the exterior wall); and **La Fonda**, which is related to Quinze Nits in the Plaça Reial and has the same effective formula – reasonably priced Catalan food, served in an attractive interior of palms and pale wood. The long queue at peak times is filled with the kind of locals you don't expect to see down this street.

Back on La Rambla you reach the spot where, in the 16th century, the city's first theatre was built. The present **Teatre Principal** replaced the old wooden theatre which was for many years the only stage in Barcelona. A 2,000-seater, it was built on the site of the historical Corral de les Comèdies, a popular early theatre, although it never appealed to the bourgeoisie. Opposite the theatre is a monument to Frederic Soler "Pitarra", founder of the modern Catalan theatre.

The few prostitutes remaining in this area choose the small square that surrounds the monument to offer their charms – almost as an epilogue to what used to be and a prologue to what is left of the **Barri Xino** (in Spanish Barrio Chino). A shadow of its former self, the area has been much cleaned up in recent years, but the neon signs of sex shops and the like are still in evidence. The square marks the beginning of the **Rambla de Santa Mònica**, the last stretch of La Rambla before it reaches the harbour.

To the waterfront

At this point the pace of the human river slows, as if reaching its delta, and the personality of La Rambla seems to fade. The Rambla Santa Mònica is lined with caricaturists, portrait painters and artisans, and a craft market is held here at the weekend. This is where, in 1895, films were first shown publicly in Spain by the Lumière brothers. Some handsome buildings have been restored and new ones built, notably on the left for the university of Pompeu Fabra.

Map on page 78

BELOW: Plaça del Portal de la Pau at the foot of La Rambla.

The Museu de la Cera (Wax Museum) is a good option for children and teenagers. Tickets are sold from a booth on La Rambla.

BELOW: the terrace café of the Centre d'Art Santa Mònica.

Contemporary art

On the right side of the street as you continue south is the **Centre d'Art Santa Mònica** ⑫ (Mon–Sat 11am–2pm and 5–8pm), a former convent redesigned as an exhibition space by the highly regarded local architects Piñón and Viaplana, who have been instrumental in much of the new Barcelona. A pleasant terrace café overlooks La Rambla while at street level an information centre provides details of cultural events in Catalonia. Opposite the centre is the **Palau March** (1780), today the Generalitat's Department of Culture.

Just before the Santa Mònica art centre, a narrow street, Santa Mònica, heads off into Barri Xino. It has an interesting range of seedy old bars, newly fashionable old bars and even techno discos. Before going too far, however, pause for some French nostalgia in the timeless **Pastis** at No. 4. An evocative French atmosphere is on offer here, except on tango nights when the bar transforms itself into a corner of Buenos Aires by playing live tango music.

Towards the end of La Rambla, on the left, an old-fashioned ticket booth sells tickets for the **Museu de la Cera** ⑬ (Mon–Fri 10am–1.30pm and 4–7pm, Sat–Sun 11am–2pm and 4.30–8.30pm; entrance charge), in the **Passatge de la Banca**. The roof of Barcelona's wax museum sports Superman, poised to leap from the top of the building, and inside are more than 360 waxworks, giving an insight into some of Catalonia's historic personalities. Children love it, especially the spooky bits, but it is probably best kept for a rainy day.

Around this part of La Rambla you'll usually find a horse and carriage waiting to whisk tourists off for a trot around town.

Our Lady of Mercy

A long street on the left, Ample, leads to the 18th-century church of **La Mare de Déu de la Mercè** ⑭, usually known simply as **La Mercè** (like many Catalan women), the patron saint of Barcelona. A dramatic statue of the Virgin and child stands on the top of the church,

creating a distinctive element in the waterfront skyline. The square was one of the first urban spaces (1983) to appear as a result of the socialist city council's long-term project of demolishing old buildings to open up dense areas.

It is at its most festive on 24 September, the day of La Mercè, when *gegants* and *castellers (see pages 42–3)* greet the dignitaries coming out of Mass, before the real *festa major* of Barcelona takes off. It is also customary for every member of the Barça football team, whatever his creed, to come and pay his respects to the Virgin after important victories, before going off to parade the trophy in front of the fans in Plaça Sant Jaume.

The last building on the left side of La Rambla has a curious history. In 1778 the foundry of the Royal Artillery, as well as its workshop, were transferred to this building, popularly known as **El Refino**. The foundry was one of the most renowned cannon factories of its time. From 1844 until 1920 it was occupied by the offices of the Banco de Barcelona (the first private Spanish bank), and, since the Spanish Civil War (1936–9), it has been converted into the offices of the military governor.

The Columbus statue

Making a challenging end to this long walk down La Rambla is the steep climb to the top of the **Monument a Colom** ⓯ (daily 9am–8.30pm in summer and daily 10am–6pm in winter; entrance charge), standing in the centre of **Plaça del Portal de la Pau**. Fortunately, it also has an internal lift as well as a great view over the city and port.

Cross the busy traffic here and you will reach the relative peace of the waterfront, where an antique market is held at weekends. From this point there is a choice of diversions: the Golondrinas for trips around the harbour or to the Olympic Port, or the Rambla de Mar, a floating extension of La Rambla that connects with the Moll d'Espanya and the Maremagnum leisure and commercial centre *(see pages 129–131)*. ❑

The Columbus statue is a useful landmark. A lift will take you to the top of the statue for far-reaching views (see below).

BELOW: views from the top of the Monument a Colom.

RESTAURANTS & BARS

Restaurants

Consider La Rambla a colourful avenue to walk down and enjoy the street life, rather than a place to eat. With just a few notable exceptions, the restaurants are only average. However, just behind the main facade, in the narrow streets of the Barri Gòtic and El Raval you will find some of the most traditional and the trendiest spots in the city (see pages 104 and 126).

Amaya
La Rambla, 20–24 (metro: Drassanes)
Tel: 93 302 6138
L & D daily. €€ (set menu Mon–Fri L €)
This well-established Basque restaurant is a traditional treasure in the midst of the cheap alternatives surrounding it. You can opt for a snack at the bustling bar or the more elegant dining room at the rear, where fish is the best option.

Ateneu
Canuda, 6 (metro: Catalunya)
Tel: 93 318 5238
L & D Mon–Sat. €
A welcome new restaurant in the atmospheric, literary surroundings of the Ateneu, in a quiet corner looking over Plaça de la Vila de Madrid. Specialises in the wholesome country food of La Garrotxa.

Attic
La Rambla, 120 (metro: Catalunya)
Tel: 93 302 4866
L & D daily. €€
Part of a chain that produces authentic Spanish cuisine on a large scale, but does so effectively. Popular with tourists. If you are not too choosy about the gourmet experience, the window tables overlooking La Rambla provide an irresistible floor show.

Bar Ra
Plaça de la Gardunya, 3 (metro: Liceu)
Tel: 93 301 4163
B, L & D Mon–Sat. €
Even in the winter this large, colourful terrace behind the Boqueria market is a sun trap, frequented by a seriously cool crowd. Good-value creative food with Oriental overtones.

Can Culleretes
Quintana, 5 (metro: Liceu)
Tel: 93 317 3022
L & D Tues–Sat. L only Sun. €€
This is the second-oldest restaurant in Spain, founded in 1785 and full of character, adorned throughout with paintings and photos of famous visitors.

Can Maxim
Bonsuccés, 8 (metro: Catalunya)
Tel: 93 302 0234
L & D Mon–Sat. €
Just off La Rambla, this restaurant serves a good-value, substantial set menu to local office workers. A far cry from the tourist traps on the main Rambla.

Central
Elisabets, 6/Plaça Vicenç Martorell (metro: Catalunya)
Tel: 93 317 0293
B & L Mon–Sat. €
A peaceful spot amid the books and music of the Central Bookshop in the former chapel of the medieval Misericòrdia complex, serving tasty, minimalist dishes and delicious home-made cakes.

Egipte
La Rambla, 79 (metro: Liceu)
Tel: 93 317 7480
L & D daily. €
Once situated behind the Boqueria market, this is a popular, lively place that has grown from being a small market restaurant into several well-decorated floors.

El Paraguayo
Parc, 1 (metro: Drassanes)
Tel: 93 302 1441
L & D daily. €
A magnet for passionate carnivores, with daily deliveries of Argentinian and Uruguayan meat, duly grilled in the inimitable Argentinian style. Always has a lively atmosphere.

Fresc Co
Carme, 16 (metro: Catalunya/Liceu)
Tel: 93 301 6837
L & D daily. €
Healthy fast food. Pile up your plates from a huge choice of salads, then gorge on the dish of the day, or pasta and pizza. Finish with ice cream if you must, or fruit. A hit with kids and adults alike. Branches in Ronda Universitat, Plaça Medinaceli and Diagonal.

Irati
Cardenal Casañas, 17 (metro: Liceu)
Tel: 93 302 3084
L & D Mon–Fri. €€ Pinchos daily. €
One of the first and best of a bevy of Basque bars that opened in the 1990s. Grab what you fancy from the great variety of pintxos (snacks on a toothpick) emerging at regular intervals from the kitchen. It's best to go a bit earlier than Barcelona lunch and dinner times, before they run out. Serious à la carte Basque food is served in the rear.

Juicy Jones
Cardenal Casañas, 7 (metro: Liceu)
Tel: 93 302 4330
B, L & D daily. €
Revive yourself on a nourishing juice in this small vegetarian/vegan restaurant just off La Rambla, with high standards and top-quality, freshly cooked dishes.

Kasparo
Plaça Vicenç Martorell, 4 (metro: Catalunya)
Tel: 93 302 2072

Daily. Closed Jan. €
Charming terrace bar in secluded square just off La Rambla. Delicious and cosmopolitan light snacks and lunch dishes, original creations of its Australian owners. There's a play area for children in the square.

Kiosco Universal
Mercat Sant Josep (La Boqueria), Parada 691 (metro: Liceu)
Tel: 93 317 8286
B & L Mon–Sat. €
Pull up a stool at the bar amid the market's stallholders and eat the freshest of produce, cooked before your very eyes.

La Verónica
Avinyó, 30 (metro: Liceu)
Tel: 93 412 1122
D Mon–Fri. L & D Sat–Sun. €
Colourful, modern space designed for a colourful, modern crowd in the heart of the old city, with a popular terrace. Delicious designer *pizzas del mercat* using seasonal vegetables, like wild mushrooms and artichokes, as well as great salads. Another branch to open soon in Rambla del Raval.

Los Caracoles
Escudellers, 14 (metro: Liceu/Drassanes)
Tel: 93 302 3185
L & D daily. €€
This old Barcelona favourite still oozes atmosphere, from the moment you walk in through the sizzling, busy kitchen and are settled in its labyrinthine interior, at a table with a crisp white cloth. Specialises in rich meat dishes like lamb and suckling pig.

La Llotja de les Drassanes Reials
Avinguda Drassanes (metro: Drassanes)
Tel: 93 317 5256
L Mon–Sat (set menu €), D only Wed–Sat. €€
A part of the medieval building in which the Maritime Museum is housed, this is a delightful setting for lunch or dinner. Also has a vegetarian menu in the evening.

Pinotxo
Mercat Sant Josep (La Boqueria), Parada 66–67 (metro: Liceu)
Tel: 93 317 1731
B & L Mon–Sat. €
A high-profile market bar, where the uptown crowd pause from their Saturday shopping for cava and oysters, or whatever the charismatic owner has selected from the season's produce at the neighbouring stalls.

Sagarra
Xuclà, 9 (metro: Catalunya)
Tel: 93 301 0604
B, L & D daily. €
Don't be off put by the formal, conventional décor – this is a good, honest, local place serving traditional dishes with a touch of flare. Excellent value lunchtime menu.

Bars & Cafés

This is a good area for cafés and *xocolateries*, with legendary meeting place **Cafè Zurich** on Plaça de Catalunya a perfect starting point for any stroll down La Rambla. Halfway down, the **Cafè de l'Opera** retains its charm despite recent facelifts, sedate and subdued in the morning but buzzing by night. Have a coffee at the *modernista* **Escribà** at La Rambla, 83 and you won't be able to resist an exquisite pastry. For real indulgence don't miss the oldest milk bar in town, **Granja Viader**, Xuclá, 4–6, a delightful spot where kids' favourite *Cacaolat* (chocolate milk) was invented. Or try **La Pallaresa**, Petritxol, 11, one of several *granjes* in this pretty street, where the *xocolata desfeta*, Catalan drinking chocolate, is not for the faint-hearted, and is often topped with lashings of cream. Two essential night-time stops are **Boadas**, Tallers, 1, a classic cocktail bar straight from the 1930s; and **Pastis**, Santa Mònica, 4, a small corner of Marseilles at the bottom of La Rambla. **Castells**, Plaça Bonsuccés, has something to offer both day and night, with good *tapes* and cool beers at the solid marble bar.

PRICE CATEGORIES

Prices for three-course dinner per person with a half-bottle of house wine:
€ = under €25
€€ = €25–€40
€€€ = €40–€60
€€€€ = more than €60

BARRI GÒTIC

There's no finer introduction to Barcelona's Golden Age than a stroll around the warren of narrow streets that constitutes the lovely Barri Gòtic, the oldest part of the city

Map
on page
94

The jewel of the Old Town, the Gothic Quarter or Barri Gòtic is a dense nucleus of historic buildings that has formed the central part of the old city since Roman times. Today it represents the centre of municipal administration and is home to the Catalan autonomous government. The oldest part of the city, it is built around **Mont Tàber**, Taber Hill, a misnomer for what is little more than a mound in an otherwise flat city. This section of the Old Town is surrounded by the remains of Roman walls. Layer upon layer of different architectural styles illustrate the different periods of Barcelona's history, from remnants of the Roman city to contemporary architectural solutions seen in renovation work and extensions to old buildings. The Gothic period predominates, reflecting the glorious medieval period when Catalonia was at its height.

A tour of the Barri Gòtic

This route is designed to take in the key sites, and constitutes an enjoyable walk through the present-day Gothic Quarter – its residents, its street musicians, its cafés and commerce. Alternatively, you can simply absorb its atmosphere by wandering aimlessly around its narrow streets, feeling the sense of history and observing the day-to-day comings and goings of the local people.

Approach from Plaça de Catalunya down **Portal de l'Angel**, a wide paved street full of shoe shops, fashion shops and the hi-tech branch of El Corte Inglés, which specialises in music, books, sport and computers, and is housed in a grandiose building reminiscent of long-ago department stores. The wide space lends itself to street performances, bound to waylay you. Bear left at the fork at the bottom,

LEFT: in the atmospheric alleyways of the Barri Gòtic.
BELOW: making a song and dance.

Statue in the Romanesque courtyard of the Palau Episcopal.

past the *modernista* gas board offices, an Aladdin's cave of a toyshop, and the **Col·legi d'Arquitectes**, the Architects' Association, a 1960s building with friezes designed by Picasso, although they were executed by Norwegian Carl Nesjar.

Plaça Nova

The street leads into **Plaça Nova ❶**, and there, in front of you, is one of the main Roman gates to the old city, the **Portal del Bisbe**, or Bishop's Gate. The towers date from the 1st century BC but the name came later, from the nearby 18th-century Bishop's Palace. The sculpted letters by Catalan artist Joan Brossa spell out "Barcino", the Roman name for the city, like a caption for this historic image.

Here Plaça Nova merges with **Avinguda de la Catedral**, newly paved and streamlined into a wide open space spreading out at the foot of the Cathedral steps. The paving hides an underground car park and successfully highlights the drama of the ancient facades, which rise theatrically above the Roman walls. Sit on one of the polished stone benches or the terrace of the **Hotel Colón** and take it all in: the constant movement of children, footballs and bicycles, the clicking and whirring of cameras, the balloon vendors and beggars. An antiques market takes place here on Thursdays, and at the weekend the gatherings of *sardana* dancers form large, impenetrable bouncing circles (6.30pm on Saturday, midday on Sunday). All this is played out against the surprisingly neo-Gothic front of the Cathedral, which was tacked onto its 13th-century origins in the 19th century.

Into the Barri Gòtic

Enter the Gothic Quarter through the Roman gate in Plaça Nova, up the slope into **Bisbe**. On the right is the **Palau Episcopal,** built in 1769

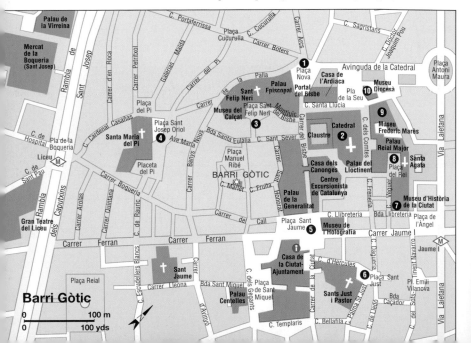

Barri Gòtic

0   100 m
0   100 yds

around a 12th-century courtyard, which is the only remaining evidence of the original palace after centuries of modifications. The frescos on the facade (facing the Carrer Montjuïc del Bisbe) date from the 18th century, while the triple recess windows and large *flamígero* window in the courtyard are from the 14th century.

Opposite the palace entrance a short street, **Santa Llúcia**, leads towards the Cathedral. On the corner is a chapel dedicated to Santa Llúcia, patron saint of the blind and, curiously, of seamstresses. Built in 1268, it is one of the oldest parts of the Cathedral and a fine example of Romanesque architecture, with images of the Annunciation and the Visitation decorating the facade capitals. The holy-water font inside the chapel is from the 14th century. A rear doorway leads into the Cathedral cloister. The **Fira de Santa Llúcia**, a Christmas arts and crafts fair, takes over the narrow streets from early December, and the Cathedral square is filled with Christmas trees of all shapes and sizes, plus everything you could possibly need to make your own nativity scene.

The cathedral precincts

Opposite the Capella de Santa Llúcia, on the other corner, is the **Casa de l'Ardiaca** (Archdeacon's Residence), built in the 15th century on Roman ruins. It has one of the most evocative patios in the city. A tall, elegant palm tree rises high above a fountain, which is decorated with flowers at Corpus Christi and the setting for a curious tradition, *l'ou com balla*, in which a fragile egg "dances" on the spouting water. The building contains the **Municipal History Archives**, a valuable collection of historical chronicles and documents. Recent extensions at the rear of the patio have opened up the building, revealing another angle on the Roman tower and part of the first city wall, dating from the 1st century BC. The outer wall, with square towers and the remains of two aqueducts (which can be seen from Avinguda de la Catedral) is from the 4th century AD.

Map on page 94

Next to the entrance of the Casa de l'Ardiaca look out for the letterbox designed by the modernista *architect Domènech i Montaner. The swallows suggest how fast the post should travel; the tortoise represents the reality.*

BELOW: the patio of the Casa de l'Ardiaca.

TIP

For a gargoyle's view of the city, take a lift to the rooftop of the Cathedral (10.30am–1pm and 4.30–6pm; closed Sat pm and Sun; entrance charge).

BELOW: the Cathedral.
BELOW RIGHT: fountain in the garden of the Cathedral's cloister.

The Cathedral

Enter the **Catedral** ❷ (daily 9am–3.30pm and 4–7.30pm) by the main door. Its glowing darkness and slightly scented air from the myriad candles are a marked but soothing contrast after the bright Mediterranean skies outside. Its traditional, ornate chapels are a far cry from the simple majesty of Santa Maria del Mar *(see page 112)*. For any kind of spiritual peace it is essential to visit in off-peak hours, such as first thing in the morning, to avoid herded groups and the accumulation of human traffic; attending Mass is no solution, as the congregation chatters loudly and moves in and out at will.

The construction of the cathedral began in 1298 under the patronage of Jaume II, on the spot where an early Christian church had been destroyed by the pillaging of al-Mansur, the vizier of Córdoba, in 985. Some signs of it can be seen in the remarkable subterranean world beneath the present Cathedral, which can be visited from the City History Museum.

The main area consists of three naves and an apse with an ambulatory beneath an octagonal dome. Two 14th- and 15th-century towers rise at each end of the transept. Beneath the main altar is the crypt of Santa Eulàlia, and of particular note are the dome's multicoloured keystones. Some say that this is one of Catalonia's three "magnetic" points.

The tomb of Santa Eulàlia, behind the altar, is an important 14th-century work of art, executed in alabaster by a disciple of Giovanni Pisano during the same period as the episcopal cathedral. The most outstanding altarpiece is that of the Transfiguration, designed by Bernat Martorell in the chapel dedicated to Sant Salvador, which was built in 1447.

The high-backed choir pews are by Pere Sanglada (1399), and the lower-backed benches were carved by Macià Bonafé towards the end of the same century. The retrochoir (the extension behind the high altar) was built at the beginning of the 16th century by the artist Bartolomé Ordóñez. The Capella del Santo Cristo de Lepanto (Chapel of

Christ Lepanto) contains the crucifix borne in the Christian flagship against the Ottomans in the battle of Lepanto. It was built between 1405 and 1454 and is considered to be the finest example of Gothic art in the cathedral.

The oldest part is that of the Porta de Sant Ivo (St Ive's Door), where some of the Romanesque windows and archways can still be seen. Although most of the cathedral's more antique furnishings are in the City Museum, there is a small collection in the **Sala Capitular** or Chapter House (daily 9am–3.30pm and 4–7pm; entrance charge).

A small pavilion beside the Porta de la Pietat shelters a 15th-century terracotta statue of St George by Antoni Claperós, and the door to the western end of the transept is made from marble taken from the earlier Romanesque cathedral.

The cathedral cloisters

On one side is the Santa Eulàlia Portal which leads to the **cathedral cloister**, a quiet haven and perhaps the most atmospheric part of the cathedral, with the sound of running water from the pretty fountain and a romantic garden of elegant palms, medlars and highly perfumed magnolia trees, all enclosed by the 15th-century wrought-iron railings. Thirteen geese are the sole residents, symbolising the age of Santa Eulàlia, co-patron saint of Barcelona, when she died.

Recommended restaurants near the cathedral include **La Cassola**, with tasty Catalan home cooking, in Sant Sever, and **Portalón** in Banys Nous. The latter, a timeless bodega, is a good bet in winter, when its warming bean stews go down well.

Plaça Sant Felip Neri

Leave the cloister through the side door which gives on to **Plaça Garriga i Bachs**. To the left notice the picturesque bridge across the street (another neo-Gothic construction), linking two departments of the Generalitat. Cross the square to **Montjuïc del Bisbe**, a narrow street leading into **Plaça Sant Felip Neri** ❸. This small square is a treasure, enclosed by heavy stone buildings

At Christmas, festive stalls in the Cathedral Square sell pessebres *(nativity scenes), Christmas trees and* tiós *(jolly-faced logs that "excrete" presents).*

BELOW: the geese that inhabit the Cathedral's cloister.

A giant shoe in the Museu del Calçat, made to fit the Columbus statue at the foot of La Rambla.

BELOW: inside the church of Santa Maria del Pi, a prime example of Catalan Gothic.

and happily neglected, which increases its historic impact.

Adjoining the 18th-century church of Sant Felip Neri is a school, so if you coincide with play-time the peace will be shattered by shrieking children and stray footballs. The children's cries echoing around the walls are a melancholy reminder that a large number of children were killed here when a bomb dropped near by during the Civil War. The pock-marked church facade tells the tale, and the eccentric **Museu del Calçat** (Shoe Museum) shares the story (Tues–Sun 11am–2pm; entrance charge). The museum was formerly in a street that used to be opposite the Cathedral, **Corríbia**, which has since been cleared to make Avinguda de la Catedral, and was moved to the *plaça*, brick by brick. An enormous shoe made to measure for the Columbus statue in La Rambla and a gold stiletto worn by Victoria de los Angeles are among the curiosities.

Take the other exit to **Sant Sever**, past the discreet new boutique hotel

Neri, and go down **Baixada Santa Eulàlia** into a world apart, with hidden courtyards behind enormous wooden doors and small dark workshops where furniture is polished and restored. At **Banys Nous**, turn right past a shop displaying night-dresses from another era. On the wall opposite, a panel of ceramic tiles explains the origin of the street's name.

Santa Maria del Pi

Where the street joins Palla (which, to the right, runs back to the Cathedral) turn left towards **Plaça Sant Josep Oriol** ❹. This lively square, dominated by the sought-after terrace of the **Bar del Pi**, is one of the most popular spots in the Old Town. Along with the adjoining Plaça del Pi and Placeta del Pi, it embraces the church of **Santa Maria del Pi**. Begun in 1322 and completed in the 15th century, this is a fine example of Catalan Gothic architecture, fortress-like on the exterior but ample and welcoming inside. The rose window is magnificent when lit from within. On weekends farmers

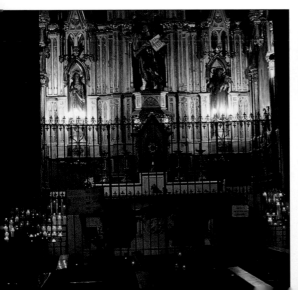

come in from the country to sell goat's cheese and honey at the market on the square (Sat 10am–8.30pm, Sun 9am–2pm). In the adjacent Plaça Plaça Sant Josep Oriol artists sell their work.

Buskers became so numerous here that local residents campaigned to have them banned, except between 6–8pm on Saturday and noon–2pm on Sunday. Guests of the popular Hotel Jardí no doubt appreciate the ruling. Before leaving the square check out the **Roca** knife shop, dating from 1911, and around the corner from it the very pretty street **Petritxol**.

The **Palau Fiveller**, at No. 4 in Plaça Sant Josep Oriol, is occupied by an Agricultural Institute with information on rural tourism. Take the narrow street **Ave Maria** that runs down its side and at the end turn right, back into Banys Nous. Even the old *granja* (milk bar) here has had the trendy treatment. One landmark, the wonderful **Obach** hat shop, remains unchanged. Turn left here and follow **Call**, the main street in Barcelona's important Jewish

quarter until 1401 *(see page 103)*, as it winds up to Plaça Sant Jaume.

Plaça Sant Jaume

The area that today forms the **Plaça Sant Jaume ❺** was inaugurated in 1823, at the same time as the streets **Ferran** and **Jaume I**. The square is considered to be the civic heart of the city, and it is from here that the **Ajuntament** (Town Hall) presides over Barcelona from the Casa de la Ciutat, and the Generalitat (Autonomous Government) presides over Catalonia. In 2003 former socialist mayor Pasqual Maragall became president, finally ousting Jordi Pujol, who had been in power since democracy returned to Catalonia and Spain. The **Palau de la Generalitat** is guarded by the *Mossos d'Esquadra*, the autonomous police force. Opposite, the town councillors are protected by the slightly dishevelled *Guàrdia Urbana*. Demonstrations wind up here, as do festive parades, Barça fans and players after major football and basketball victories, and, of course, visiting dignitaries. This is where

Top of the Palau de la Generalitat, seat of Catalan government, on the Plaça Sant Jaume.

BELOW: festivities marking La Mercè in the Plaça Sant Jaume.

President Tarradellas was given a clamorous reception on his return from exile to attend the birth of the new democracy.

Both buildings are of Gothic origin and can be visited on key public holidays (such as Sant Jordi, 23 April) or at weekends by prior arrangement (tel: 93 402 4600 for the Generalitat, and 93 402 7364 for the Casa de la Ciutat). Each has some fine elements: the oldest part of the Casa de la Ciutat is the **Saló de Cent**, created by Pere Llobet in 1373; the Gothic facade tucked down the side street **Ciutat** is the most delicate. The **Pati dels Tarongers** (a 16th-century courtyard full of orange trees) is perhaps the most famous part of the Palau de la Generalitat and the scene of many official photographs. From the square you can glimpse the painted ceilings of a large reception room.

There is a tourist information office in the Town Hall, on the corner of La Ciutat (Mon–Fri 9am–8pm, Sat 10am–8pm, Sun 10am–2pm). Take La Ciutat out of the square and immediately turn left into Hercules,

Each year, from early December until after the fiesta of Els Reis (the Kings) on 6 January, the Plaça Sant Jaume is taken over by the largest nativity scene in town – and the queue to visit it.

BELOW: remains of the Roman city, accessed via the Museu d'Historia de la Ciutat.

a quiet street leading to **Plaça Sant Just ⑥**. This is an interesting, often overlooked corner of the Barri Gòtic with a strong sense of identity. The *plaça* has all the elements of a village: a church, a *colmado* (grocer's shop), a restaurant, a noble house, and children playing football. The streets off here are also worth exploring, notably **Palma Sant Just** for the bodega and its breakfasts with wonderful omelettes, and **Lledó** for its neglected medieval houses.

The church of **Sant Just and Sant Pastor** was an ancient royal chapel until the 15th century. According to legend, it is built on the site of Barcelona's first Christian temple. The Café de l'Acadèmia spills out onto the square, serving excellent Catalan nouvelle cuisine.

Royal palace

Follow **Dagueria** past a feminist bookshop, a cheese shop and over Jaume I turning right into Baixada Llibreteria until you arrive at the **Museu d'Història de la Ciutat ⑦** on the corner of Veguer (Tues–Sat 10am–2pm and 4–8pm, all day in

Map on page 94

summer, Sun 10am–3pm; entrance charge). Its eclectic collection, not all on show, includes maps, models, Roman portraits, guild paraphernalia and an anarchist's bomb that damaged the Liceu in 1893. The entrance to the palace complex *(see below)* is through the musum.

The museum also gives access to the excavations of the Roman city that flourished between the 1st and 7th centuries. Covering 4,000 sq. metres beneath the Plaça del Rei, it offers an intriguing insight not only into Roman building methods, but also into commercial and domestic life.

The **Plaça del Rei ❽** is a fine medieval square, a living testimony to the nobility of the ancient city of Barcelona, and was a cattle-fodder market for three centuries. It was here that all the flour brought into the city in payment of taxes was collected. The sculpture is by the Basque artist Eduardo Chillida.

At one end is the **Palau Reial Major**, with vast vaulted ceilings, 13th-century triple-recess windows and 14th-century rose windows. The silhouette of the box-shaped Renaissance tower of **Rei Martí** *(see page 102)* is an outstanding feature of the palace. Built like a dovecote, it has fine views over the royal complex.

The main room of the palace, the great **Salò del Tinell**, was built by Guillem Carbonell, the architect to Pere III ("the Ceremonious") in 1359. Its six unreinforced arches span an unprecedented 15 metres (50 ft). It was later converted to a baroque church, only to recover its original appearance after restoration works were carried out during and after the Civil War.

During the 15th century the Inquisition held court in the Salò del Tinell. Legend has it that the walls of the tribunal cannot bear a lie to be told and that, when this occurred, the ceiling stones would move, adding further to the terror of the victims. Today, the salon functions as an exhibition area.

Next door is the **Capella Reial de Santa Agata** (Royal Chapel), built for Jaume II (1302–12) using the Roman wall as its north side. The decorated ceiling timbers are by

TIP

Concerts and exhibitions are held in the Salò del Tinell. Look out for details of upcoming events in listings or in the Palau de la Virreina information centre *(see page 83)*.

BELOW: the Palau Reial Major exemplifies the Catalan Gothic style.

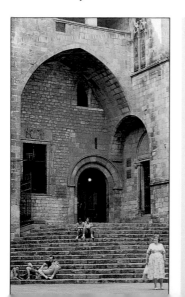

The Royal City

The royal palace of the count-kings of Barcelona-Aragón, begun in the 11th century, lies between the Cathedral and the northern Roman wall. Its courtyard is now the Plaça del Rei and beneath it you can see the foundations of the Roman episcopal palace from which it grew.

A single wall-painting is the palace's only remaining decoration, and the original layout of the complex is not immediately clear, but the surviving public buildings give a glimpse of the power and prosperity of Catalonia during this period. At its core is the great hall, the Saló del Tinell, that has served as throne room, banqueting hall, parliament and inquisitors' court. When the crown slipped from Barcelona's grasp and the palace decayed, Madrid's appointed viceroy had his residence built on the left-hand side of the square. On the right is a 16th-century Gothic mansion, brought here brick by brick to house artefacts from the city's history that had been amassed for display at the 1929 Universal Exposition. While re-siting the building, the Roman city beneath was discovered and since then the complex has been gradually restored.

Map on page 94

In summer, a delightful and peaceful café operates in the courtyard of the Museu Frederic Marès.

BELOW: the cool courtyard of the Museu Frederic Marès.
RIGHT: the Palau del Lloctinent and the tower of Rei Martí.

Alfonso de Córdoba, the beautiful Epiphany altarpiece was painted by Jaume Huguet in 1465, and the Taule de Santa Agata in the Queen's Chapel is from around 1500. It also houses the stone on which the saint's breasts were mutilated.

The **Torre de Martí I**, sometimes called a mirador because of its views over the city, can be reached by steps that begin behind a small door in the south side of the royal chapel (not usually open to the public). The tower was built by Antoni Carbonell and is named after Martí I ("the Humanist", 1396–1410), last in the 500-year dynasty of Barcelona count-kings.

Opposite the chapel is the **Palau del Lloctinent**. When the kingdoms of Catalonia and Aragón were joined with that of Castile, Carlos V created the office of Deputy (*Lloctinent*) for the court's representative, and this palace, the official residence, was built in 1549 by Antoni Carbonell. The facade is typically Catalan-Gothic; however, the exquisite inner courtyard is one of the few extant examples of Renaissance architecture left in the city. Until recently the headquarters of the **Arxiu de la Corona d'Aragó** (Archive of the Crown of Aragon), it is now undergoing a major restoration.

Follow Comtes down the side of the Cathedral to a tiny square, **Sant Iu**, which leads into the lovely courtyard of the **Museu Frederic Marès** ❾ (Tues–Sat 10am–7pm, Sun 10am–3pm; entrance charge). This private collection, donated by the sculptor Marès in 1946, includes an important display of Spanish sculpture, with medieval pieces in the crypt. The **Museu Sentimental**, on the upper floors, gives an insight into daily life in Barcelona in the 18th and 19th centuries.

Comtes comes out into the **Pla de la Seu**, the small space in front of the Cathedral. On the right is a simple but beautiful Gothic building, the **Pia Almoina**. Once the place where 100 meals were given out to the poor daily, it now houses the **Museu Diocesà** ❿ (Tues–Sat 10am–2pm and 5–8pm, Sun 11am–2pm; entrance charge), which has a small but varied collection of religious objects and paintings. ❑

The Jewish City

Throughout Catalonia the Jewish quarter of a town or city is known as the *call*, from the Hebrew *qahqal* or "meeting". The most important *call* was in Barcelona. Situated west of the Roman metropolis in what is now the Gothic Quarter, it reached its peak of importance during the Middle Ages and had a remarkable cultural reputation. Many famous philosophers, writers, astronomers and intellectuals lived here between the 9th and 12th centuries, including the poet Ben Ruben Izahac, philosophers Abraham Ben Samuel Hasdai, Rabbi Salomon Arisba and the Biblical scholar Joseph Ben Caspí.

For centuries the only university institution in Catalonia was the "Universidad Judía" or "Escuela Mayor". This community also had a talent for finance and monarchs were known to apply for loans. Their knowledge was so advanced that they were made ambassadors at court. But their display of wealth and their superior lifestyle created great jealousy.

The fortunes of the Jews began a slow decline in 1243 when Jaume I ordered the separation of the Jewish quarter from the rest of the city and made Jews wear long hooded capes with distinguishing red or yellow circles. Fights began to break out, and became worse when a rumour spread that the Jews were responsible for bringing the Black Death to Spain. Full-scale rioting erupted in several cities in 1391, provoked mainly by a group from Seville who encouraged the population to storm houses in the Jewish quarter and murder their occupants.

These riots began in Valencia in July 1391 and spread to Mallorca, Barcelona, Girona, Lléida and Perpignan. But those in Barcelona were by far the most violent; the *qahqal* was virtually destroyed and about 1,000 Jews died. The survivors were forced either to convert to Christianity or flee, despite the efforts of the national guard who defended the lives and properties of the persecuted as best they could.

RIGHT: inside Sinagoga Mayor, Carrer Marlet.

Joan I ordered the arrest and execution of 15 Castilians responsible for the uprising, but despite the monarch's good intentions the *call* was never rebuilt. By 1395 the flow of anti-Semitism had reached such proportions that the synagogue on the street then called "Sanahuja" was converted into a church (today the Església de Sant Jaume, in Carrer de Ferran). In 1396, the principal synagogue was rented to a pottery maker.

The *call* disappeared in 1401 when the synagogues were abolished and Jewish cemeteries destroyed. It was not until 1931 that the first new Spanish synagogue was established, on the corner of Balmes and Provença. It was shut down during the Civil War, and reopened in 1948, in the Avinguda de Roma. It later moved to its present site in Carrer d'Avenir.

Today the only evidence of the prosperous era of the *call* are certain stretches of the Carrer de Banys Nous and the Carrer del Call, the Jewish quarter's main street. A 13th-century synagogue, Sinagoga Mayor, possibly built on the site of an earlier synagogue, was recently excavated and can be visited at Carrer Marlet, 5 (tel: 93 317 0790; www.calldebarcelona.org). Guided tours (in Spanish, English and Hebrew) can be booked in advance via the website. ❑

RESTAURANTS & BARS

Restaurants

Modern restaurants designed within medieval buildings, fusion food in old local bars, one of the best Japanese restaurants in town, creative pizzas eaten on a sunny terrace and economic family-run establishments – this historic quarter has it all.

Agut
Gignàs, 16 (metro: Jaume I)
Tel: 93 315 1709
L & D Tues–Sat. L only Sun.
€€
Bustling, noisy, traditional restaurant with heaps of atmosphere and walls lined with paintings. Good for getting the "Barcelona feel" and for succulent Catalan specialities.

Buenas Migas
Baixada de Santa Clara, 2 (metro: Jaume I)
Tel: 93 319 1380
B, L & D daily. €
This picturesque branch of the successful little *focacceria* chain is tucked behind the Cathedral. Great for a quick break from sightseeing, the savoury pies with

spinach or artichoke are delicious. Perhaps the only place in Barcelona selling apple crumble.

Cafè de l'Acadèmia
Lledó, 1 (metro: Jaume I)
Tel: 93 315 0026
B, L & D Mon–Fri. €€
Delicious new interpretations of classic Catalan dishes have made this low-key, attractive place one of the best options in town. Tables in the medieval square, shaded by umbrellas in summer. Popular with politicians from nearby Plaça Sant Jaume.

Cafè d'Estiu
Plaça Sant Iu, 5–6 (metro: Jaume I)
Tel: 93 310 3014
Tues–Sun, Mar–Sept. €
Delightful summer café serving refreshments and light snacks in a shady, peaceful courtyard next to the Museu Frederic Marès entrance.

Can Fly
Baixada de Viladecols, 6 (metro: Jaume I)
Tel: 67 561 8473
Tues–Sun. €
Attractive new bar squeezed into a corner overlooking one of the Roman towers. Delicious snacks, unusual salads, *torrades* (large slices of toast rubbed with oil and tomato, served with cheese or ham). Try the best olives ever, marinated according to the owner's grandmother's secret formula.

El Gran Café
Avinyó, 9 (metro: Liceu/Jaume I)
Tel: 93 318 7986
L & D daily. €€ (set menu €)
A splendid, classic old restaurant with Parisian overtones, quite expensive unless you order the set lunch.

El Portalón
Banys Nous, 20 (metro: Liceu)
Tel: 93 302 1187
L & D Mon–Sat. €
Barrels, pitchers of wine, nicotine-stained walls and old men playing dominoes – this place oozes atmosphere, and the set menu chalked on a blackboard is excellent value. Don't miss their *potajes* (bean or chick pea stews) in winter.

El Salón
Hostal d'en Sol, 6–8 (metro: Jaume I)
Tel: 93 315 2159
D only Mon–Sat. €
Inspiring and delicious food which draws from a variety of sources, resulting in imaginative combinations. A warm and pretty candlelit space, with old-style Spanish furniture. Some outdoor tables in the shadow of a Roman tower.

Els Quatre Gats
Montsió, 3 (metro: Catalunya)
Tel: 93 317 3022
B, L & D daily. €€ (set menu Mon–Sat L €)
The house Puig i Cadalfach built, made famous

by Picasso and his friends. Risk being a tourist for the sake of eating here; the food is very acceptable but not a priority.

Freud B'Art
Baixada de Sant Miquel, 4 (metro: Liceu/Jaume I)
Tel: 93 318 6629
D Tues–Sat. €€
Try a cocktail before one of Gianni Fusco's inspired dishes in the laid-back atmosphere of this stylish gallery-cum-restaurant.

Gaucho's
Baixada de Sant Miquel, 6 (metro Liceu/Jaume I)
Tel: 93 318 9900
L & D daily. €
Argentinian to the core, including the imported meat, which is cooked *a la parrilla*, that is on the grill, in Gaucho style.

Il Panetto
Tapineria, 4 (metro: Jaume I)
Tel: 93 268 3004
B, L & D daily. €
A hole-in-the-wall snack bar with delicious sandwiches, soups and juices, plus home-made cakes. Relaxing atmosphere with good music and reading material.

La Cassola
Sant Sever, 3 (metro: Jaume I)
Tel: 93 318 1580
L & D Mon–Fri. €
Family-run restaurant, with regular clientele from nearby offices who enjoy good home-made Catalan food.

PRICE CATEGORIES

Prices for three-course dinner per person with a half-bottle of house wine:
€ = under €25
€€ = €25–€40
€€€ = €40–€60
€€€€ = more than €60

La Verónica

Avinyó, 30 (metro: Liceu)
Tel: 93 412 1122
D Mon–Fri. L & D Sat–Sun. €
Colourful, modern space designed for a colourful, crowd, with a popular terrace. Delicious *pizzas del mercat* using seasonal vegetables, like wild mushrooms and artichokes, and great salads. Another branch will open soon in Rambla del Raval.

Les Quinze Nits

Plaça Reial, 6 (metro: Liceu)
Tel: 93 317 3075
L & D daily. €
The only way to beat the queues for this sought-after, elegant restaurant serving cheap Catalan food is to follow a northern European timetable (lunch at 1pm, dinner at 8.30pm). The dishes are effective, even if mass-produced, and sitting on a terrace overlooking this majestic square is a treat.

Living

Capellans, 9 (metro: Jaume I/Catalunya)
Tel: 93 412 1370
B, L & D Mon–Sat. €
Hidden from the madding shopping crowds of Portal de l'Angel is this peaceful, well-designed restaurant with a terrace on the quiet square. Creative dishes in the lunchtime set menu and an outdoor cinema on summer evenings.

Matsuri

Plaça Regomir, 1 (metro: Jaume I)
Tel: 93 268 1535

L & D Mon–Fri. D only Sat. €
Filling a gap in the market, this good-looking restaurant specialises in South-East Asian food, which is given a personal interpretation by its creative chef.

Peimong

Templaris, 6 (metro: Jaume I)
Tel: 93 318 2873
L & D Tues–Sun. €
A small, very simple restaurant just behind Plaça Sant Jaume, serving authentic *ceviche* (raw fish marinaded in lemon juice with coriander and spicy peppers) and other Peruvian specialities, including Peruvian beers and Inca Kola.

Shunka

Sagristans, 5 (metro: Catalunya/Jaume I)
Tel: 93 412 4991
L & D Tues–Sun. €
Tucked into a quiet street near the Cathedral this newcomer to the growing ranks of Japanese restaurants in the city is impressive enough for the renowned chef Ferran Adrià to be a regular customer.

Taxidermista

Plaça Reial, 8 (metro: Liceu)
Tel: 93 412 4536
L & D Tues–Sun. €
No prizes for guessing the not-too-distant origins of this elegant addition to the line-up of restaurants in Plaça Reial. Stylishly renovated from its former role into a luminous space where unconventional Catalan dishes are served.

Vinissim

Sant Domènec del Call, 12 (metro: Liceu/Jaume I)
Tel: 93 301 4575
L & D Tues–Sat. D only Mon. €
Hidden in a forgotten square, this new restaurant serves delicious and unusual Catalan food and has an excellent selection of wines by the glass. Attractive decor and peaceful surroundings.

Bars & Cafés

Favourite squares for coffee or drinks are the Plaça del Pi and the adjoining Plaça Sant Josep Oriol, where there are several cafés, including the enticing terrace of the popular **Bar del Pi**. Serious coffee enthusiasts should not miss the **Mesón del Café**, Llibreteria, 16,

something of a curio in today's designer city. Nearby **Can Conesa**, Llibreteria, 1, in a corner of the Plaça de Sant Jaume, is a traditional sandwich bar making some of the best toasted *bocatas* in town, as the queue testifies. With its cool music and stylish deco interior, **Ginger**, Lledó, 2, has rapidly become an essential stop on the night scene, while timeless, cavernous **Glaciar** is still one of the best bars in Plaça Reial.

Taste the boutique hotel experience without the bill by having a drink on the terrace of the **Neri Hotel** in the charming Plaça Sant Felip Neri, or jostle your way to the counter to select *tapes* in one of the many bars in Carrer Mercè near the port.

RIGHT: Els Quatre Gats, a haunt of Picasso.

LA RIBERA, BORN AND PARC DE LA CIUTADELLA

The narrow streets and grand mansions of La Ribera resound with reminders of medieval commerce, but the focus is switching to a vibrant bar and restaurant scene

The *barri* of La Ribera is loosely defined as that part of the Old Town which is separated from the Barri Gòtic by Via Laietana. There is a very beaten track to the door of its star museum, the Museu Picasso, but the area has many other charms which should not be overlooked. Technically speaking, La Ribera lies between Princesa and the waterfront, and the modish Born area is within La Ribera. However, we'll take the long way round to get there and enjoy discovering this district with its many contrasts, from the present-day rag trade to medieval merchants' houses, from new social and urban developments to the most beautiful church in Barcelona, from contemporary artists' studios to carpenters' workshops.

Like so many of the city's *barris*, La Ribera is a richly woven texture of contrasts. Nothing is more representative of this than the **Palau de la Música Catalana ❶** (guided tours daily 10am–3.30pm; entrance charge), an extravaganza of a concert hall designed by leading *modernista* architect Domènech i Montaner in 1908 *(see pages 170–1)*, and declared a World Heritage building by UNESCO. The only concert hall in Europe to be naturally lit, in all its ornate splendour it was cramped uncomfortably between dull neigh-bours. However, in a major renovation plan by Oscar Tusquets, architect of an earlier extension, it has been liberated and a new chamber for concerts, the Petit Palau, and offices have been constructed.

Locals rush past dismissively, busy about their day-to-day routine, while visitors queue patiently for a tour of the building. Tours are often accompanied by the sounds of a soprano in an upstairs rehearsal room practising her scales. Visits are possible now that the resident

Map
on page
108

LEFT: the sumptuous Palau de la Música Catalana, designed by Domènech i Montaner.
BELOW: playing to an audience in La Ribera.

orchestra, the Orquestra Simfònica de Barcelona i Nacional de Catalunya (OBC), has moved to the grand new **Auditori**, near Glòries. Don't miss the chance to see inside the Palau de la Música, though perhaps the best way is to attend one of the concerts in its busy classical season, or even a jazz concert during the International Jazz Festival.

Rags to riches

Keeping the colourful kaleidoscope of stained glass and mosaics in mind, continue along the street Sant Pere Més Alt through the heart of today's rag-trade district. This is the wholesale end of Catalonia's once great textile industry. On weekdays it is buzzing with commercial activity, particularly around the 19th-century arcades, like the Passeig Sert, birthplace of the painter Josep Maria Sert (1876–1945), where old warehouses have been converted into desirable lofts.

The street emerges into the comparative tranquillity of **Plaça Sant Pere ❷**, with the much renovated 10th-century church, **Sant Pere de les Puel·les**, a former Benedictine monastery. In the middle of this triangular square is a delicate *modernista* drinking fountain, designed by Pere Falqués, famed for his benches-cum-lamp-posts on Passeig de Gràcia. Follow Basses Sant Pere down past stray dogs, drunks and local bars with a firm grip on rucksacks and cameras to **Plaça Sant Agustí Vell ❸**. Signs of urban cleansing are evident, but thankfully new social housing and created *plaças* have not wiped out local colour altogether. There are several terrace bars, but hold out for the **Bar Mundial**, a 1950s time warp famed for its seafood *tapes*.

From here, one option is to take Carders, rapidly becoming Dominican territory (there is a great musical atmosphere on Saturday and

Poised outside the Palau de la Música Catalana.

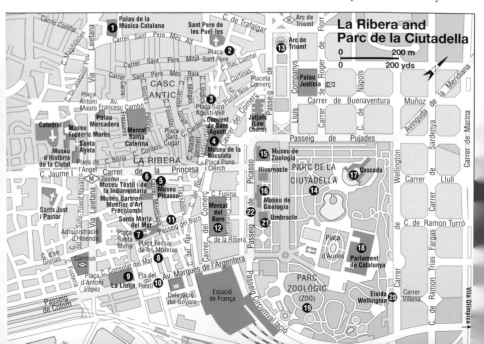

Sunday evenings), to the delightful Romanesque chapel of **Marcús**, where post horses were blessed on the main route out, being just beyond the city walls and the Portal Major. Turn left into Montcada for the Museu Picasso.

Another option is to meander a little longer down Tantarantana, passing more urban rehabilitation to the former **Convent de Sant Agustí** ❹. Now a civic centre, and highlighted by the Ruta del Gòtic as a 14th-century building, it also houses the **Museu de la Xocolata** (Mon and Wed–Sat 10am–7pm, Sun 10am–2.30pm; entrance charge), which is mildly interesting for children and chocolate buffs.

Just before Princesa, turn right into **Assaonadors**, which immediately on the right opens into a long *plaça*, **Allada-Vermell**, a typical Barcelona "hard" square. Created by the demolition of a row of housing, it brings light and space into the dense *barri*, and provides a recreation area for local residents. The **Espai Escènic Joan Brossa**, an alternative theatre with its own

company, whose productions tend to be in line with artist-poet Brossa's thinking and interests is well worth checking out. One of Brossa's visual poems sets the scene: the horizontal B (for Brossa) on the roof has "lost" one of its curved pieces, which is lying on the ground to provide an open-air stage.

Continue along Assaonadors, taking the first left which leads into **Princesa**. The Parc de la Ciutadella *(see page 114)* is at the end of the road, but turn right towards the city centre again. It is a busy, narrow street full of lorries unloading goods "made in China" and taxis unloading tourists by Montcada. Many of the buildings are being restored to a bygone elegance and sold off expensively as studio flats by rich developers. The pavements are crowded with Asian shopkeepers on mobile telephones and tourists looking for the Picasso Museum.

On the corner before turning into Montcada be tempted by a *roque de Montserrat*, speciality of the *patisseria* **Brunells**. If these boulders, looking remarkably like meringues,

Map on page 108

Street theatre of all kinds is endemic in the old quarter of Barcelona.

BELOW: street life in La Ribera.

*Pablo Picasso
(1881–1973) began
his art studies in
Barcelona but spent
most of his career
outside Spain,
passing his formative
years in Paris. His
work always retained
its Spanish links, as
in his most famous
painting,* Guernica
(1937).

BELOW:
the courtyard of the
Picasso Museum.

from the sacred mountain of Montserrat don't appeal, there is a wide choice of refreshments in the café behind the shop.

Street of museums

Montcada has become museum street supreme since the local authorities started renovating its medieval palaces in 1957, but it is a lot more besides and can be enjoyed on many levels. Named after the fallen during the conquest of Mallorca, it was the city's most elegant district from the 12th to the 18th centuries. It linked the waterfront with the commercial areas, when Catalonia's trading in the Mediterranean was at its height. The rich merchants' palaces reflect this former prosperity. As you jostle with the crowd in the narrow street, glance up at the menacing gargoyles and elegant medieval arches on top-floor terraces. And pause between exhibitions to sit in one of the peaceful patios, where the past is palpable in the stones and fine masonry.

The **Museu Picasso ❺** (Tues–Sat including public holidays 10am–

8pm, Sun 10am–3pm; entrance charge) at Montcada Nos. 15–23, opened in 1963, now occupies five palaces: Palau Berenguer d'Aguilar, Baró de Castellet, Meca, Casa Mauri and Finestres. The last two, opened in October 1999, are for temporary exhibitions; the main entrance is through the 15th-century Aguilar palace. Its beautiful court-yard, with a surrounding first-floor gallery and pointed archways rest-ing on slender columns, was designed by Marc Safont, best known for the inner patio of the **Generalitat** building.

The museum has the most complete collection of Picasso's early works, including sketches in school books and a masterly portrait of his mother done when he was only 16. The Blue Period (1901–4) is also well represented. It is an absorbing collection although there are only a limited number of Picasso's later works, apart from the fascinating studies of *Las Meninas* from the 1950s.

Opposite is the **Museu Tèxtil i de la Indumentària ❻** (Tues–Sat 10am–6pm, Sun 10am–3pm;

entrance charge), housed in another noble Gothic palace, the Marquès de Lliò. The museum has a small collection, with fabrics from the 14th century to the present day, some notable *modernista* and Balenciaga creations, and tools from the 19th-century Catalan textile industry. In truth, it is perhaps more visited for the attractive café that spills onto the courtyard, serving snacks until late in the evening, and for its inspired gift shop.

Adjoining it is the **Museu Barbier-Mueller d'Art Precolombí** (Tues–Sat 10am–6pm, Sun 10am–3pm; entrance charge), which has a small but prestigious collection of pre-Colombian art, representing most styles of pre-Hispanic American civilisations, bequeathed to Barcelona by the Geneva Museum. The gift shop has some beautiful contemporary Indian work, albeit at Western prices.

Continuing down the street there is the avant-garde **Sala Montcada** at No. 14, run by the highly regarded prosperous cultural foundation of La Caixa, the affluent Catalan savings bank. On the other side in the Palau Cervelló, No. 25, is the **Galeria Maeght** (closed lunchtime). Both are guaranteed to have worthwhile exhibitions.

Bars and boutiques

Reeling from these cultural riches, pop into the marble-and-tile haven **El Xampanyet** for a glass of wonderful sparkling wine and some anchovies. Here the street opens into **Plaçeta Montcada**, which contains an exotic palm tree, and **Euskal Etxea**, one of the most authentic establishments to emerge in the recent trend for Basque bars. You must arrive at aperitif time (around 1pm or 8pm) to catch the best *tapes*, or else you'll have to opt for a full meal in the restaurant.

Souvenir and "arty" shops abound here, and are beginning to eclipse the originals selling blue overalls and the like. Wander through the labyrinth of streets off Montcada to get closer to the true local atmosphere. There are many attractive new shops, bars and studios, too, worth visiting and useful for gift ideas.

Map on page 108

The café at Museu Tèxtil i de la Indumentària.

BELOW: Euskal Etxea, top for *tapes*.

Sun streams through one of the lovely stained-glass windows in Santa Maria del Mar.

BELOW:
Santa Maria del Mar.

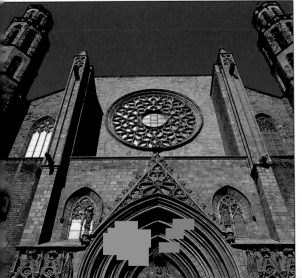

Santa Maria del Mar

One such street is **Sombrerers** on the right (named, like many in the area, after the medieval guilds, in this case the hatters'), just before reaching the Passeig del Born. Follow its shade, with the towering edifice of Santa Maria del Mar on the left, past an exquisite grocery specialising in nuts, a local barber and the gossip of the chicken shop, to reach the **Plaça Santa Maria**, once the church's graveyard. The Gothic fountain is one of the oldest in the city, dating from 1402. On reaching the square, stand back and take in the Gothic facade of the **Església de Santa Maria del Mar** ❼ (daily 9am–1.30pm and 4.30–8pm; free), considered by many – and justly so – to be the most beautiful church in Barcelona. Its soaring majesty is uplifting, and should not be missed.

The church was built relatively quickly, between 1329 and 1384, resulting in a purity of style which ranks it as the most perfect example of Gothic church architecture in Catalonia. All the local corporations collaborated in the building and it became a symbol of the economic and political power of Catalonia in this period. The facade exhibits all the characteristics of the Catalan Gothic style: "prevalence of horizontal lines; flat terraced roofing; wide open spaces; strong buttresses and octagonal towers ending in terraces", according to Alexandre Cirici, the Catalan art historian. It is a much more down-to-earth style than Northern European Gothic, lacking the decorative filigree and pointed spires of the latter. As the critic Robert Hughes says in his book *Barcelona*: "The mass counts for more than the opening … Catalan architects did not want to imitate the organic profusion of detail in northern Gothic. They liked a wall."

The rose window is 15th-century, the original having been lost in the earthquake of 1428. The interior is breathtaking in its simplicity and elegance. The church is built in what is known as the "salon" design, with three lofty and almost identical naves, which contribute to the sense of space. Ironically, the drama of more recent history has also contributed to this purity: fire during the Civil War destroyed a great deal of the interior, which left it free of over-ornate decoration. The octagonal columns are 13 metres (43 ft) apart, a distance no other medieval structure was able to achieve. Robert Hughes sums up this extraordinary beauty: "There is no grander or more solemn architectural space in Spain than Santa Maria del Mar."

The old commercial district

Leave through the side door of the church, which takes you to the **Plaça Fossar de les Moreres** ❽, a memorial to the fallen in the 1714 siege of Barcelona *(see page 23)*, who are buried here in the former cemetery. Restored in 1986 by Carme Fiol, one of the leading architects in Barcelona's urban space programme, it is a favourite venue for Catalan nationalists to meet on 11 September, La Diada, the day the siege ended.

Return to Plaça Santa Maria, passing a shop selling the most creative *botifarras* (sausages) imaginable, and turn left into **Canvis Vells.** If you want to be sidetracked, one of the widest selections of Catalan and Spanish wines is just down **Agullers** in the Viniteca. If not, continue to Consolat del Mar, and the large volume of **La Llotja ❾**, the former stock exchange (now in Passeig de Gràcia). Its core is from the 14th century, but the outer shell was completed in 1802. The Chamber of Commerce occupies most of the building and organises occasional visits (tel: 93 319 2412), although part of the Acadèmia de Bellas Artes, where Picasso and Miró studied, is still on an upper floor.

The main facade of La Llotja (not used as an entrance) looks over **Plaça del Palau ❿** where a royal palace once stood. Now devoted mostly to restaurants, it was the political centre of town for a period during the 18th and 19th centuries

under the dominant viceroy. There are several good restaurants to choose from, but you could walk past the most famous without even knowing it, **Passadís d'en Pep** at No. 2, hidden away down a private-looking corridor.

Keeping on the same pavement, walk through to **Plaça de les Olles** (Square of the Cooking Pots), a charming little square with pleasant terrace cafés. In the far corner turn into Vidrieria. An ancient glass shop at No. 8 befits this street of "glaziers", selling all manner of glassware and run by the twelfth generation of the same family.

Glass and tin fairs used to be held in the **Passeig del Born ⓫** at the end of the road, as well as jousts and tournaments from the 13th to the 17th centuries. Take time to wander along this boulevard and its adjoining streets, where the bars, shops and art galleries change hands and style with remarkable frequency, but where a few stalwarts remain, like the *colmado* selling *legumbres*, delicious ready-cooked lentils and beans.

At the end, in Plaça Comercial,

Map on page 108

TIP

Santa Maria del Mar is a popular venue for concerts (as well as for fashionable weddings), so check local listings for a recommended opportunity to sit back and enjoy this sacred corner of Barcelona.

BELOW: the courtyard of La Llotja.

Medieval Guilds

Wandering around the *barri* of La Ribera, you get a real sense of history from the names of its narrow streets, particularly those named after trades, a throwback to the medieval boom when guilds were formed to look after the interests of the different craftsmen.

At their height, between the 13th and 15th centuries, there were 135 *gremis* (guilds), and 52 streets still carry their names. Watch out for Sombrerers (hatters), Flassaders (blanket weavers), Mirallers (mirror makers), Argenteria (silversmiths), Assaonadors (tanners), Agullers (needle makers) and Semoleres (pasta makers). A few medieval *tallers* (workshops) also remain.

In some streets a niche in the wall indicates where the devoted saint of the respective guild, usually dedicated to its patrons, would stand. The Museu d'Història de la Ciutat *(see page 100)* has a room dedicated to the guilds, with documents and paintings pertaining to the craftsmen and their work. The Museu del Calçat (Shoe Museum) in Plaça Sant Felip Neri is housed in the guildhall of the shoemakers, the first guild to be formed and the last to be disbanded – not until the 20th century, in fact, when the Civil War broke out.

The 19th-century Mercat del Born, once the city's main fruit-and-veg market.

there are several good cafés and restaurants, any of which would make a good stopping point and a fine place to contemplate the magnificent wrought-iron **Mercat del Born** ⓬, designed by Fontseré and Cornet in 1873. The building functioned as Barcelona's central wholesale fruit-and-vegetable market from 1876 until 1971. Recent excavations have revealed valuable archaeological remains, so plans for a library have been halted.

The whole area takes on a different atmosphere at night when the many small bars and hidden restaurants come to life. International and Catalan cuisines abound, with a range to please all tastes, from Brazilian cocktails to cuban *frijoles* (beans) and, of course, Catalan *pa amb tomàquet* (bread with tomato).

Parc de la Ciutadella

Just beyond this area is Barcelona's oldest and most visited park, the Parc de la Ciutadella, which is also one of the city's most attractive. It is easy (and therapeutic) to while away half a day here, simply walking in the fresher air, or enjoying some of the diverse activities on offer. Located between the Old Town and the new Vila Olímpica, it lies on the eastern side of the Mercat del Born, just across the Passeig de Picasso, where there are two entrances.

However, one of the most interesting approaches, which also gives the park its historical perspective, is from the northern end of Passeig de Lluís Companys, next to the **Arc de Triomf** ⓭ (easily reached by the metro of the same name, or by bus). This enormous brick arch served as the entrance to the 1888 World Exposition site *(see page 25)*, which was held on the redeveloped land previously occupied by the fortress. From the top of Passeig de Lluís Companys you can look down towards the park or up along **Passeig Sant Joan** – a typical Eixample street with architectural echoes of Passeig de Gràcia, including some fine *modernista* houses – towards the Collserola range.

The clear light and sense of space around the Arc de Triomf are truly representative of Barcelona. Designed by Josep Vilaseca, the arch includes sculptures by Josep Llimona, among others. It is easy to imagine visitors to the Exposition sweeping down this elegant route to the showground, past the magnificent street lamps. Today's palms are some of the most attractive of the many species growing in the city. In front of the monumental Law Courts on the left, old men play *petanca* (a southern European form of bowls), while rollerbladers vie for space with retired couples who sit on pieces of cardboard playing card games. A large tent on this promenade is the temporary home (for several years) of the Santa Caterina market, until the new market in La Ribera is completed. Just behind this is the main entrance to the **Parc de la Ciutadella** ⓮

(daily 8am–9pm in summer, 8am–8pm in winter; free).

A turbulent history

The name, La Ciutadella (which means citadel, or fortress), has its origins in the use to which Felipe V put this land. After the fall of Barcelona in 1714, following a siege by Franco-Spanish troops, he ordered a fortress to be built that was capable of housing 8,000 soldiers, with the intention that they would control the city in his name. To do this it was necessary to demolish 40 streets and 1,262 buildings. Barceloneta was built to accommodate the evicted residents. For many years after the Civil War the citadel was used as a political prison.

In 1869 General Prim ceded the land to the city for conversion into a public park; the town hall issued a public tender for the landscaping and construction of the gardens, which went to Josep Fontseré. His plan was approved in 1873 but it was not until 1888, the year of the World Exposition, that the park began to be a reality, emerging in a shape later to be damaged by bombing in the Civil War.

Interesting buildings remain from its military past and from its glorious time as the Exposition showground, but the most remarkable aspect of the park is its refreshing tranquillity. It is a real city park, full of skateboards and footballs, prams and toddlers. There are bicycles made for six for hire, as well as rowing boats on the lake. On Sunday large families parade in their best outfits before lunch. Yet it is still peaceful. Constantly tended by municipal gardeners, it is verdant, scented and shady, a soothing place to walk in all seasons.

Old-fashioned charm

On the right as you enter is the **Museu de Zoologia** ⓯ (Tues–Sun 10am–2pm, Thur 10am–6.30pm; entrance charge; combined ticket with Museu de Geologia available) in a building designed by Domènech i Montaner, the Castell dels Tres Dragons (Castle of the Three Dragons). It was intended to be the restaurant of the 1888 Exposition,

Map on page 108

fountain in the Parc de la Ciutadella.

BELOW LEFT: a model of a woolly mammoth provides a photo opportunity.
BELOW: relaxing by the boating lake.

Barcelona's zoo has a good reputation, particularly for its lowland gorillas and dolphin show.

BELOW: the Cascada forms the centrepiece of the Parc de la Ciutadella.

though it never opened as such. However, it was one of the first *modernista* projects in Barcelona and the architect's studio for years. Its collections of zoological specimens and impressive skeletons are well housed amid the 19th-century marble and polished floors.

Behind is the beautiful **Hivernacle**, an elegant greenhouse bursting with tropical plants, which has been well restored to include a restaurant. Jazz and classical concerts are held here on summer evenings. In line with these two buildings is a more classical-looking structure built to be a museum in 1878, the first public one in Barcelona. Now the **Museu de Geologia** ⑯ (opening times are as for the Museu de Zoologia), it has collections of rocks, minerals and fossils, notably from Catalonia and the rest of Spain, and the same old-world charm as the Museu de Zoologia. These are a different breed from the new generation of state-of-the-art museums in other parts of the city.

Cross over the inner road and follow signs to the **Cascada** ⑰, the monumental fountain and artificial lake designed by Fontseré in 1875; both the cascade and the lake were intended to camouflage a huge water deposit in the central section of the waterfall, which can be reached by two flanking, symmetrical stairways. Curiously, Gaudí worked on this project as a young architectural student. Something of a landmark and meeting place, its esplanade is often used for concerts, shows or fairs.

Reminders of the citadel

With your back to the Cascada, follow the boating lake round either way to the **Plaça d' Armes**, where there is a serene, oval formal garden designed by French landscape architect, J. C. N. Forestier. The statue in the lake is *El Desconsol*, one of Catalan sculptor Josep Llimona's most highly regarded pieces. This square is bordered by the remnants of the citadel era: the Governor's Palace, now a secondary school, the chapel and the arsenal.

This last is now where the **Parlament de Catalunya** ⑱ sits, guarded by the Catalan police, the *Mossos d'Esquadra*. Until recently, part of the building housed the Museu d'Art Modern, with its large collection of Catalan painting, drawing, sculpture and decorative art. This has been rehoused in the Museum of Catalan Art (MNAC) on Montjuïc.

Follow the paved road towards the park gates to find the zoo or **Parc Zoologic** ⑲ (daily May–Aug 9.30am–7.30pm, Sept–Apr 10am–5pm; entrance charge). Founded in 1892, its most famous inmate was Floquet de Neu (Snowflake), the only albino gorilla in captivity, who died amid much lamenting in 2003, succeeded by various non-albino descendants. Other highlights include the Aquarama dolphin show.

From within the zoo the **Wellington exit** ⑳, which leads to the street of the same name, takes you to the

Vila Olímpica and its beaches *(see page 137)*. A new tramline starts from this street, connecting, at Plaça de les Glòries, with another route down to the Forum site. Alternatively, the metro is also close by, but for further exploration take **Avinguda Icària** into the Olympic Village, or head for the Hotel Arts (the right-hand skyscraper) passing through a small, modern park, **Parc Cascades**, above the Ronda Litoral. Complete your day with a swim on Barceloneta beach and dinner in the Olympic Port. If this sounds appealing, but the zoo doesn't, there is another exit from the park on Pujades, behind the Cascade. Turn right and follow Wellington past the haunting brick structure, the **Diposit de les Aigües**, which stored water on its roof. Part of this building has been impressively restored as the library of the nearby University Pompeu Fabra. This street links up with the zoo exit.

However, if you prefer to do full justice to the Ciutadella, from the main entrance to the zoo (inside the park), take the road that leads past the Plaça d'Armes on the right and meander through to the **Umbracle ㉑** on the far side of the park. This is a beautiful arched building of brick and wood, with fine iron columns, also designed by Fontseré. It offers much-needed shade for the more delicate species in the park. The dim light inside is reminiscent of a jungle.

Passeig de Picasso

A small gate by the Umbracle leads out of the park to the **Passeig de Picasso ㉒**. The handsome arcaded apartment blocks that line this side of the park were designed by Fontseré as an integral part of his plans for redevelopment of the site. Some good bars and a useful bike-rental shop are located under the arches at this end. A large modern sculpture in a transparent cube on the boundary of the park is by leading Catalan artist Antoni Tàpies and was designed as a homage to Picasso *(Homenatge a Picasso)*. Old men in berets play *petanca* alongside it.

The heavy traffic thunders past here on its way to the port, turning the corner into **Marquès de l'Argentera**. Spain's first railway line was inaugurated here in 1848 with a route that ran from Barcelona to Mataró. The railway station was little more than a shack near today's **Estació de França** (halfway down the avenue) which, at the time of its opening in September 1929, was the largest station in Europe. It was closed for several years while the tracks were buried underground to make way for the Olympic Village. The station has now been restored to formidable splendour, and looks more like a grand hotel than an international railway station. Occasionally, exhibitions are held here in its marble, polished expanse. Whether it forms part of your journey or not, be sure to visit it to capture the romance of train journeys from an earlier epoch. ❑

Map on page 108

The Aquarama show takes place three times a day in the Parc Zoologic.

BELOW: a new tram runs from Wellington through Plaça de les Glòries to Diagonal Mar and beyond.

RESTAURANTS & BARS

Restaurants

At the hub of this area is the trendy Born district whose recent spectacular rise to fame has resulted in a constant turnover of bars, cafés and restaurants, so there's plenty of choice, especially of the alternative variety. There are also many old, established favourites as well as new stars that are here to stay, where you need to book, or join the queue, from Thursday to Saturday.

Abac
Rec, 79–89 (metro: Jaume I/Barceloneta)
Tel: 93 319 6600
L & D Tues–Sat. D only Mon. €€€€
Michelin-starred chef Xavier Pellicer has quickly converted this sleek modern restaurant in the Park Hotel into an essential stop for international foodies.

Bascula
Flassaders, 30 bis (metro: Jaume I)
Tel: 93 319 9866
B, L & D Mon–Sat. €

PRICE CATEGORIES

Prices for three-course dinner per person with a half-bottle of house wine:
€ = under €25
€€ = €25–€40
€€€ = €40–€60
€€€€ = more than €60

A new kind of restaurant, run as a cooperative by people from many different countries, in a former sweet factory in the labyrinth of streets behind the Picasso Museum. Delicious snacks as wll as wholesome meals using organic produce, mostly vegetarian.

Cafè Kafka
Fusina, 7 (metro: Jaume I)
Tel: 93 310 0526
L & D daily. €
Sophisticated space with relaxing atmosphere and alternative food with Oriental influences. Located just behind the Born market but slightly removed from the usual bustle. Open for drinks until 3am.

Cal Pep
Plaça de les Olles, 8 (metro: Jaume I/Barceloneta)
Tel: 93 310 7961
L & D Tues–Sat. D only Mon. €€€
Jostle and queue to sit at the bar where you can witness the chefs tossing and flipping fat prawns and succulent squid. Mediterranean cooking at its simplest and very best, with atmosphere to match.

Carpanta
Sombrerers, 13 (metro: Jaume I)
Tel: 93 319 9999
L & D Tues–Sat. L only Sun. €€
Well-established favourite in this area

where businesses open and close overnight. Here you can be sure of a good Mediterranean meal in attractive art nouveau surroundings.

Comerç 24
Comerç, 24 (metro: Arc de Triomf)
Tel: 93 319 2102
L & D Tues–Sat. €€€
One of the leading lights in new-wave Catalan cooking, chef Carles Abellán, inspired by several years working in the laboratory-kitchen of El Bullí, has opened his own designer-smart restaurant where the tasting menu, the *Festival de tapas,* is a trip for the taste buds.

Comme Bio
Via Layetana, 28 (metro: Jaume I)
Tel: 93 319 8968
B, L & D daily. €
A vegetarian emporium with two restaurants (daytime and evening) upstairs, and downstairs an eat-as-much-as-you-want buffet. There are also two shops: one for organic groceries and one that is open until late. Another branch, Comme-Bio II, is just off Rambla Catalunya in Gran Via, 603.

Dionisos
Av. Marquès de l'Argentera, 27 (metro: Arc de Triomf/Barceloneta)
Tel: 93 268 2472
L & D daily. €
A genuine taste of

Greece in pleasant surroundings looking over the Parc de la Ciutadella. Ideal for a light lunch after a walk or cycle ride in the park.

El Passadís del Pep
Pla de Palau, 2 (metro: Jaume I/Barceloneta)
Tel: 93 310 1021
L & D Tues–Sat. D only Mon. €€€€
This is a place for people "in the know", the kind of place you walk past if you are not. Be prepared to spend a lot, but otherwise relax; you don't even have to choose from a menu; food is simply brought to you.

Espai Sucre
Princesa, 53 (metro: Jaume I/Arc de Triomf)
Tel: 93 268 1630
D only Tues–Sat. €€€
"Dinner" is not quite the word in this very Barcelonan restaurant serving nothing but *postres.* And we're not talking apple crumble but creations that play with the palate, like lychee soup with celery, apples and eucalyptus. Excellent range of dessert wines to accompany the 3- or 5-course pudding menu.

Euskaletxea
Placeta Montcada, 1–3 (metro: Jaime I)
Tel: 93 310 2185
L & D Tues–Sat. D only Mon. €€€ (*tapes* €)
A stronghold of Basque

cuisine just two minutes from the Picasso Museum, where you can be sure of a good meal. Discover a range of Basque specialities by opting for *cazuelitas*, small portions served in casserole dishes. If you prefer *tapes* get there early to catch the fresh *pintxos* at the bar.

Hofmann
Argenteria, 74–78 (metro: Jaume I)
Tel: 93 319 5889
L & D Mon–Fri. €€€€
Food by cordon bleu chefs for serious gourmets, served in a set of cosy rooms on the first floor, next to the adjoining cooking school. Essential to book in advance.

L'Hivernacle
Passeig de Picasso, Parc de la Ciutadella (metro: Jaume I/Arc de Triomf)
Tel: 93 295 4017
B, L & D Mon–Sat. L only Sun. €
To eat under the glass and ironwork of this tropical plant house right in the park is a treat, especially on a warm summer evening when you may catch one of their regular jazz concerts.

Mirador
Palau de la Música Catalana, Sant Pere Més Alt (metro: Urquinaona)
Tel: 93 310 2433
L & D daily. €€€
An elegant option for taking a closer look at the amazing *modernista* concert hall, as this restaurant is in the new extension. Under the

watchful eye of Michelin-star chef Jean-Luc Figueras the immaculate dishes are Catalan with French influences. Open after concerts.

Mosquito
Carders 46, baixos 2a (metro: Arc de Triomf/ Jaume I)
Tel: 93 268 7569
D only. Wed–Sun. €
The delightful English owners define their food as "exotic tapas", which is a modest assessment of the delicious, original Asian dishes they create personally. It's rare to find such good Oriental cuisine in Barcelona. What's more, it's open from 7pm, which is handy for early dinners with kids.

Mundial
Plaça Sant Agustí Vell, 1 (metro: Arc de Triomf/ Jaume I)
Tel: 93 319 9056
Tapes Tues–Sun. €
May the Mundial never change. A stalwart of traditional, Spanish bars, fast fading in this up-and-coming district, its solid marble bar is piled with fresh, simple seafood *tapes*.

Pla de la Garsa
Assaonadors, 13 (metro: Jaume I)
Tel: 93 315 2413
D only daily. €
This tastefully restored medieval stable with attractive decor is a peaceful option for an evening meal. Enjoy Catalan specialities, especially their range of cheeses, patés and

embotits (cured sausages, ham and typical pork products).

Rodrigo
Argenteria, 67 (metro: Jaume I)
Tel: 93 310 3020
B, L & D Wed–Mon. L only Tues. €
Endearing, busy, family-run restaurant. Delicious food at very economical prices. Cramped and chaotic but fun, especially if you begin with the house *vermut*.

Santa Maria
Comerç, 17 (metro: Jaume I/ Arc de Triomf)
Tel: 93 315 1227
L & D Tues–Sat. €€
Young, creative chef Paco Guzman pioneered this unusual way of eating in the city. On the menu are extremely dainty but delectable little plates of Oriental and Mediterranean extraction. Gourmet food at manageable prices in this trendy but workmanlike space.

Senyor Parellada
Argentería, 37 (metro: Jaume I)
Tel: 93 310 5094
L & D daily. €
A mixture of unusual and classic Catalan dishes in a pleasant, sophisticated environment, run by the Parelladas, a well-known family of restaurateurs. Half-portions are available, which is a welcome innovation.

Set Portes
Passeig Isabel II, 14 (metro: Barceloneta)
Tel: 93 319 3033
L & D daily. €€

Over 160 years old and still going strong. Sympathetically restored, recapturing the original atmosphere, this classic remains popular, especially for family Sunday lunches. Specialises in rice dishes, one for each day of the week. Also has the advantage of remaining open through the afternoon and evening until 1am.

Têxtilcafè
Montcada, 12 (metro: Jaume I)
Tel: 93 268 2598
B, L & D Tues–Sun. €
Even if you don't visit the textile museum it's worth dropping in to its appealing courtyard for a coffee, snack or candle-lit dinner. Light, delicious meals are served.

Bars & Cafés

There are now numerous terraces on pavements and in small squares for cool drinks or coffee, plus an explosion of late-night bars – just follow the crowd. Don't miss the district's gem, **El Xampanyet**, Montcada, 22, a pretty, ceramic-tiled bar, with its intoxicating, fizzy white wine and house anchovies. From **La Vinya del Senyor**, Plaça Santa Maria, 5, a tiny, designer wine bar with an extensive choice of interesting wines by the glass, you can gaze at the wonderful Santa Maria del Mar church.

EL RAVAL

Contemporary art, music, design and cultural centres plus a new Rambla are rejuvenating the historic but long neglected quarter of El Raval

Walking down La Rambla from Plaça de Catalunya, the section of the Old Town to the right-hand side is known as El Raval. Enclosed by **Ronda Sant Antoni** and **Ronda Sant Pau**, in the 1930s this area was one of the most densely populated urban areas in the world, when it became derogatively known as the Barri Xino (Chinese Quarter). It is still given a wide berth by many of Barcelona's inhabitants. However, it is one of the districts of the city with the most potential, and a stimulating area in which to wander and observe. Although some areas are still run-down and at times menacing, some of the most interesting cultural activities in the city are now taking place here.

Religious past

In its medieval past the area was heavily populated by convents and religious institutions. With the advent of industrialisation in the late 18th century the emphasis switched to factories, and dense urbanisation began. Relics of the religious past still stand out in today's bustling El Raval.

From La Rambla, turn down the second road on the right, Bonsuccés, which opens into the **Plaça Bonsuccés**. The large, handsome building dominating the square is a

former convent dating from 1635, now used as district council offices. The adjoining modern archway leads into **Plaça Vicenç Martorell**, a square where the convent cloisters would have been. In the far corner in the arches, the popular bar, **Kasparo**, provides delicious alternative snacks; relax on its shady terrace and watch children playing in the central park. Behind the newspaper kiosk the long-neglected **Casa de la Misericòrdia** (1583), formerly a hospice for

Map on page 123

LEFT: enjoying a flavour of North Africa with a pot of mint tea on the Rambla del Raval.
BELOW: getting a haircut in Sant Pau.

An Arab woman in El Raval, wearing the characteristic jellabah *of North Africa.*

abandoned children, has been cleverly restored, complete with interior palm tree, to make more council offices. If you look closely you will see a small wooden circle in the wall, where babies were pushed through and received by nuns on the other side until as recently as 1931.

Return to Plaça Bonsuccés and turn into **Elisabets**, by the restaurant of the same name (good for hearty winter dishes and atmosphere), heading towards the **Convent dels Angels**, which forms an evocative backdrop at the end of the street. There is a good bookshop in the lofty space of the Misericòrdia chapel and some wonderful tall palms in a secret garden bounded by lush wisteria. **Doctor Dou** on the left has some interesting bars, good value restaurants and modern art galleries. Just past a fashion designer's shop on Elisabets is another well-renovated chapel, part of an orphanage dating back to 1370.

State of the art MACBA

At this point you emerge into the **Plaça dels Angels**, which opens up into the unexpected space dominated by the breathtaking **Museu d'Art Contemporani de Barcelona** (MACBA) ❶ (Mon, Wed–Fri 11am–7.30pm, Sat 10am–8pm, Sun 10am–3pm; entrance charge). Designed by US architect Richard Meier and opened in 1995, the building is dazzling against the blue Mediterranean sky and gigantic within the context of the humble buildings beyond. The social and urban significance of the architecture in this once declining area has been almost more of a talking point than the collection inside, which comprises Catalan, Spanish and some international art, mostly from the second half of the 20th century. The museum also hosts temporary exhibitions.

Its large forecourt has evolved into a popular public space for skate-boarding and football matches. Filipino families who live in the narrow streets around **Joaquín Costa** often gather here with picnic suppers on warm evenings: the square is a fascinating melting pot of local residents and cosmopolitan visitors.

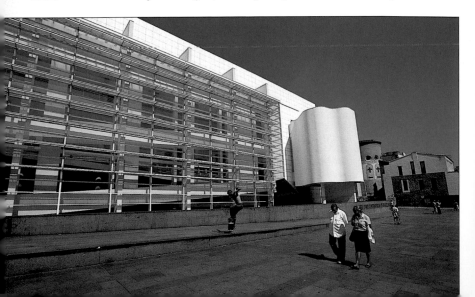

Centre for performance art

The museum was built in the grounds of the enormous Casa de la Caritat (poorhouse), which once provided a home for thousands of children (part of it still stands around the corner in Montalegre). The former 18th-century hospice has been transformed into the **Centre de Cultura Contemporània de Barcelona (CCCB) ❷** (Tues, Thur, Fri 11am–2pm and 4–8pm, Wed, Sat 11am–8pm, Sun 11am–7pm; entrance charge), a series of exhibition spaces for diverse cultural activities, including dance, music, film, video and seminars.It also has great views from its Sala de Mirador. The complex – a wonderful renovation by prestigious architects Piñon and Vilaplana – rivals MACBA for its architectural interest.

The ripples of urban renewal have spread to the surrounding streets where galleries and designers' studios are rapidly opening. Go through the central Patí de les Dones of the CCCB, past its excellent bookshop, into the **Plaça Joan Coromines** which links it with the art museum. Part of the Ramon Llull University also looks over this square. A glass door leads into the older part of the Casa de la Caritat and its ceramic tiled courtyard, Patí Manning. This area is sometimes used as a theatre or dance space, but primarily houses cultural offices.

Hospital de la Santa Creu

Return down Montalegre and continue along as it becomes Angels, a pleasant tree-lined street. When it reaches Carme turn left and cross the road into the **Hospital de la Santa Creu ❸**, a large Gothic complex which was a hospital until the 1920s (open daily). On the left is the 18th-century Academy of Medicine and Surgery, and on the right the **Institut d'Estudis Catalans** in the hospital's **Casa de Convalescència**, which is

The CCCB, a lively arts venue, occupies an 18th-century hospice.

BELOW: the Hospital de la Santa Creu.

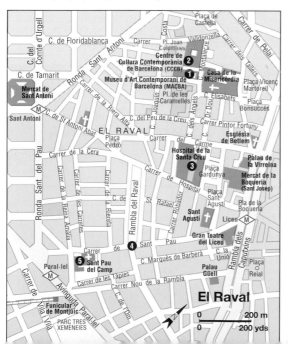

currently being restored. Wander through the atmospheric cloistered patio, although it is lamentably neglected and a favourite meeting place for lonely down-and-outs. The Biblioteca de Catalunya occupies much of the old hospital, along with the Massana art school.

As you emerge into Hospital, check if there is an exhibition in **La Capella** (Tues–Sat noon–2pm and 4–8pm, Sun 11am–2pm), once the hospital's chapel, which promotes experimental artists and has interesting work on display.

Multicultural El Raval

With your back to La Rambla, follow Hospital deeper into El Raval. This is a busy commercial street, even on Sundays, reflecting the increasing number of shops run by Pakistanis, the most recent immigrant group in the district. Tandoori restaurants sit side-by-side with Halal butchers, Arab pastry shops, cheap bazaars and old established tailors selling uniforms for the catering business. A sign above a narrow doorway, squeezed between

two shops, indicates the entrance to a *mezquita*, the main city mosque, though a new one is being built elsewhere in the city.

An arcade on the left, **Passatge Bernardí Martorell**, leads to one of Barcelona's most traditional and recommendable fish restaurants, **Casa Leopoldo**, run by Rosa, the granddaughter of the founder, in the dubious-looking **Sant Rafael**. Trendy second-hand clothes shops are another new thread in this multicoloured fabric. **Riera Baixa**, a short pedestrian street on the right, has some wacky shops and an outdoor market on Saturday.

Turn left at Cadena and be dazzled by the sunlight in the new broad Rambla that leads down to **Sant Pau ❹**, part of the city council's policy of forging through dense urban areas. Old housing has been demolished and new blocks built to create this pleasant **Rambla del Raval**. Old residents and new immigrants are finally coming out into the sunshine to enjoy the space, and it is fast becoming a venue for lively outdoor markets

BELOW:
Rambla del Raval.

and concerts. The prostitutes and junkies are retreating to the narrower streets behind, where the darker side of urban life – sickness, decadence and desperation – is still evident. An unusual abundance of chemists' shops reflects its poor state of health.

The city's oldest church

A left on Sant Pau leads back to the Liceu on La Rambla, but turn right to reach the Romanesque **Església de Sant Pau del Camp ❺** (Mon–Sat 10am–1pm and 5–8pm, Sun 10am–4pm; free), generally considered to be the oldest church in Barcelona. Surrounded by greenery, including an olive tree, a cypress and a palm, as well as a modern park which sweeps around it protectively, it is a true survivor in this long beleagured area.

Much of the former industrial activity was in this lower part of El Raval – the new park was created after a fire burned down a factory – and the tall chimney is a fitting memorial to the area's industrial past. Another old factory, now **Can**

Xatarra, is a training centre for young people.

Sant Pau del Camp is a fine example of Romanesque architecture, quite rare in the city. The present building dates from the 12th century but it incorporates elements of an earlier church that was built in 912. Its small cloister, with unusual carvings, is a gem and exquisitely peaceful. On the exterior above the main door, look for the simple carving of the Hand of God and a winged creature, a symbolic representation of one of the evangelists.

Continue along the last block in Sant Pau, which brings you back into the late 19th–early 20th century: decorative mirrored shopfronts proclaim an old grocer's shop, **Ultramarinos Casa Victor**, and **La Confiteria**, a pastry shop turned stylish bar.

At the end of Sant Pau, just south along the Avinguda Paral·lel, is the Funicular de Montjuïc, which will take you up to the Parc de Montjuïc, not far from the Fundació Joan Miró (see page 152). ❑

Map on page 123

The magnificent Romanesque doorway of Sant Pau del Camp.

BELOW: Sant Pau del Camp, Barcelona's oldest church.

RESTAURANTS & BARS

Restaurants

This once-forgotten neighbourhood is rapidly becoming fashionable. The only difficult aspect of finding a place to eat is making the choice. There is a wide range for all tastes, tending towards new ideas of fusion, or new concepts in eating, though there's no shortage of genuine local places, plus some ethnic options.

Anima

Àngels, 6 (metro: Catalunya)
Tel: 93 342 4912
L & D Mon–Sat. €
A peaceful pavement near the MACBA plus indoor tables in the designer interior are a good setting for the delicious dishes presented like artworks by the young, creative chef. Evident influences from his travels around the world. Good-value set menu.

Biocenter

Pintor Fortuny, 25 (metro: Catalunya)
Tel: 93 301 4583
L Mon–Sat. €

PRICE CATEGORIES

Prices for three-course dinner per person with a half-bottle of house wine:
€ = under €25
€€ = €25–€40
€€€ = €40–€60
€€€€ = more than €60

This was one of the first vegetarian restaurants in the city. You can choose between an enormous, nutritious *menú del día* (four courses) or a substantial *plato combinado* (one dish with accompaniment). Either way you will enjoy a hearty meal, in surroundings where everyone always seems to be in a good mood.

Ca l'Isidre

Les Flors, 12 (metro: Paral·lel)
Tel: 93 441 1139
L & D Mon–Sat. €€€€
A family-run business which has grown into one of the city's most acclaimed restaurants. The well groomed clientele appreciate the meticulous attention to detail in food, decor and service. Classic Catalan dishes exquisitely prepared, using whatever's in season in the nearby Boqueria market.

Camper Food Ball

Elisabets, 9 (metro: Catalunya)
Tel: 93 270 1363
L & D daily. €
A first for food culture. Ground-breaking Spanish shoemaker Camper has brought us "food balls", supposedly a complete, balanced and totally natural meal in one simple ball. A choice of savoury balls can be followed by a

sweet ball, accompanied by healthy juices.

Can Lluís

Cera, 49 (metro: Paral·lel/Sant Antoni)
Tel: 93 441 1187
L & D Mon–Sat. €
This is the kind of genuine Catalan restaurant you would hope to find in a small village. Delicious food amid noise and bustle, and no pretensions. Excellent value for money.

Casa Leopoldo

Sant Rafael, 24 (metro: Liceu/Paral·lel)
Tel: 93 441 3014
L & D Tues–Sat. L only Sun. €€€€
Just off Rambla del Raval, a family-run Barcelona classic with great atmosphere. Particularly known for its fish and its own version of the Catalan staple, *pa amb tomàquet*.

Dos Trece

Carme, 40 (metro: Catalunya/Liceu)
Tel: 93 301 7306
L & D Tues–Sun. €
Fashionable place with laid-back attitude: eat, drink, listen to DJs or live music in the basement, have brunch on the terrace (Sunday only). Unconventional dishes show the influence of owner's Mexican/LA background.

El Fortuny

Pintor Fortuny, 31 (metro: Catalunya)
Tel: 93 317 9892

B, L & D Tues–Sun. €
The easy-going atmosphere of a student café belies the high standard of French-influenced dishes.

Elisabets

Elisabets, 2 (metro: Catalunya)
Tel: 93 317 5826
L Mon–Sat. D Fri. €
You have to fend for yourself in this bustling, smoky local bar, but it's worth it for one of their hearty winter stews and good-value set menu.

Es

Doctor Dou, 14 (metro: Catalunya)
Tel: 93 301 0068
L & D daily. €
The whiter-than-white spacious interior of Es is extremely soothing, the complete antithesis of a traditional local bar. Likewise the food, with delicate portions of subtly flavoured Mediterranean dishes with an international edge, or a salad buffet.

Hotel España

Sant Pau, 9 (metro: Liceu)
Tel: 93 318 1758
L & D daily. €
This is not really a place to come for great food, but having a cheap *menú del día* is a great way to see the extravagant *modernista* interior of this hotel. Designed by architect Domènech i Montaner, the dining room is the lavish high point.

Mam i Teca

Lluna, 4 (metro: Liceu/Sant Antoni)
Tel: 93 441 3335
L & D Wed–Mon. D only Sat. €
Mama i Teca is easy to miss, but don't. It offers excellent home-made Catalan food, with different dishes daily according to the chef's inspiration. Sample dishes include baby broad beans with wild mushrooms and prawns, or perfectly cooked *bacalao* (salt cod). Also offers a surprising range of wines and spirits.

Mama Cafè

Doctor Dou, 10 (metro: Catalunya)
Tel: 93 301 2940
L & D Mon–Sat. €
This place is neither strictly vegetarian nor strictly organic but a wide selection of both options are available. An aesthetically pleasing place, in line with what's in fashion in other major cities. Open for lunch – when you can get a *menú del día* – and evenings, either for supper or just a drink.

Organic

Junta de Comerç, 11 (metro: Liceu)
Tel: 93 301 0902
L & D daily. €
One of the latest new-wave vegetarian restaurants, and possibly the largest. Good choice of wholesome organic food in an impressive space. Re-emerge feel-ing healthy, especially if you opt for the shiatsu massage which is also on offer.

Plats

Carretes, 18 (metro: Paral·lel/Sant Antoni)
Tel: 93 441 6498
D Tues–Sat. €
Plats is located in deepest El Raval but don't be deterred by that: it's well worth venturing down the narrow street to this small, cosy restaurant where the well-travelled cook produces unusual Catalan food fused with Indian influences.

Rita Blue

Plaça Sant Agustí, 3 (metro: Liceu)
Tel: 93 412 3438
L & D daily. €
A glossy, colourful bar/restaurant named after the saint of the impossible in the adjoining church. They have coined the phrase "Tex-Med" to describe their signature fusion food of light snacks and main dishes. After a meal you can chill out in the basement.

Romesco

Sant Pau, 28 (metro: Liceu)
Tel: 93 318 9381
L & D Mon–Sat. €
The dazzling fluorescent lighting and formica-topped tables deter no one. Popular prices for good food. Famous for its *frijoles*: black beans, rice, minced meat, fried egg and fried banana, all on one plate.

Shalimar

Carme, 71 (metro: Liceu)
Tel: 93 329 3496
L & D Wed–Mon. D only Tues. €
Above-average (for Barcelona) Pakistani and Indian cooking, at very reasonable prices.

Silenus

Angels, 8 (metro: Catalunya)
Tel: 93 302 2680
L & D Mon–Sat. €€ (set menu Mon–Fri L €)
A good-looking, comfortable and arty café/restaurant with a selection of Mediterranean and international dishes. In warm weather, tables are set up outside in the pretty, tree-lined street near MACBA.

Bars & Cafés

This area now buzzes day and night as more terrace cafés open in small squares or wherever the pavement is wide enough. The light, sunny space of Rambla de Raval is practically lined with bars and places for *tapes*, such as the **Fragua**, at No. 15, and the bars in the MACBA square always attract a colourful crowd. **Oliva**, Pintor Fortuny, 22, is a stylish new café fitted out with pale wood, and **Iposa**, Jardins del Dr Fleming, has tables out on the square and lots of atmosphere inside (good food, too).

The night scene in and around Joaquín Costa is popular, with a mixture of old favourites, like the *modernista* **Almirall**, at No. 33, and some trendy newcomers, like **Benidorm**, at No. 39.

RIGHT: one of numerous bars in El Raval.

THE WATERFRONT

Rejuvenated for the Barcelona Olympics in 1992, the waterfront area has added an exciting new dimension to the city. Bold development is continuing, with the creation of Diagonal Mar and the Forum on land reclaimed from the sea

I t is perhaps ironic that Barcelona, a city on the shores of the Mediterranean with a large industrial port and strong maritime tradition, gained a "waterfront" only in the last decade of the 20th century. As the popular saying went, Barcelona lived with its back to the sea, which meant that although a great deal of the city's trade depended upon the water, the attitude of its residents was directed inland.

Inevitably, because of the geographical limitation of the sea, the city's residential and commercial areas expanded inland, first with the construction of the 19th-century Eixample and then by moving further up the hill towards Collserola during the 20th century. Investment tended to be linked with this movement, and as a result the Old Town and Barceloneta were neglected. In the 19th century factories had mushroomed along the shoreline extending north to the River Besòs, with only humble housing provided for the workers.

Impetus for change

The rediscovery of the waterfront began in the 1980s as part of the socialist city council's vision, but the 1992 Olympics were the vital catalyst. The development, perhaps the most radical transformation of

any city in Europe, represented an investment of some 400 billion pesetas (€3 billion). Some 5 km (8 miles) of beaches were renovated or newly created, landscaped and equipped with facilities. The Vila Olímpica was built, creating what is now a new residential district. The old city wharves, once hidden under tumbledown sheds, emerged, blinking, into the sun. Barceloneta was transformed. And since 1992 the momentum has been sustained: more developments have been completed

Map on page 130–131

LEFT: Port Vell, Barcelona's Old Port.
BELOW: Bogatell beach, one of a string of lively *platges* running north of the centre.

Inspecting a wooden submarine invented by the Catalan Narcís Monturiol.

and, for better or worse, there are more to come.

For energetic walkers or those on bicycles, this route could be one long itinerary right along the walkable parts of the front. However, to be able to enjoy the walk and fully appreciate the extensive renovations, to take in the many colourful details and have time to pause in the right places (such as the fish restaurants in Barceloneta), the route should be split into two (or more) days. What's on offer on Barcelona's waterfront is something quite extraordinary for a large cosmopolitan European city.

The Museu Marítim

A good place to begin is the Maritime Museum, which provides a vivid sense of Catalonia's seafaring past. The **Museu Marítim** ❶ (daily 10am–7pm; entrance charge) is housed in the **Reials Drassanes** (Royal Shipyards), at the foot of La Rambla just before it meets the port. It is half a minute from the metro Drassanes. One of the most imposing aspects of the museum is the building itself – the magnificent Gothic shipyards dating from the 13th century are a fine and rare

example of civil architecture from that period. The art critic Robert Hughes, in his book *Barcelona,* describes this stunning building as "perhaps the most stirring ancient industrial space of any kind that has survived from the Middle Ages: a masterpiece of civil engineering".

The entrance to the museum is along the side, where there is an inviting terrace café in a shady garden with a lily pond, as well as a restaurant. Before starting your visit, it is worth picking up the multilingual audiotour.

The collection includes real fishing boats from the Catalan coast, representing the importance of both fishing and boat-building in the country's history, and models of vessels from all ages. Also on display is a modern Olympic winner, and maps, instruments, paintings and more are well presented. The highlight is the full-scale replica of the 16th-century galley in which Don Juan of Austria led the Christian fleet to defeat the Turks in the Battle of Lepanto in 1571. Like so many vessels over the centuries, it was built in Barcelona in one of the slipways on the water's edge.

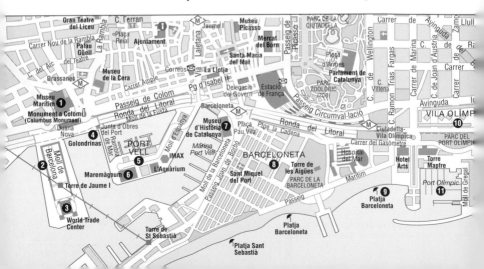

The port of Barcelona

Today you have to cross a wide road, full of traffic leading to the Ronda Litoral, before reaching the water. Leaving the Monument a Colom to your left, go down the side of the rather overbearing building that is the **Duana Nova** (New Customs House), built between 1895 and 1902 from a project drawn up by Enric Sagnier and Pere García. Crowned by a massive winged sphinx and other mythical flying beasts (Barcelona's port buildings seem to specialise in fine rooftop silhouettes), the Duana Nova is designed in the form of the letter "H", the most practical design for processing cargoes.

To the left of the Columbus statue is the **Junta d'Obres del Port** (Port Authority Building), designed by the engineer Julio Valdés and built in 1907. Its original use was as the reception for passengers arriving in the city from the sea. The interior is somewhat eclectic in style, and rather ornamental for its present mundane function. A recent external facelift has much improved the outward appearance of the building.

To the right, the **Moll de Barcelona ❷** and, beyond it, the **Moll de Sant Bertran** are the centre for ferry services to the Balearic Islands, including a new high-speed space-age catamaran, the so-called Buquebus, which reaches Palma in 2½ hours. The jetty also has the 119-metre (390-ft) **Torre de Jaume I** link for the cross-harbour cable car, which comes from Montjüic and goes to the tower on the other side of the harbour, the **Torre de Sant Sebastià** (an alternative route to the beach). The cable car has hardly changed since its introduction in 1931 – unlike the spectacular views it affords of the city and port, which are constantly changing.

After years of discussion, financial crises and local resistance, the **World Trade Center ❸** has now been completed at the end of the Moll de Barcelona. Designed by the world-famous architect I. M. Pei, it makes a loud statement in the middle of the port, looking remarkably like the luxury cruisers regularly moored alongside it. Unlike most new developments on the waterfront, this building is not used for social or leisure activities by the

The controversial World Trade Center, designed by architect I. M. Pei.

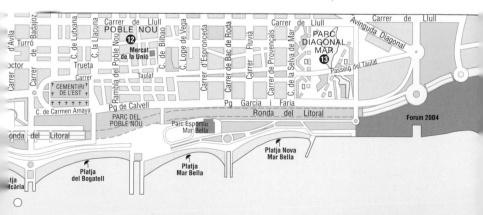

MEDITERRANEAN SEA

Waterfront

0   500 m

0   500 yds

The Golondrinas wait to take passengers around the harbour. Their name means "swallows".

BELOW: Port Vell.

citizens of Barcelona: it is a commercial centre with offices, a smart restaurant and a very grand hotel.

Of course, the port of Barcelona plays an important commercial role: it covers a huge expanse, winding south below Montjüic towards the airport, and it is undergoing further enlargement. The authorities' much vaunted aim is to establish it as "Europe's southern port", tying in with the city's aspiration to be regarded as the "capital of the Mediterranean". During the summer months enormous white cruisers are a daily sight, moored against the far sea wall, the **Moll Adossat**, from where coachloads of passengers are disgorged into La Rambla for a day on shore.

The serious business of large cargo ships and containers goes on in an area where no visitors are welcomed. A glimpse of the industrial port is possible, however, if you take a trip around the harbour in one of the historic pleasure boats, the **Golondrinas** ❹ (ferries) which, apart from a pause during the Civil War, have been plying these waters

since the 1888 Exposition. The ferries wait patiently in the **Moll de Drassanes**, the jetty opposite the Columbus monument. Half-hour trips take you out to the sea wall and back again, although you can disembark there and have a drink before catching a return boat. Be sure to choose one of the older, more elegant Golondrinas with names like *Mercedes*, *Lolita* and *Encarnación*.

As the ferry chugs through the working port you get a different perspective on the waterfront, seeing the enormity of the surrounding vessels and the battering they take in high seas. The same company also offers a longer trip as far as the **Port Olímpic** beyond Barceloneta beach, in a slick catamaran.

Waterfront leisure complex

The Golondrinas mark a divide between the industrial port and the leisure areas encompassed in **Port Vell** ❺, the old port. If you visit this area at the weekend, or on summer evenings, you will see from the noisy crowds that the Barcelonans are enjoying their newfound waterfront.

An architect-designed walkway and footbridge, the **Rambla de Mar**, leads across the water to the large commercial complex in the middle of the harbour on the **Moll d'Espanya**.

Alternatively, you can continue on the mainland along the **Moll de la Fusta**, a promenade built in the 1980s on the site of the old wooden cargo sheds, already redesigned since its brief life offering restaurants and nightlife was not entirely successful.

Better to look to the sea, where an exhibit from the Maritime Museum can be visited. The *Santa Eulàlia* (Tues–Fri noon–5.30pm, weekend 10am–5.30pm) is an old sailing boat, restored by the museum to its original glory from the beginning of the 20th century when it took cargo to the Americas.

Inevitably the crowds head over the Rambla de Mar to **Maremàgnum ⑥**, **L'Aquàrium** and the **Imax** cinema. Take heed of the warning signs to mind your step at the start of the walkway, as the designers take no responsibility for sprained ankles. The undulating design of the Rambla de Mar fits in well with the maritime environment, and is a great concept for crossing the harbour, but the subtle "waves" and changes in level can sometimes catch you out.

Cross over above yachts and yacht clubs to the Maremàgnum shopping and eating emporium, where you can shop until 11pm every day of the year. A selection of bars and restaurants seems to be dominated by fast-food outlets – a new phenomenon in Barcelona – but there are some old favourites like **El Salmonete**, a fish restaurant that used to be located on Barceloneta beach before the redevelopment. Despite the commercial context, a few *tapes* in the spring sunshine while watching the maritime traffic or looking across the harbour at Barcelona's Gothic towers and 19th-century chimneys takes some beat-

ing. The place throbs at night with salsa music and tacky discotheques.

Ultra-modern aquarium

Wander through Maremàgnum towards **L'Aquàrium** (daily 9.30am–11pm in summer, 9.30am–9pm in winter; entrance charge). Not long ago this area was taken up by disused warehouses. Old-timer tenants include the Reial Club Nautic and the Reial Club Marítim, two of the city's most elite sports clubs. The wharf has now been landscaped and leisure opportunities abound: the **Cines Maremàgnum**, with eight screens, rooftop mini-golf, the Imax cinema (with a semi-circular screen) and the spectacular Aquarium. Holding over 5 million litres (1 million gallons) of water, this is the largest aquarium in Europe. Since opening in 1995 it has become the largest crowd-puller in Barcelona, beating the Sagrada Família into second place. The much vaunted shark tunnel is a disappointment, however.

Pass the historic submarine and follow the path that leads up to the **Mirador del Port Vell** (a slightly

Map on page 130–131

The Rambla de Mar footbridge, leading to the Moll d'Espanya.

BELOW: the Maremàgnum leisure complex, containing shops, cinemas, mini-golf and the Aquarium.

Look out for Roy Lichtenstein's El Cap de Barcelona *(Barcelona Head).*

BELOW: people-watching on the Passeig Marítim.

raised lookout point) and down towards the *Barcelona Head*, an unmistakable Roy Lichtenstein sculpture. Inland from the sculpture, on the corner of Via Laietana, is the headquarters of **Correus** (the post office), a rather pompously grand building completed in 1927. The enormous vestibule was decorated by the prestigious *noucentiste* artists (from the 1900s) Canyellas, Obiols, Galí and Labarta. It is easier to buy stamps in an *estanc*, but not nearly as interesting. It is not hard to see why the facade has been used by filmmakers as a stand-in for American law courts.

On the sea side of **Passeig d'Isabel II** is a neoclassical arcade known as the **Porxos d'en Xifré**, built by the "Indiano" (a name given to anyone who left Spain to make their fortune in the Americas) Josep Xifré between 1836 and 1840. One of these apartments was the first home of the Picasso family in 1895 when they arrived in Barcelona from Málaga.

Historic restaurant

The arcade is also the site of one of Barcelona's most historic restaurants, the **Set Portes**, first established in 1838 by Josep Cuyás. Set Portes was the first bar in Barcelona to have an outdoor terrace set with tables and chairs and was among the city's leading café-theatres. Both features now form part of its long history, but its elegance and atmosphere remain. Specialising in rice dishes, a different one for each day of the week, it is the kind of place every first-time visitor to Barcelona should try. On the other side of Plaça del Palau is the **Delegació del Govern**, Madrid's central government foothold in Catalonia. It was built in the 18th century as a customs house.

Return to the harbour by **Reina Cristina**, a street full of bazaars behind the Set Portes restaurant. Towards the end, a popular *cava* bar on the right sells sparkling wine at rock-bottom prices and is much frequented by locals and tourists alike. Just beyond it is the first Galician seafood restaurant to open in Barcelona, **Carballeira**. If you are passing when the *arròs a la banda* (a delicious rice-and-seafood dish) is coming out of the kitchen, cancel all other plans: stand at the bar, request a *tape* of it with *allioli* (garlic mayonnaise) and a glass of Galician *vino turbio*.

Back on the quayside, the promenade sweeps on round, past a floating bar, to the **Moll Dipòsit** and the **Moll de la Barceloneta**. These once busy working quays now shelter the **Marina Port Vell**, where some of the most exclusive motor and sailing yachts in the Mediterranean winter or pass through on their way to the Balearics or the Caribbean. In 1992 the former warehouse complex, the Magatzem General de Comerç (1878) by Elias Rogent, was transformed into the Palau de Mar. This is a handsome building, very well renovated, and part of it now houses the fascinating **Museu d'Història de Catalunya ❼** (Tues–

Sat 10am–7pm, Wed until 8pm, Sun 10am–2.30pm, extended opening times in summer; entrance charge). True to its name, it elucidates Catalan history but also serves as a generic history museum with various bits of technical wizardry and plenty of interactive spaces – try walking in a suit of armour, or building a Roman arch – which kids of all ages love.

There are a couple of government offices in the back of the building, but the main focus here is on the restaurants that line the front. Sunday lunch in the Palau de Mar has become an institution for those who can afford it. This is an attractive place to sit and watch the world go by, and sheltered even in winter. The restaurants are new and glossy, not famed establishments, but the charms of outdoor eating often outweigh the gastronomic shortcomings. As long as you don't expect haute cuisine you will be spoilt for choice along here, from Palau de Mar along the whole length of **Passeig Joan de Borbó**. Even for Barcelona residents it is a thrill to eat on a pavement in the December sun. Serious eaters, however, tend to go into the backstreets of **Barceloneta** ❽ that form a grid between Marina Port Vell and the open sea.

Above the Moll de la Barceloneta is another landscaped, broad promenade with benches and palm trees. A favourite spot for rollerbladers, cyclists and dog-walkers, it was until comparatively recently covered in crumbling *tinglados* (sheds), and the decision to knock them down to bring this area into line with the new-look Barcelona of the 1990s was met with outrage. However, people are evidently making the most of the vacated space, and the seafood restaurants on Joan de Borbó are happy to have been given their own view of the harbour.

At the end of the promenade is an expensive but excellent fish restaurant called **Barceloneta**, with great harbour views, and just beyond are glimpses of the hard-working fishing boats moored up against the **Moll de Pescadors** (Fishermen's Wharf). The distinctive clock tower, **Torre del Rellotge**, started life as a lighthouse. Close by is the fish market (first opened in 1924), where auctions are held twice a day on weekdays.

Towering above the scene is the Torre de Sant Sebastià, whose 78-metre (257-ft) height marks the end, or the beginning, of the route of the cable car, which completes its 1,292-metre (4,200-ft) journey at Miramar, on Montjuïc.

At the foot of the tower, **Club Natació Atlètic Barceloneta** (also known as Banys Sant Sebastià) has an excellent heated outdoor pool which is open to the public and overlooks the beach of Sant Sebastià. Beyond the beach, major building works have begun: the sea wall is being extended to make way for a new entrance to the port. Further large-scale development of the

Map on page 130–131

TIP

For a table with a view, the restaurant at the top of Torre de Sant Sebastià is hard to beat. The lofty setting is matched by the high prices.

BELOW: dominoes on the beach.

The characterful back streets of Barceloneta.

BELOW: a waiter at work on the Passeig Marítim.

area, including a gigantic hotel designed by Ricardo Bofill, are under discussion. Meanwhile, there are worries that the city is losing sight of the intelligent town planning of the 1980s for which Barcelona has been justly renowned.

Origins of Barceloneta

Town planning in the 18th century was also of questionable merit. The rigidity of Barceloneta's street plan gives a clue to its origin. Misleadingly called the Fishermen's Quarter, this area was in fact born of a political, military decision. It was to this area that the inhabitants of La Ribera were relocated when their homes were demolished to make way for the building of the fortress, La Ciutadella, after the siege and conquest of Barcelona by Felipe V. The plans for Barceloneta were based on the construction of 15 short, identical streets, giving rise to a series of narrow, rectangular blocks all facing in the same direction (towards La Ciutadella), facilitating easy military control.

During the second half of the 19th century the lack of living accommodation in the city and pressure from the local proprietors resulted in the buildings of Barceloneta being raised to three storeys.

New beach development

By cutting through the streets of Barceloneta to the **Passeig Marítim**, or wandering along from Platja Sant Sebastià, you get to **Platja Barceloneta** ❾. The wooden walkways, palms and designer-showers of the post-Olympic seafront were ravaged by storms in 2001, but are gradually being replaced at vast expense. The six beaches along this stretch are easily accessible by public transport, and both the sand and the water's surface are cleaned daily, with weekly sanitary checks on top of that. Many fondly remember the *xiringuitos*, colourful restaurants, no more than huts, where you could eat good fish with your toes in the sand. They were bulldozed in the early 1990s under a cloud of controversy but reputedly because of a ruling by the national coastal authority.

No one can deny the obvious

pleasure the people of Barcelona derive from these wide open beaches. Every morning, locals come down in their towelling dressing gowns to swim in all weathers, play cards, gossip and get fit. In summer the beaches get very crowded and noisy by midday, but then comes the lunchtime exodus. If you can't make it in the early morning, wait until the early evening sun brings a new tranquillity – an eight o'clock swim here is sheer bliss.

The Vila Olímpica

Walk towards the unmistakable **Vila Olímpica ⑩**, distinctive by virtue of its two skyscrapers and the copper fish sculpture (*Pez y Esfera* by Frank Gehry) rippling in the sun. A new park just before the Hospital del Mar does justice to the *modernista* **Watertower** (1905) by Josep Domènech i Estapà, virtually the only original industrial building left in this area. The formerly gloomy hospital underwent a metamorphosis for the Olympics and is now more reminiscent of an international airport than a major public hospital. At beach level is a bike-rental shop.

Nearing the Olympic Village, the bars and restaurants proliferate, with entrances on the promenade above: some of these are excellent, as in the Port Olímpic, but it's not as classy as it was in 1992 when gold medallists lived in the village and the Spanish royal family supported the yachtsmen in the port. Inevitably, brash commercialism has played a part.

You can wander beneath Frank Gehry's awesome fish and imagine the heady view from the exclusive rooms in the **Hotel Arts** that towers above, but the canned music filling the air will bring you safely down to earth. Down at ground level, what was once an exclusive shopping area is now home to the **Barcelona Casino** (against many wishes).

The strikingly designed **Port Olímpic ⑪** is a pleasant place to walk, particularly out of season. At the end of the **Moll de Gregal**, jutting out to sea, is the municipal sailing school, offering courses for the public.

Map on page 130–131

An evocative sculpture by Rebecca Horn marks the spot where Barceloneta's traditional beach restaurants (xiringuitos) once stood. Called Estel Ferit (Wounded Star), it shows the xiringuitos piled on top of each other and lit from within.

BELOW:
Passeig Marítim, with Frank Gehry's copper fish sculpture in the distance.

BELOW: acrobatics at Diagonal Mar.

Architect-designed village

It is worth taking time to go inland a block or two, to see the architectural feats of the Olympic Village. Built according to a master plan developed by architects Mackay, Martorell, Bohigas and Puigdomènech, on land formerly occupied by 19th-century ramshackle warehouses and tumbledown factories, the flats accommodated athletes in 1992 and since then have been gradually sold. It was a major undertaking, and a vital part of Barcelona's wider plan of achieving long-overdue improvements to the city's infrastructure. In order to assimilate the village into the city, the major railway lines into Estació de França, the international train terminus, had to be buried below ground.

The 200 new buildings cover 74 hectares (183 acres), and are in 200 different designs. The area has not become a new neighbourhood of Barcelona overnight, but with the help of the many new parks and gardens it is now looking more established, and even beginning to merge with the remaining buildings of Poble Nou that surround its outer limits. In the midst of a clinical, totally un-Spanish shopping mall is one of the few magnetic points that attracts people in the evenings: the 15-screen cinema complex, **Icària Yelmo**, which specialises in *v.o.* (original-language) films.

A string of beaches

Return to the front to walk along the series of new beaches that begins after the Port Olímpic. Tons of sand were imported to create **Platja Nova Icària** (named after the original industrial neighbourhood), **Bogatell**, **Mar Bella** and finally **Nova Mar Bella**, reclaiming a seafront that had been cut off by railway lines, yards and warehouses. The strategic Ronda Litoral (ring road) runs all along here but at a lower level, and is cleverly hidden beneath parks, playgrounds and bridges that connect with the residential areas behind.

Poble Nou

Just after the cemetery behind Bogatell beach, make a detour inland to visit the centre of **Poble Nou** ⑫

and have a drink on its Rambla. It was the "new village" in the mid-19th century, built to accommodate the factory workers of what was known as the "Catalan Manchester". Scant industry remains today, and many of the old factories have been converted into loft apartments or artists' studios.

The predicted metamorphosis of Poble Nou into a trendy place to live is slowly happening. Much of its original character and charm has been retained and a village atmosphere prevails. A good time to visit is during the Festa Major in mid-September. It is to be hoped that the remnants of its industrial past will continue to be resurrected as studios or civic centres, like the impressive **Can Felipa** (an old textile factory converted in 1978, which has a swimming pool) near the metro in Pallars.

Diagonal Mar

Moving on towards **Selva de Mar**, many old buildings have fallen prey to Barcelona's latest mega-development, **Diagonal Mar** ⓭.

This is a project to bring Avinguda Diagonal all the way down to the sea, and has created a new district within the city's bounds. The landscape here changes daily: old buildings and areas of wasteland are being transformed into vast, square apartment blocks. Several hotels and a huge shopping centre have opened, with further hotels still to come. This is intended to link up with the city's latest development, the **Forum**, the legacy of the The Universal Forum of Cultures, held in Barcelona in the summer of 2004 with the aim of promoting cultural diversity, world peace and a sustainable urban environment.

Where Avinguda Diagonal meets the sea a huge showground was constructed, comprising exhibition areas and a port. Though some of these features were demolished after the event, the Convention Centre, designed by acclaimed Swiss architects Jacques Herzog and Pierre de Meuron, is being used for conferences and is the hub of an ongoing architectural project that will include a new marina and an aquatic zoo. ❏

Map on page 130–131

TIP

One of the most interesting features of Diagonal Mar is its open-air park designed by the late Enric Miralles. A sustainable park, irrigated by recycled water, it includes fun, creative games for children.

BELOW: Parc Diagonal Mar.

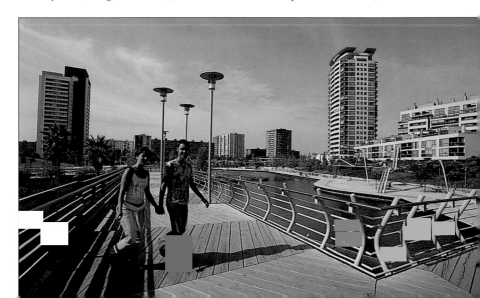

RESTAURANTS & BARS

Restaurants

The 4 km (2½ miles) of waterfront makes an endlessly tempting place to walk, meet, eat and drink, especially in the winter when there is nothing like the luxury of eating a paella outdoors. Sea views are a treat that sometimes require a sacrifice, either financially or in food quality, but are often worth it. However, don't miss some of the best options hidden in the backstreets of Barceloneta and Poble Nou.

Agua
Passeig Marítim, 30 (metro: Vila Olímpica)
Tel: 93 225 1272
L & D daily. €€
This stylish, relaxed

restaurant, serving modern Mediterranean food, is virtually in the sand near the Vila Olímpica. The combination is bliss, especially at lunchtime, so book days in advance for the terrace, especially at weekends.

Barceloneta
L'Escar, 22 (metro: Barceloneta)
Tel: 93 221 2111
L & D daily. €€€
Its outdoor terrace in a privileged position, jutting out above the fishing boats and smooth yachts of the marina Port Vell, makes this one of the most perfect places to have standard seafood dishes.

Barlovent
Rambla Poble Nou, 21 (metro: Poble Nou)

Tel: 93 225 2109
B, L & D Tues–Sun. €
A great corner bar, just inland from the waterfront on the bustling Rambla Poble Nou. The *tapes* are genuinely home-cooked and good enough to meet with local residents' approval.

Bestial
Ramon Trias i Fargas, 2–4 (metro: Vila Olímpica)
Tel: 93 224 0407
L & D daily. €€
The name is perhaps an exclamation of admiration (at the sea views, the minimalist interior, the multi-levelled outdoor terrace, the beautiful staff) rather than a reference to the graphic beasties crawling all over the glass entrance, designed by Federico Amat. More of a place to be in than to eat in, though their unusual risottos and pasta dishes of Italian inspiration are good.

Can Majó
Almirall Aixada, 23 (metro: Barceloneta)
Tel: 93 221 5818
L & D Tues–Sat. L only Sun.
€€€
This is one of the best and most established of the Barceloneta fish restaurants, where it's worth paying a little bit extra to be sure of a good paella.

Can Solé
Sant Carles, 4 (metro: Barceloneta)
Tel: 93 221 5012
L & D Tues–Sat. L only Sun.
€€
In the heart of Barceloneta, literally and metaphorically, and a favourite with local people. Great seafood and fish at traditional marble tables.

Carballeira
Reina Cristina, 3 (metro: Barceloneta)
Tel: 93 310 1006
L & D Tues–Sat. L only Sun.
€€€
Excellent Galician fish dishes in old-style restaurant. At lunchtime try a simple *tape* of *arròs a la banda* (delicious rice cooked in fish stock) at the bar. Accompany it with a glass of Ribeira (Galician white wine); in particular, the cloudy variety, *turbio*.

El Pòsit
Ramon Trias i Fargas, 2 (metro: Vila Olímpica)
Tel: 93 224 0088
L & D Mon–Sat. L only Sun.
€€€€
Offspring of the renowned Pòsit in Arenys de Mar, this sophisticated newcomer to the seafront near the Vila Olímpica guarantees top-quality seafood.

El Suquet de l'Almirall
Passeig Joan de Borbó, 65 (metro: Barceloneta)

LEFT: there are cafés galore along the waterfront.

Tel: 93 221 6233
L & D Mon–Sat. L only Sun.
€€€
This comfortable, tastefully decorated restaurant with a small terrace overlooking the Port Vell is in a different league to its neighbours. Young chef Quim Marqués has given new interpretations to Mediterranean favourites like rice dishes and *suquet* (fish stew), with excellent results.

Els Pescadors
Plaça Prim, 1 (metro: Poble Nou)
Tel: 93 225 2018
L & D daily. €€€
This elegantly designed, friendly restaurant specialising in seafood and game is a complete surprise, tucked in a pretty square amid the former textile factories and new developments of Poble Nou and the waterfront. Worth tracking down.

Kaiku
Passeig Joan de Borbó, 74 (metro: Barceloneta)
Tel: 93 221 9082
L Tues–Sun. €
A nicely down-to-earth local restaurant, great for *pescaditos* (small fried fish) or *calamarcitos* (baby squid) in one of the most sought-after spots in Barceloneta, overlooking open beach.

La Oca Mar
Espigó Bac de Roda, Platja Mar Bella (metro: Poble Nou/Selva de Mar)
Tel: 93 225 0100
L & D daily. €€
Here you can wine and dine virtually in the sea. This spectacular restaurant, jutting out to sea on the breakwater, serves good seafood and local seasonal dishes.

L'Elx al Moll
Local 9, Maremàgnum (metro: Drassanes)
Tel: 93 225 8117
L & D daily. €€
As a close relative to the Elx in the Paral·lel, known for its rice dishes since 1959, you can be sure of a good rice dish here. Try the *pica-pica* (assorted starters) followed by the rice of your choice. A cut above most places in this commercial centre, with magnificent harbour views.

Puda Can Manel
Passeig Joan de Borbó, 60–61 (metro: Barceloneta)
Tel: 93 221 5013
L & D Tues–Sun. €
A good, middle-range fish restaurant on this parade bursting with restaurants, many of which are best avoided. Well established with a pretty terrace overlooking the Port Vell.

Ruccula
World Trade Center, Moll de Barcelona (metro: Drassanes)
Tel: 93 508 8268
L & D Mon–Sat. L only Sun.
€€€
A slick, enormous restaurant in the new business area where everything is done on a large scale, catering for company events and tourists from oversized cruise ships moored alongside. Despite this, the international cuisine manages to keep a fresh, creative edge and the view is equally grand.

Sal Café
Passeig Marítim (metro: Barceloneta/Vila Olímpica)
Tel: 93 224 0707
L & D Tues–Sat. L only Sun–Mon. €
Down on the Barceloneta beach near the climbing frame is this slick restaurant-cum-bar, the trendiest *xiringuito* around. A resident DJ presides over the relaxed scene until 3am on Friday/Saturday, a bit earlier on other nights.

Talaia Mar
Marina, 16 (metro: Vila Olímpica)
Tel: 93 221 9090
L & D Tues–Sun. €€€
Probably the best restaurant in the Olympic Port (certainly the best view), with a guaranteed high standard of creative cooking from chefs who all trained at El Bullí.

Torre d'Altamar
Passeig Joan de Borbó, 88 (metro: Barceloneta)
Tel: 93 221 0007
L & D Tues–Sat. D only Mon.
€€€€
This newcomer to the restaurant scene, perched 75 metres (246 ft) above the port in Torre Sant Sebastià, competes with L'Orangerie (*see Above Diagonal*) for the title of "best dining room with a view". The gourmet experience does not quite measure up to such heights, but the panorama is quite spectacular.

Xiringuito Escribà
Avinguda del Litoral, 42 (metro: Vila Olímpica)
Tel: 93 221 0729
L & D daily (summer). L only Tues–Sun (winter). €€
One of the more elegant *xiringuitos* (beach bars), serving good fish and other dishes on its sunny terrace. As it's part of the famed pastry-making Escribà family, there are predictably high-class desserts.

Bars & Cafés

Bars and cafés galore along the waterfront, in the streets behind and even in the sea, like the comfortable floating bar **Luz de Gas Port Vell**, Moll del Dipòsit. **Can Paixano**, Reina Cristina, 7, with its cheap *cava* and tasty sandwiches, is a popular student dive; while nearby **Vaso de Oro**, Balboa, 6, is a hidden treasure, serving beer chilled to perfection and excellent *tapes* to the crowd crammed into its long, narrow space. The **Fastnet Bar**, Passeig Joan de Borbó, 22, is popular with sports fanatics for its televised events, to say nothing of the curry and Guinness.

PRICE CATEGORIES

Prices for three-course dinner per person with a half-bottle of house wine:
€ = under €25
€€ = €25–€40
€€€ = €40–€60
€€€€ = more than €60

MONTJUÏC

The lofty setting for the 1992 Olympic Games has superb views of the city, two world-class museums, a brand-new cultural centre and the Poble Espanyol

The small hill of Montjuïc is only 213 metres (699 ft) high, but has an undeniable physical presence that is noticeable from most parts of the city: from along the waterfront it marks the end of the port, and from the Ronda Litoral it acts like a barrier between the inner residential area of the city and the industrial sprawl of the Zona Franca, the gateway to the south. From high points around Barcelona you can see how densely packed a city this is – the result of its growth having been contained within the natural limits of the River Besòs, the Collserola range and Montjuïc.

Past and present

The rocky promontory of Montjuïc has also featured in some of the key events in Barcelona's history. A pre-Roman civilisation made a settlement here, preferring its rough heights to the humid plain that the Romans later opted for. The Romans did, however, build a temple to Jupiter here, which is thought to explain the origin of the name: Mons Iovis eventually evolved into Montjuïc.

In 1929 the hill was landscaped and used as the grounds of the Universal Exposition. More recently, it was seen by millions of people worldwide as it hosted the opening and closing ceremonies and core

events of the 1992 Olympic Games. It was regarded as the "nerve centre" of the Games.

Today it is a large city park offering a wide range of cultural, leisure and sporting activities – a playground used by both residents and tourists. It is a wonderful space for walking dogs and allowing children to run wild, or just for clearing the head and getting a bird's-eye view of Barcelona, especially its maritime area. Apart from the cable car that crosses the harbour, this is the

Map on page 144

LEFT: the Torre de Calatrava.
BELOW: the view from Montjuïc.

TIP

Pick up an "M-card", the new pass to all activities on Montjuïc, from bike rental to theatre tickets, available from tourist offices and the information centre in La Font del Gat (see page 148).

only place where you can piece together the waterfront at a glance, and watch the comings and goings of the busy industrial port.

One of the best approaches to Montjuïc is from **Plaça d'Espanya ❶**, which has good metro and bus connections. (If you are heading for a specific destination, such as the Fundació Joan Miró or the castle, the funicular from Paral·lel metro station is a better option.) Plaça d'Espanya is a large, noisy junction at the southern end of town. It is glaring and hot, surrounded by an incoherent mixture of buildings and,

with little or no shade, is not a place to linger.

Spare a brief moment, however, to look at the statue to Spain in the middle of the square's roundabout, commissioned for the 1929 Universal Exposition. The most intriguing thing about it is that Josep Jujol was the sculptor: it is difficult to reconcile this monumental piece with the same artist's brilliant ceramic serpentine bench in Parc Güell (see page 175), built at least 15 years earlier. The explanation for the two opposing styles was that the Primo de Rivera dictatorship in Madrid

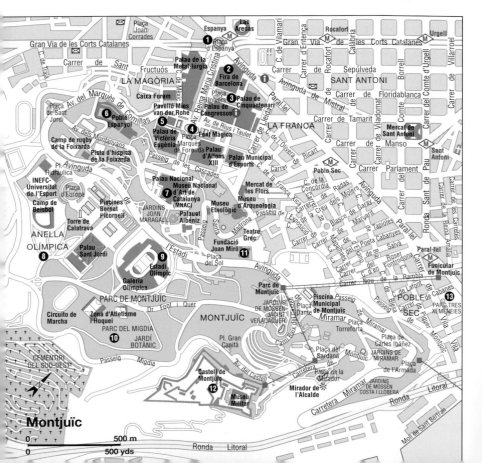

Montjuïc

controlled the design of Jujol's monument to Spain.

The disused bullring, **Las Arenas**, on the other side of the square opened in 1900 with a capacity for 15,000 spectators. Weeds now push through the ground where bulls once stamped, but there are plans in the pipeline for the British architect Richard Rogers to convert the bullring into a commercial centre. In 2004, city councillors became the first in Spain to declare their opposition to bullfighting, the first step towards an outright ban in the city. Meanwhile, fights still take place at the Monumental bullring.

The Palau Nacional

Turning your back on the roundabout, head past the twin Venetian-style towers, designed by Ramon Reventós, that formed the main entrance to the Universal Exposition of 1929. Most of the buildings here were designed for this event, with a sweeping vista up to the **Palau Nacional**, the enormous, rather overbearing building at the top of the steps. The Exposition, opened by King Alfonso XIII, had as its themes industry, art and sport, and was a political *tour de force* for the Primo de Rivera dictatorship. The hillside was landscaped in accordance with a plan drawn up by Forestier and Nicolau Maria Rubió i Tudurí. Some 15 palaces were built, as well as national and commercial pavilions, a stadium, a swimming pool, the Poble Espanyol (Spanish Village), ornamental fountains, the Greek Theatre, several towers and the access avenue.

It still looks very much like a showground, and today acts as the main headquarters of the Barcelona Trade Fair organisation, the **Fira de Barcelona ❷**, a complex with 180,000 square metres (2 million square ft) of exhibition space and 2 million visitors a year. If a trade fair is being held, you may be swept through the gates with the crowds.

The exhibits, mostly in the pavilions lining Avinguda Maria Cristina, are sometimes displayed in the open air, notably in the **Plaça Univers ❸**, a large square created between the main pavilions on the left. The statue in the middle is by Josep Llimona.

Ascending the hill

The upper esplanades are reached by escalator; the system of escalators that covers Montjuïc was created for the 1992 Olympics, the next major event to bring enormous change to this district. The imposing **Font Màgica ❹**, designed by Carlos Buigas in 1929, has recently been restored; the dancing fountain, which is creatively lit, delights thousands of visitors several times a week during the *son et lumière* shows (May–Sept Thur–Sun 8pm–midnight, Oct–Apr Fri–Sat 7–9pm). The hill is floodlit at night.

Before going up, don't miss the **Pavelló Mies van der Rohe ❺** across the esplanade (daily 10am–8pm; entrance charge). Built by

Map on page 144

TIP

The spectacular *son et lumière* shows at the Font Màgica take place several times a week and last around 15 minutes.

BELOW: Font Màgica.

Giants at a festival in the Poble Espanyol (Spanish Village), a kitsch but very popular attraction on Montjuïc.

Ludwig Mies van der Rohe as the German Pavilion for the 1929 Exposition, it was later dismantled, but, at the instigation of some leading architects, rebuilt in 1986 to celebrate the centenary of the architect's birth. Its clean lines and simplicity are quite breathtaking, and help one to understand the beauty of minimalism *(see picture on page 47)*. The contrast with some of the other, pompously ornate, buildings constructed at the same time is extraordinary. Mies van der Rohe's professor wrote at the time: "This building will one day be remembered as the most beautiful of those built throughout the 20th century."

Across the road is a fascinating former textile factory, **Casaramona**, built by Puig i Cadafalch in 1911. Another gem of *modernista* industrial architecture, it has been overlooked for years but has now been rescued by the Fundació "la Caixa", which has converted it into their new cultural centre the **CaixaForum** (Tues–Sun 10am–8pm; free). It is a wonderful space, with an entrance designed by Isozaki. Apart from its own contemporary collection, it holds temporary exhibitions, concerts, debates and festivals.

Kitsch corner

Just up the road, in the norhwest corner of Montjuïc, is the **Poble Espanyol ❻** (Sun 9am–midnight, Mon 9am–8pm, Tues–Thur 9am–2am, Fri–Sat 9am–4am; entrance charge), also built for the 1929 Exposition. The shady green of **Avinguda del Marquès de Comillas** is a welcome relief after the exposed areas of the Fira. The Poble Espanyol is pure kitsch, but provides many diversions both day and night, from a *tablao*, where you can watch flamenco dancing, to "The Barcelona Experience", an audio-visual show. It is not just "family" entertainment: teenagers flock here for the night scene and retired folk arrive in busloads. The village is one of the most popular venues in Barcelona, welcoming year after year more visitors than even the Sagrada Família or the major museums.

It was built as a showpiece for

regional architecture, handicrafts, and cultural and gastronomic styles from all over Spain. It has a Plaza Mayor, typical of many squares you might find in any part of the country, where popular *fiestas* take place. The square is seen in its best light when it stages jazz and rock concerts during the **Grec** summer festival. The entrance is through San Vicente de Avila Portal; Javier Mariscal, one of Barcelona's most popular designers (he was responsible for the Olympic mascot), put the Poble Espanyol into the limelight in the early 1990s by creating a trendy bar within the gateway, the **Torres de Avila**. It was briefly fashionable but is now a dance club open at weekends only.

There are two museums in the village: one, the **Museu d'Arts, Indústries i Tradicions Populars**, is devoted to popular arts and crafts; the other is the **Museu de les Arts Gràfiques**, documenting graphic design since the 19th century (visits by prior arrangement only; tel: 93 426 1999).

The MNAC

From here, you can either walk up the hill, following signs to the Palau Nacional, or take a longer walk up Avinguda de l'Estadi straight to the Olympic Stadium. The easiest route, however, is to go back down Avinguda del Marquès de Comillas and then take the escalator up. The museum in the Palau Nacional should not be missed.

In some lights, or at a distance, this massive building can look imposing and quite dramatic, but on the whole it looks somewhat out of place in Barcelona. The front steps are full of tourists trying to spot their hotels in the panorama in front of them.

Since 1934 the Palau Nacional has housed the **Museu Nacional d'Art de Catalunya ❼** (MNAC) (Tues–Sat 10am–7pm, Sun 10am–2.30pm;

entrance charge), which has the most important Romanesque art collection in the world, including murals that were peeled from the walls of tiny churches in the Pyrenees in the province of Lleida and brought down by donkey. There is also an excellent Gothic collection and a small selection of Renaissance and baroque art *(see picture story, page 156–7)*.

The building has undergone major renovation work over the last decade under the direction of the Italian architect Gae Aulenti but has now reopened to show a millennium of Catalan art. The original collection has been complemented by the 19th- and 20th-century works from the former Museu d'Art Modern, which includes work by Casas, Rusiñol, Nonell and Fortuny, and the decorative arts, including pieces by Gaudí and Jujol. The museum also houses the Thyssen collection, formerly in the Monestir de Pedralbes, a coin collection, drawings, engravings and photography.

From the front steps of the Palau turn right if you want a detour to the

Map on page 144

TIP

There is no charge for entry to the Poble Espanyol after 9pm from Sunday to Thursday. In the evenings, this part of Barcelona is a lively entertainment hotspot, with bars, discos and restaurants.

BELOW: detail on the exterior of the Museu Etnològic.

Greek figure in the Museu d'Arqueologia de Catalunya.

museums of archaeology and ethnology on Passeig Santa Madrona. The **Museu Etnològic** (Tues–Sun 10am–2pm; entrance charge) has collections from all over the world, notably Latin America and the Philippines. A section on Japan, the *Espai Japó*, is an indication of the new cultural (and commercial) exchange between Catalonia and Japan.

Tourist information

On the same street and in the midst of lovely gardens, the **Jardins Laribal**, is a small and pretty café and restaurant, La Font del Gat. In the same building is the administrative centre organising all events held on Montjuïc, and an information desk. Here you can find out about all activities and pick up an "M-card", a day pass costing €20, which is valid for museums and other activities on the mountain. It is also available from tourist offices.

Further down the hill is the **Teatre Grec**, also built for the 1929 Exposition. Inspired by a model of Epidaurus, the theatre's backdrop is a solid wall of rock which was part of an old abandoned quarry. During the Grec summer festival it is an important venue for plays and concerts. Just beyond it is the **Museu d'Arqueologia de Catalunya** (Tues–Sat 9.30am–7pm, Sun 10am–2.30pm; entrance charge), with interesting discoveries from the first inhabitants of Catalonia, including the Greek and Roman periods.

This route will bring you down the hill as far as the so-called **Ciutat del Teatre**, home of several municipal theatres including the **Teatre Lliure**, **Mercat de les Flors** and **Institut del Teatre**. The productions here are generally interesting and of a good standard. However, if your main goal is to check out the Olympic legacy on Montjuïc, this detour should be left for another day as it takes you a long way down the hill.

Sporting Barcelona

The **Anella Olímpica** ❽ (Olympic Ring) is spread across the hillside behind the Palau Nacional and easily accessible from there by escalator. The buildings here appear to be sculpted out of the ridge, with wide

open views to the south dropping down behind them. Despite the passage of time, they are quite dazzling in the abundant light of Montjuïc.

There are eight Olympic-standard sports centres and three athletics tracks in the area, but if you stick to the road you will see only a fraction of what was created: fortunately, a walkway on the inland (downhill) side of the main stadium gives access to the central square.

The **Estadi Olímpic ❾** (daily 10am–8pm in summer, 10am–6pm in winter; free) was actually built for the 1929 Universal Exposition, following a design by Pere Domènech. Its opening football match was a victory for the Catalan side against Bolton Wanderers – a little-known fact. It remained open until the Mediterranean Games in 1955, then fell into disrepair. Extensive works for the 1992 Olympics involved lowering the arena by 11 metres (36 ft) to create the extra seating needed for 55,000 spectators. Most of the track events and the opening and closing ceremonies were held here. You can relive the excitement of

Barcelona's glory in the **Galeria Olímpica**, an exhibition space at the rear of the stadium (Mon–Fri 10am–2pm and 4–7pm in summer, Mon–Fri 10am–1pm and 4–6pm in winter; entrance charge).

Below and west of the stadium stretches the immense **Olympic Terrace**, lined with pillars. In the middle of the main terrace is a lawn with an artificial stream flowing through it; on the left is a small forest of identical sculptures. The terrace drops down to a second level in the middle distance, and then to a third – the **Plaça d'Europa** – which is a circular colonnaded area built on top of a massive water tank containing 60 million litres of drinking water for the city. The whole has the atmosphere of a re-created Roman forum.

Olympic installations

On each side of the terrace are key installations: to the left is the **Palau Sant Jordi**, to the right the **Piscines Bernat Picornell**. In the far distance the **INEFC Universitat de l'Esport**. All this is as planned, but there is

Map on page 144

The Piscines Bernat Picornell. In high summer this swimming pool operates an open-air cinema. Films are shown at 10pm, followed by a refreshing dip.

BELOW:
the Olympic Stadium.

The Barcelona Olympics

On 17 December 1986, in Lausanne, the president of the International Olympic Committee, Juan Antonio Samaranch, announced that the 25th Olympic Games would be held in his native Barcelona. This much-anticipated news was greeted with jubilation in Spain, particularly by Barcelonans and Catalans. It was the fourth time the city had pitched for the Games and the Catalans were quick to recognise that it was a golden opportunity to attract long-overdue investment in the city. Neglected infrastructure could be repaired, and it could become, some believed, a major city of the 21st century.

This vision took some battering in the following six years of upheaval, and there were serious doubts about whether too much was being attempted in too short a time. However, when the 25th Olympiad opened on 25 July 1992, the confident Catalans were proved right. The Games were a display of great organisational skills, from the moment a burning arrow taken from the torch was unleashed to light up the Olympic flame in the renovated stadium on Montjuïc, to the departure of the last athlete from the reconstructed airport.

It was also, being Barcelona, something of a "designer-Olympics". Everything looked good. Key elements of the infrastructure were designed by leading national and international architects – the Communications Tower on Collserola by Sir Norman Foster, the one on Montjuïc by Calatrava, the Palau Sant Jordi indoor stadium by Isozaki, the Vila Olímpica by the Barcelona firm Mackay, Martorell, Bohigas and Puigdomènech. With everything from the starting blocks to the medal bearers' uniforms being designed by Barcelona's top fashion designer Toni Miró, the sporting events were meticulously staged for the maximum visual effect, with an eye on the 3½ million viewers around the world.

The 500,000 people who came to the city saw it spruced up with new roads, renovated squares, freshly painted facades, urban sculptures and newly opened vistas. There were four centres of activity located in the four corners of the city, and 16 subsidiary centres, some outside the city. The key Olympic area in Barcelona itself was the hill of Montjuïc, where the original stadium, built for the 1929 Universal Exhibition, was renovated to accommodate 55,000 spectators, and the Palau Sant Jordi indoor stadium, the INEF (University of Physical Education) and the Picornell swimming pools were constructed. The hill was landscaped and a system of escalators was installed to make access easier. The Olympic Gallery in the stadium today recaptures the atmosphere and excitement of the Games through thousands of photographs, sound recordings and videos.

The other areas of Barcelona to benefit were around the football club on Diagonal, the Vall d'Hebron and, most spectacular of all, the Parc de Mar, built on former industrial land by the sea. This incorporated the Olympic Village (now a desirable area of seaside apartments) and the Olympic Port, where dozens of new restaurants buzz every evening and at weekends.

At the closing ceremony on 9 August it was an even prouder Juan Antonio Samaranch who declared that Barcelona had hosted one of the most successful Olympic Games ever. ❏

LEFT: signalling the start of the 1992 Games.

Map on page 144

one highly visible landmark in the whole which caused great controversy at the time, not least with the architects who created the whole Olympic ring: the great white **Torre de Calatrava** communications tower (188 metres/616 ft), designed by Spanish architect Santiago Calatrava, known for his elegantly engineered bridges. Olympic architects Frederic Correa, Alfonso Milá, Joan Margarit and Carles Buxadé hated the tower project, and rallied dozens of intellectuals to their cause, Nevertheless the Telefònica tower went ahead, and the result is quite stunning.

Palau Sant Jordi

Other than the stadium itself, the installation most in the public eye is the **Palau Sant Jordi** (Sat and Sun 10am–6pm, except when hosting an event), an indoor stadium designed by Japanese architect Arata Isozaki. The ultra-modern design in sleek steel and glass can seat 15,000, with not a pillar in sight. The roof, which measures 160 metres (525 ft) by 110 metres (360 ft), was built on the

ground *in situ*, covered in ceramic tiles then raised agonisingly slowly using hydraulic pistons. It took 10 days to reach its final height of 45 metres (148 ft). Since the Olympics, the Palau has proved popular for concerts and exhibitions as well as sporting events.

Green spaces

Just beyond the stadium a road winds behind it. This expanse of hillside is known as the **Parc del Migdia ⑩**. Here, after years of expectation among the local population, the new botanical garden has opened, the **Jardí Botànic** (daily, Oct–June 10am–5pm, Jul–Sept 10am–8pm; entrance charge), a sustainable garden in keeping with Barcelona's aspirations for the new century. The many new plants and trees are slowly becoming established. Looking to the top of the hill, you can see how the niches from the enormous cemetery, which drops down to the sea on the other side of the ridge, are beginning to creep over the ridge.

Returning to the Avinguda de l'Estadi, opposite the stadium are

A cheeky cherub in the Jardins de Joan Maragall.

BELOW: the ultra-modern Palau Sant Jordi.

The Fundació Joan Miró has one of the largest collections of the artist's work.

the smaller, more peaceful and elegant gardens of Joan Maragall surrounding the **Palauet Albéniz**. This *palauet* – or "little palace" – is now the official residence of visiting dignitaries to Barcelona. It was built as a Royal Pavilion for the 1929 Exposition and during the years of self-government in Catalonia – from 1931 until the end of the Civil War – it was used as a music museum.

Fundació Joan Miró

With the stadium on your right, follow the main road until it becomes **Avinguda de Miramar**. On the left is the **Fundació Joan Miró ⑪** (Tues, Wed, Fri and Sat 10am–7pm, Thur 10am–9.30pm, Sun 10am–2.30pm; entrance charge), an understated yet powerfully impressive gem on this sporting hill. Designed by Josep Lluís Sert, eminent architect and friend of Miró, the gallery has been open since 1974 *(see picture on page57)*.

A Mediterranean luminosity floods the striking building and shows Miró's work in its best light.

One of the largest collections in the world of Miró's work, it includes paintings, drawings, sculptures and tapestries as well as his complete graphic work. It also contains the mercury fountain designed by Alexander Calder for the Spanish Republic's Pavilion in the 1937 Paris Exhibition. It seems fitting that this should be here now: the Spanish Pavilion was intended as a political statement, coinciding as it did with the Civil War, and was designed by Sert and included Miró's work and Picasso's *Guernica*. Contemporary exhibitions and concerts are also held here regularly.

Just before the municipal swimming pool on the left, scene of Olympic diving in 1992, is the funicular station, Parc de Montjuïc, with the **Jardins de Mossèn Cinto Verdaguer** close by. Continue along the road for magnificent views of the port from the **Jardins de Miramar**, where there are several bars serving food and refreshments, and the impressive **Jardins Mossèn Costa i Llobera**. Once a strategic defence point for the city,

the Buenavista battery, this is now a cactus garden, described by the *New York Times* as one of the best gardens in the world. It has cacti from Mexico, Bolivia, Africa and California. A 5-star hotel is to be built up here, part of a major plan for redeveloping and landscaping Montjuïc. Alternatively, catch the funicular back down to Paral·lel metro station, or complete the Montjuïc experience and catch the cable car up to the Castell de Montjuïc for an even better view. The cable car, the *teleférico*, is a great way to reach it, but it is closed for renovation until 2006. In the meantime, a bus will take you to the top if you don't want to walk.

Castell de Montjuïc

The **Castell de Montjuïc** ⑫ (daily 9.30am–8pm, winter 4.30pm; entrance charge) was built in the 17th century during the battle between Catalonia and Spain's Felipe IV, known as the "War of the Reapers". At the beginning of the 18th century Bourbon troops ransacked the castle; it was rebuilt between 1751 and 1779. The new fortress was in the form of a starred pentagon, with enormous moats, bastions and buttresses. It has little appeal for Catalans, as it represents hated oppression from the central government in Madrid, and is a place where torture and executions took place over many years. It was here that beloved leader **Lluís Companys**, president of the Generalitat, was shot in 1940 *(see page 26)*. A statue of Franco on his horse was removed from the castle's courtyard soon after democracy was restored to Spain, following his death in 1975. Today the castle houses the **Museu Militar**, with a collection of weapons, lead soldiers and military uniforms. Keen climbers spend their weekends abseiling down the castle walls.

The route down

Descending the hill on foot, you pass through the **Plaça del Sardana** with its circle of stone dancers, sculpted by Josep Cañas in 1966. Nearby is the Mirador de l'Alcalde (the Mayor's Lookout point) with

Map on page 144

There are several attractive gardens on Montjuïc, including the Jardins de Mossèn Cinto Verdaguer near the Parc de Montjuïc funicular station.

BELOW: visiting the Castell de Montjuïc.

Map on page 144

panoramic views over the water-front. A new walkway, the Camí del Mar, runs from here to the Mirador de L'Anella Olímpica, giving a new perspective southwards over the delta of the River Llobregat. Return to Plaça d'Espanya by the escalators or from the castle take the scenic route down by catching the *transbordador aeri* from the Plaça Armada, in the area known as Miramar, and cross to the port.

Alternatively opt for the funicular from near Plaça Dante, which is another relic of the 1929 Exhibition, though greatly refurbished. The rail descends a distance of 760 metres (2,500 ft) and disembarks at Avinguda Paral·lel, not far from the church of Sant Pau *(see page 124)*.

Avinguda Paral·lel

Avinguda Paral·lel was originally the Calle Marqués del Duero, in honour of the man himself. Then, in 1794, a Frenchman, Pierre François André Méchain, discovered that the avenue's pathway coincided with the navigational parallel 44°44'N. In honour of this discovery a local

cook opened a tavern which she called "El Paralelo". The popularity of the place ensured that the name was adopted as the street name.

This area has always been known as the centre of variety theatre and vaudeville. Its most famous theatre was El Molino, a colourful music hall which, sadly, after several attempts at resuscitation, has been closed down indefinitely. Some large theatres remain, usually showing musicals or farces which attract coachloads of people from out of town.

Parc Tres Xemeneies ⑬, just down the avenue towards the sea, is dominated by three enormous 72-metre (235-ft) chimneys. This is a fine example of a "hard" urban park, with interesting design ideas. The chimneys are the remains of the "Grupo Mata", an electricity-producing plant dating from the turn of the 20th century. They are now integrated into the pristine glass premises of FECSA, the electrical company.

Paral·lel is a good departure point for heading into the Old Town through El Raval, or going down to the waterfront. ❑

BELOW: *sardana* dancers in Plaça del Sardana, on the walk down from the castle.

RESTAURANTS & BARS

Restaurants

This is more of a wide open space for picnics than a place to go out for dinner, but the cultural centres on this hill have decent cafeterias, and the Miró restaurant is great for lunch. During the Grec festival in July and August an attractive open-air restaurant operates near the amphitheatre, and wandering down the hill to the Paral·lel and Poble Sec districts there are plenty of decent local restaurants.

Can Margarit
Concòrdia, 21 (metro: Poble Sec)
Tel: 93 441 6723
D Mon–Sat. €
Everyone's idea of a medieval tavern, with long tables, enormous barrels of wine and raucous company, this is a good place to go with a crowd. Unchanged for years, the atmosphere is welcoming from the moment you are encouraged to serve yourself a glass of wine from the barrel. The

PRICE CATEGORIES

Prices for three-course dinner per person with a half-bottle of house wine:
€ = under €25
€€ = €25–€40
€€€ = €40–€60
€€€€ = more than €60

grilled meats with mongetes (white haricot beans) and lashings of allioli are as succulent as ever.

El Pa i Trago
Parlament, 41 (metro: Poble Sec)
Tel: 93 441 1320
L & D Tues–Sun. €
A typical Catalan restaurant with well-prepared traditional dishes, rustic-style decor and a jolly atmosphere.

Elche
Vila i Vilà, 71 (metro: Paral·lel)
Tel: 93 441 3089
L & D daily. €€
Famous for its paella and other rice dishes since 1959 when the parents of the present owners brought the traditional recipes from Valencia, the birthplace of Spain's most famous dish.

Fundació Joan Miró
Avinguda Miramar, 1 (metro: Paral·lel and funicular)
Tel: 93 329 0768
L only Tues–Sat. €
Select menu of original pasta, wok and Indian dishes in the attractive, luminous setting of the Miró museum.

Kasbah
Vila i Vilà, 82 (metro: Paral·lel)
Tel: 93 329 8384
L & D Tues–Sat. €€
Textiles, cushions and low tables create the right atmosphere for deli-

cious Arabic food, predominantly Moroccan (couscous, tajin), but also Syrian and Lebanese specialities.

La Tomaquera
Margarit, 58 (metro: Paral·lel)
L & D Tues–Sat. L only Sun.
€€
No phone, no reservations, no credit cards, but always packed. This is a rough-and-ready no-nonsense restaurant where large portions of grilled meat are served with the essential dollop of allioli and house wine. Snails are the speciality.

Quimet i Quimet
Poeta Cabanyes, 25 (metro: Paral·lel)
Tel: 93 442 3142
L & D (tapes) Mon–Sat midday. €
Wall-to-wall wine bottles (unusually wide choice by the glass) and excellent tapes (try the combinados, a special selection) in this tiny, authentic bar now run by the third generation of "Quims".

Rías de Galicia
Lleida, 7 (metro: Espanya)
Tel: 93 424 8152
L & D daily. €€€
A well-known, typically Galician, family-run restaurant with fresh, top-quality seafood delivered daily. Smart and serious, with matching quality. Particularly good is the fish, such as

dorada (gilthead bream) or merluza (hake).

Tablao de Carmen
Poble Espanyol, Av. Marquès de Comillas, 13–27 (metro: Espanya)
Tel: 93 325 6895
D Tues–Sun. €€€ (includes show)
One of several restaurants in the Poble Espanyol (Spanish Village), which verge on the touristy but can usually be fun if you get in the right mood. This one in particular has a good flamenco show twice a night, with a set dinner, although you can choose from several starters, main courses and desserts.

Bars & Cafés

One of the city's most famous orxaterias is in this area, the **Sirvent**, at Parlament, 56, where you can join the crowds on hot summer days to try this remarkably refreshing (non-alcoholic) drink from Valencia made from xufas (tiger nuts). Amid the rather dreary selection of cafeterias along the Paral·lel it comes as a relief to stumble upon **La Confiteria**, Sant Pau, 128, an attractive bar in a former pastry shop which has well-preserved modernista fittings, and a comfortable, laid-back atmosphere.

THE HOME OF CATALAN ART

The Palau Nacional is home to the Museu Nacional d'Art de Catalunya (MNAC) and the Museu d'Art Modern, tracing 1,000 years of Catalan art

At the end of 2004, after a decade of refurbishments, the Palau Nacional opened its doors for the first time to the fully integrated collections of Catalan art in the city.

The original collection of the umbrella museum, MNAC (Museu Nacional d'Art de Catalunya), runs from Romanesque through to baroque and has the finest assemblage of medieval art in Europe. To this has been added the collection of the Museu d'Art Modern that until recently had its own home in the Parlament de Catalunya in the Parc de la Ciutadella, where the main art collection was also once housed.

The Palau Nacional was designed to house the Catalan national art collection after relinquishing its function as host centre for the Universal Exposition of 1929.

Unmissable above the exhibition halls and shooting fountains of Montjuïc, the imposing neo-baroque "palace" is lit up at night by nine anti-aircraft searchlights. Behind its large galleries, the architects Enric Català i Català and Pedro Cendoya Oscoz included an enormous Oval Hall which is hired out for private and public events.

ABOVE: *Immaculada Concepció* by Francisco de Zurbarán.
LEFT: the museum includes many magnificent chests, caskets, screens and crucifixes.

ABOVE: a 13th-century retable depicting *The Martyrdom of St James*.
BELOW: a depiction of the 13th-century *Assault on the City of Mallorca.*
BOTTOM: one of a number of Ramón Casas paintings.

THE HIGHLIGHTS

Romanesque The greatest collection of Romanesque art in Europe includes many wall paintings from churches in the Pyrenees, rescued from decay at the beginning of the 20th century. Dating from the 11th to the 13th centuries, these paintings, along with altar screens, chests, madonnas and crucifixes, are brightly coloured and executed with a powerful simplicity that has inspired many modern Catalan painters.

Gothic Catalonia's exceptional period of architecture was also rich in fine art. From the 13th to the late 15th centuries religious paintings by Jaume Huguet, Bernat Martorell and many others in the collection is complemented by sculpture, metal and enamel work and other decorative arts.

Renaissance and Baroque Between the 14th and the 19th centuries, Catalonia had no artists of international standing. This is a Europe-wide collection, with works of art from Italy and the Netherlands as well as from Spain, with paintings by El Greco, Goya, Velázquez and Zurbarán.

Museu d'Art Modern The collection of modern Catalan art runs from the early 19th century until the Civil War (1936), and is important for anybody who wishes to understand *modernisme* and *Noucentisme*, the driving art forces of the modern city. *Modernista* furniture, decorative arts and interiors can also be seen.

Other Collections MNAC also oversees a collection of Numismatism, Prints and Drawings from the 17th to the 20th centuries, and a Department of Photography, with both historical and contemporary prints that form temporary exhibitions.

ABOVE: *Poble Escalonat* (Terraced Village; 1909) painted by Joaquim Mir (1873–1940).

THE EIXAMPLE

Cerdà's 19th-century grid system of streets allowed the city's wealthy elite to commission some of the most innovative buildings of the age, including Gaudí's fabulous Sagrada Família

The Eixample is one of the most characteristic districts of Barcelona, and has some of its most distinctive elements, such as the Sagrada Família and much of the city's famed *modernista* architecture. It stands as a symbol of the 19th-century boom that initiated the city's modern era, and today is the most populated district in the city. After the narrow, irregular streets of the Old Town, where history has left layer upon layer of building styles, the Eixample can feel like a new town. Its regular structure forms a repeated pattern. Ttaffic roars down one street and up another in a well-structured one-way system, all the way from its southern boundary by Plaça d'Espanya to its northern limit leading up from Plaça de les Glòries.

Plaça de les Glòries itself is the axis for three main roads crossing the city: La Meridiana, Gran Via and Avinguda Diagonal where a recently introduced tramline takes you down to another new shopping centre, Diagonal Mar, the site of the Forum, and out to Sant Adrià.

Also at Plaça de les Glòries is the latest addition to Barcelona's skyline, the Torre Agbar, headquarters of a water company (*see picture, page 74*). Designed by the French architect Jean Nouvel, it has an outer casing of glass vents reflecting 40 colours.

An expanding city

In a sense, the Eixample *was* a "new town": it grew from the need to expand out of the old city in the middle of the 19th century. *Eixample* means "enlargement" (*ensanche,* the Castilian word, is still used) and was to extend over the areas between the old city centre and the equally historic municipalities of Sants, Sarrià, Sant Gervasi de Cassoles and Gràcia. Although criticised by some, this exceptional piece of town planning is deeply admired by architects, who

Map on page 160

LEFT: among the spires of the Sagrada Família.
BELOW: shopping on the Passeig de Gràcia.

One of the modernista street lamps designed by Pere Falqués on the Passeig de Gràcia.

still come from far and wide to see it.

Its designer, Ildefons Cerdà i Sunyer, was a liberal-minded civil engineer. He planned a garden city in which only two of the four sides of each block would be built on. The other sides, together with the central open space, were to have been attractive, shady squares and the *xamfrans* (angled street corners) were meant to be open spaces, not packed with double-parked vehicles as they are today. Work began in 1859 but Cerdà's plan was not adopted in its entirety for a number of different reasons. His "utopian socialism" did not appeal to the more conservative elements in the city, causing widespread controversy.

The Eixample is broken into two halves, *la dreta* (right) and *l'esquerra* (left) on either side of **Balmes** as you look inland towards the summit of Tibidabo. Within the two halves are well-defined neighbourhoods, such

as those of the **Sagrada Família** and **Fort Pius** (on the right) and **Sant Antoni** and a *barri* near the old municipal slaughterhouse called **L'Escorxador** (on the left).

Most of Barcelona's *modernista* landmarks can be found in *la dreta*, while *l'esquerra* is more modern and residential. Since the 1960s *la dreta* has undergone a profound transformation. With the earlier inhabitants moving to uptown districts, the larger houses have been converted into offices and flats.

The best way to appreciate the Eixample is to wander aimlessly, to be led by the green pedestrian lights at junctions, zig-zagging up, across and down these fascinating streets. Peep into doorways to see *modernista* lamps and ceramic tiles, look up at balconies and stained-glass *tribunes* (enclosed balconies), notice the decorative facades, as well as the plants, washing and other elements of real life that go on inside these

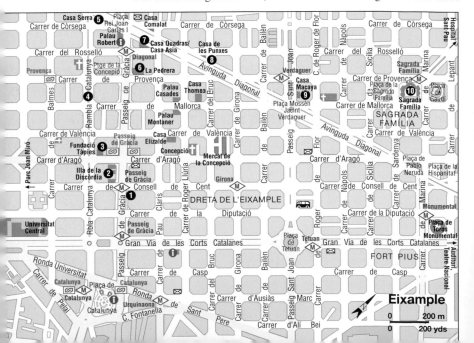

museum pieces. Take time to visit the art galleries that abound, to notice old shop signs, to shop in ancient *colmados*.

Whenever possible, catch a glimpse of the inner patios of these *illas*, the name of each four-sided block of buildings: sadly not used for the greater good, as Cerdà would have wished, but mostly for car parks, commercial or private use. They still make fascinating viewing, particularly the backs of the elegant houses and some well-established private gardens.

Passeig de Gràcia

This itinerary will focus on the central area and some key areas leading off it. Using Plaça de Catalunya as a pivotal point, cross over to **Passeig de Gràcia ❶**. This wide, tree-lined avenue originally linked the old city and the outlying neighbourhood of Gràcia even before the ancient walls of the city were torn down. Cerdà increased its width to 60 metres (200 ft), which makes it distinctive from the uniform streets of the rest of the Eixample; more recently, the pavements have been widened. The beautiful wrought-iron street lamps, which are incorporated with mosaic benches, were designed by Pere Falqués in 1906.

Notice the hexagonal pavement tiles designed by Gaudí and unique to the Passeig de Gràcia. Everywhere you look there are fascinating buildings to admire and details to observe.

Designer-label shopping

On the *xamfrà* at **Casp** you will find Gonzalo Comella, with designer-labels for men and women, and towards **Gran Via**, another classic, Furest, for the well-dressed Catalan man about town (and country). Next come the flagship premises of **Zara** in the highly desirable building at the very visible junction with **Gran**

Via. Galicia-based Zara is a phenomenon in the fashion world, with shops all over Barcelona, Spain and internationally.

Gran Via is a broad, busy thoroughfare that brings traffic from the airport and the south right through town to the motorways heading north and up the coast. The fountains in the middle and the impressive buildings around prevent it from being merely a major through-road, however. As you cross over and continue up Passeig de Gràcia, don't miss the jeweller J. Roca, a fine, subtle example of 1930s architecture by Sert.

Consell de Cent, one of the streets cutting across, demands a detour. Cross Passeig de Gràcia and wander a block or two, to see some of the best art galleries as well as **Antonio Miró**, the latest shop of Barcelona's ingenious and always intriguing fashion designer. One of the first designers to bring fame to Catalan fashion in the 1970s, he remains supreme. Apart from his twice-yearly collections, he is often brought in to advise on important

Map on page 160

TIP

In Casp, on the right-hand side as you begin your walk up Passeig de Gràcia, is one of the best spots in town to have a coffee, Bracafé, which has much the same character as when it opened in 1932.

BELOW: romance on the Passeig de Gràcia.

Inside the curvaceous Casa Batlló, a house that Gaudí remodelled for José Batlló y Casanovas, a Barcelona textiles manufacturer.

BELOW: Casa Lleó Morera, the Illa de la Discòrdia (Block of Discord).

institutional fashion decisions: he designed the uniforms for the *Mossos*, the Catalan police force, and various Olympic and Forum uniforms. The new Liceu opera house *(see page 85)* also has a Miró label on its velvet designer stage curtain.

Illa de la Discòrdia

The most famous, and no doubt most visited, block on Passeig de Gràcia is between Consell de Cent and Aragó. The block, formerly known as the Mansana de Discòrdia is now called the **Illa de la Discòrdia** ❷ (both names means the same – the Block of Discord). It gained its name because of the close juxtaposition of three outstanding buildings, each of which is in a conflicting style, although they are all categorised as modernist.

Casa Lleó Morera, designed by Lluís Domènech i Montaner and decorated with the sculptures of Eusebi Arnau, is on the corner, with an exclusive leather shop occupying the ground floor. Slightly further up is the **Casa Amatller** by Josep Puig i Cadafalch, and next door to it is **Casa**

Batlló, which was remodelled by Gaudí in 1906. Unfortunately, the first two can not be visited, but you can still enjoy their splendid facades and take a peek at the extraordinary ceramic work inside the entrance to Lleó Morera, or wander into the ground floor of the Casa Amatller with its stained-glass ceiling and lamp details. The big treat is that Casa Batlló (daily 9am–8pm; entrance charge), considered the ultimate Gaudí masterpiece *(see cover image)*, has recently opened to the public for the first time in its history, despite the upper floors being occupied.

Tàpies showpiece

Around the corner in noisy Aragó is something completely different: **Servicio Estación**, an emporium of a hardware store. Opposite it is another Domènech i Montaner work, built in 1886 for publishers Montaner i Simón and now skilfully converted to become the **Fundació Tàpies** ❸ (Tues–Sun 10am– 8pm; entrance charge). Observe the building from this side of the street to get the full perspective, and pick out the chair in

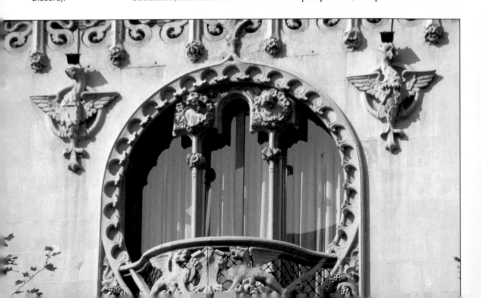

Map on page 160

the Tàpies sculpture which crowns it, *Núvol i Cadira* (Cloud and Chair; *see picture on page 55*).

Reputedly the first *modernista* building, it seems rather workmanlike after the ornate facade of Casa Batlló. The interior spaces make a good setting for the large collection of work by Antoni Tàpies, who is considered to be Spain's greatest living artist. Temporary exhibitions of modern art are also held here.

After the Tàpies museum continue to the next corner and turn right into **Rambla de Catalunya** ❹, which runs parallel with Passeig de Gràcia, one block away. It is like an elongation of the Old Town's La Rambla through the central part of the Eixample. The atmosphere, though, is quite different: the central boulevard is quiet and sedate, fewer tourists stroll here and the pavement cafés are patronised by smart, middle-aged Catalans or their offspring. The shopping is sophisticated – there is not a souvenir in sight – and it's expensive, as are the elegant galleries.

Enjoy the gentle walk up towards Diagonal, pausing at every horizontal crossing to look at the houses on the chamfered corners and the streets leading off, to get into the rhythm of the structure. If you need a break, dive down a few steps into an old wine bar, **La Bodegueta**, at No. 100, welcomingly down to earth in the midst of all this sophistication. Alternatively, go with the flow, and a little further on have a genteel snack in **Mauri** on the corner of **Provença**, with its unusual chocolate hedgehogs and tempting pastries, or a take-away lunch from its mouth-watering delicatessen counter.

Crossing the Diagonal

At the end of Rambla de Catalunya, the Eixample meets the Diagonal and there is another change of gear as a new residential district begins. On the right is **Casa Serra** ❺, built by Puig i Cadafalch in 1908 and controversially adapted to accommodate the **Diputació de Barcelona**, the central government body which occupied the Palau de la Generalitat in Plaça Sant Jaume during the Franco regime, and had to be relocated with the return of

TIP

The Casa Amatller is the centre for information on a do-it-yourself tour of *modernista* buildings in the area.

BELOW: *modernista* curves on the Rambla Catalunya.

Just outside the Palau Robert, a delightful fountain depicts a child catching a frog.

BELOW: the facade and chimneys of La Pedrera.

democracy. In the complex designed by Milà and Correa the new steel building seems like a large shadow of the older one.

There are very few outward signs of the red tape that must proliferate inside; only the presence of some chatting guards suggests anything to do with officialdom. Walk along the short stretch of **Còrsega**, and turn right into the gardens of the **Palau Robert**, a cool haven in mid-summer.

The house was built by a French architect and would not look out of place in a French provincial city. It houses the Generalitat tourist offices, with information on the whole of Catalonia and occasional exhibitions about the different regions.

Cut through the side entrance to return to Passeig de Gràcia, at the busy junction of **Plaça Rei Joan Carles I**, where a constantly traffic-filled Diagonal runs across the top of the Eixample, up to Plaça Francesc Macià and the upper reaches of the city, and down towards Diagonal Mar, where it meets the sea; above it the district of Gràcia begins.

Off the Eixample

Heading down towards Plaça de Catalunya on the same pavement, cross **Rosselló** and halfway along the next block you will come to another characteristic feature of the Eixample – a passageway running through the inner part of the block. This one, called the **Passatge de la Concepció**, has decorative iron gates across it, but it is open to the public.

Even if you do not have the time or the budget to eat at **Tragaluz**, take a look at what is one of the chicest restaurants in Barcelona. The word *tragaluz* means skylight, and you will see that this makes sense when you go upstairs.

La Pedrera

Follow the passage until it comes out into Passeig de Gràcia, and turn right to the end of the block. Pause on this corner to give yourself time to take in the extraordinary spectacle of Gaudí's **Casa Milà**, more often known as **La Pedrera ❻** (the Quarry) (daily 10am–8pm; entrance charge) because of its rippling grey stone facade.

This splendid building has been cleaned, refurbished and polished up by its new owners, the foundation of the Caixa de Catalunya.

At the time of its construction in 1910 it was the subject of passionate debate between enthusiasts and denigrators. For many years it was left to fall apart, but UNESCO declared it a monument of world interest and the Caixa de Catalunya stepped in. Take time to visit this exceptional building, which has the *Espai Gaudí*, an enlightening exhibition of the architect's work, in the attic, a spectacular roof whose chimneys have been dubbed the "witch scarers", and *El Pis*, one of the flats now open to the public and decorated as it would have been when the building was first occupied. Major temporary exhibitions are held regularly on the first floor *(principal)* and are open to the public free of charge. A bar and inspiring shop are on the ground floor.

Just up from La Pedrera, at No. 96, is another feast for designer eyes – **Vinçon**, where you can buy everything you desire for the home, and always be confident that the design divas of the day will approve. Based in the former home of 19th-century painter Ramón Casas *(see pages 156–7)*, this growing empire is quietly taking over the block, so you can actually cut through the shop to **Pau Claris** or **Provença**. Before leaving, have a look at the inner patio of the block from the *principal*, including a rear view of La Pedrera. If you don't take the short cut, return to Passeig de Gràcia and along Provença to Pau Claris, back up to Diagonal.

More modernist creations

At No 373 Diagonal is Puig i Cadafalch's **Casa Quadras** ❼. Built for Barón de Quadras in 1904, it has been modernised to become Casa Asia (Mon–Sat 10am– 8pm, Sun 10am–2pm; free), a cultural centre linking Spain with Oriental countries. It holds exhibitions, conferences and has a restaurant named Zen.

Walk down the Diagonal a short way to see another building by Puig i Cadafalch, the **Casa Terrades** (1903–5), also known as the **Casa de les Punxes** ❽ ("House of Spikes"),

Map on page 160

Tragaluz, in the Passatge de la Concepció, is one of the smartest restaurants in town.

BELOW: many shops and restaurants bear *modernista* trademarks.

The pinnacles of the Sagrada Família are encrusted with mosaics in characteristic Gaudí style.

Avinguda Diagonal, N0s 416–420. Sadly, it is not possible to go inside, but the exterior is impressive enough. Like Casa Quadras and Casa Serra, it displays Nordic neo-Gothic influences.

One option here is to continue down Diagonal until it meets **Passeig de Sant Joan** to visit an earlier (1901–2) Puig i Cadafalch house, the beautiful **Casa Macaya** at Passeig de Sant Joan, No 106 *(see below)*. Or take the longer way round to see some more Eixample gems. To do the latter, go down Bruc and turn right into Mallorca to **Casa Thomas** (No. 293), designed by Domènech i Montaner, and visit **b.d.**, the shop in its basement, which is like an exhibition of 21st-century furniture design. At the end of the block turn left into Roger de Llúria and on the next corner left again into València. On the opposite corner is **J. Murria**, an exceptional delicatessen frozen in time, which is worth visiting for the sheer aesthetics of the place to say nothing of is mouth-watering display of hams, cheeses and fine wines. Go along València, past **Navarro's**, the

best flower shop in town, until you reach the **Mercat de la Concepció**. This is a fine example of a 19th-century market, remodelled in late 20th-century style with striking results.

Now make your way to **Casa Macaya** ❾ and wander into its courtyard to see the details of Puig i Cadafalch's architecture.

Gaudí's celebrated temple

And so to the **Sagrada Família** ❿ (9am–8pm in summer, 9am–6pm in winter; entrance charge), the symbol of Barcelona for many, and the reason the name Antoni Gaudí spread around the world. Here, in the centre of this bustling, ordinary neighbourhood, it is a staggering sight.

This extraordinary building is best tackled in the morning rather than at the end of a long day's sightseeing, as there is much to see *(see the picture story, pages 172–3)*.

The temple was actually begun in 1882 as a neo-Gothic structure under the direction of the architect Francesc P. Villar. Gaudí took over the project a year later, using Villar's plans as a starting point, but greatly

expanding their scale and originality. It became Gaudí's main project for the rest of his life. He realised long before he died that he would not live to see its completion, admitting: "It is not possible for one generation to erect the entire temple."

At the time of his death in 1926 only the crypt, apse, part of the Nacimiento facade and one tower had been completed. Today, nearly 80 years after Gaudí's death, work progresses under the control of Jordi Bonet Armengol, the son of one of Gaudí's long-standing aides.

Along Avinguda de Gaudí is the much less known *modernista* complex, the **Hospital Sant Pau** (1902–12). Made up of over 20 buildings, it is the work of the prolific Domènech i Montaner. As it is a public hospital, you can wander through into the garden and pavilions behind.

Parc Joan Miró

Venturing beyond the central part of the Eixample is a good way to complete the picture of Barcelona from the mid-19th century to the millennium. On the extreme left of the Eixample you will find one of the first parks to be created in the 1980s as part of the new Barcelona. Covering four Eixample blocks above Plaça d'Espanya where Diputació and Aragó meet Tarragona (metro Espanya or Tarragona), the **Parc Joan Miró** is also known as the **Parc de l'Escorxador** because it was the location of the municipal slaughterhouse until 1979. It is a great area for kids to run wild in. The 22-metre (70-ft) Miró statue, *Dona i Ocell* (Woman and Bird), is striking in its simple setting on a small island in the middle of a pool in the park. One of Miró's last works, it was unveiled in 1983, just a few months before he died.

You could link a visit to the park with a trip to Montjuïc *(see page 143)*. Alternatively, combine it with a walk along Gran Via or one of the streets parallel to it to get a sense of the day-to-day real life of the city. The apartment blocks along this route follow the Cerdà plan, even though, on the whole, they grew up later and are more modest than earlier buildings in the Eixample.

Map on page 160

TIP

Directly below Hospital San Pau and above Plaça de les Glòries is the proposed site for the AVE high-speed train terminal connecting Barelona with Madrid and France. It is set to open in 2007.

BELOW: Joan Miró's *Dona i Ocell* (Woman and Bird) in the Parc Joan Miró.

Plaça de les Glòries

At the extreme right of the Eixample, just beyond the Monumental bullring on Gran Via, is Plaça de les Glòries Catalanes. What seems a no-man's land occupied by a roundabout and flyovers actually hides a nucleus of activities: a civic centre in an impressive old flourmill, **La Farinera**, and the much-frequented **Els Encants**, a sprawling flea market, which opened in 1928.

The city's latest landmark, the soaring Torre Agbar by Jean Nouvel, overshadows the nearby cultural complex, the **Teatre Nacional de Catalunya** (TNC) and **L'Auditori**, the National Theatre and the Concert Hall. The theatre is in the neoclassical style of its architect Ricardo Bofill. Its three stages ofer a varied programme, mainly in Catalan, of classic and experimental theatre and dance. This is the Generalitat's protégé, unlike the Ciutat de Teatre near Montjuïc, which is the domain of the municipal cultural department. L'Auditori, designed by Rafael Moneo, is the home of the Barcelona Orchestra (OBC) and will eventually house the Music Museum and a music conservatory.

RESTAURANTS & BARS

Restaurants

Stretching to the left and right of Passeig de Gràcia as its central axis, the Eixample covers a lot of ground, taking in several markets and different neighbourhoods. As a busy commercial and residential area, nearly every block has several bars-cum-restaurants where you can be sure of having a standard lunchtime set menu, along with the local office workers and residents at remarkably economical prices. It also includes some of the city's top restaurants and is home to some of the new wave Catalan chefs.

Alkimia
Industria, 79 (metro: Sagrada Familia)
Tel: 93 207 6115
L & D Mon–Fri. D only Sat.
€€€
A shining example of the new talent in Catalan cuisine, young chef Jordi Vilà is the alchemist in question, working wonders on ordinary Catalan dishes and converting them into something quite delicious. Fast becoming one of Barcelona's leading restaurants.

Casa Amalia
Passatge Mercat, 4 (metro: Girona)
Tel: 93 458 9458
L & D Tues–Sat. L only Sun.

€€ (set menu L Tues–Fri. €)
This bustling, local spot serves the freshest food straight from the attractive Concepció market nearby. Excellent value *menú del día*.

Casa Calvet
Casp, 48 (metro: Urquinaona)
Tel: 93 412 4012
L & D Mon–Sat. €€€
Satisfy gourmet and culture-vulture needs in one fell swoop at this top-class restaurant, housed in former textile offices designed by Gaudí and full of his characteristic details.

Cata 1.81
València, 181 (metro: Passeig de Gràcia)
Tel: 93 323 6818
D (from 6pm) Mon–Sat. €€
The main point of this sophisticated little bar is to taste different wines (*cata* is a tasting), with an excellent range, served in quarter-litre decanters. However, the tiny accompanying dishes have taken on equal importance and come in a wild mixture of flavours in true new-Catalan style.

Drolma
Hotel Majestic
Passeig de Gràcia, 68 (metro: Passeig de Gràcia)
Tel: 93 496 7710
L & D Mon–Sat. €€€€
One of the first Barcelona hotels to place due importance on its dining room, the

Majestic launched the highly regarded Drolma with its equally respected chef, Fermin Puig, only a few years ago. It has risen rapidly and is now considered one of the most luxurious restaurants in Spain. This is top-notch international cuisine in sumptuous surroundings at heady prices.

El Caballito Blanco
Mallorca, 196 (metro: Passeig de Gràcia/Hospital Clínic)
Tel: 93 453 1033
L & D Tues–Sat. L only Sun. €€
This is an old-fashioned, popular place that always has a large number of international and Catalan dishes to choose from. The fresh ingredients are selected from what is in season. It's a relief to find places like this have escaped being redesigned and relaunched in 21st-century Barcelona.

Gorría
Diputació, 421 (metro: Monumental)
Tel: 93 245 1164
L & D Mon–Sat. €€€€
As genuine as the first day the Gorría family opened this Basque restaurant nearly 30 years ago. Daily deliveries of fish from the north make it the perfect place to eat *bacalao a la vizcaína* or other traditional Basque dishes.

Jaume de Provença
Provença, 88 (metro: Entença)
Tel: 93 430 0029
L & D Tues–Sat. L only Sun.
€€€
It rose to fame in the 1980s with Jaume Barguès's inspired interpretations of classic Catalan and international dishes, and is still regarded as one of the city's best restaurants.

José Luis
Diagonal, 520 (FGC: Provença)
Tel 93 200 8312
B, L & D daily. €€
Elevated prices that are worth paying for sophisticated, well-prepared *tapes* that are eaten in the company of an up-town crowd.

Koyuki
Còrsega, 242 (FGC: Provença)
Tel: 93 237 8490
L & D Tues–Sat. D only Sun.
€
This is one of the simplest but best Japanese restaurants in the city, less expensive than most and frequented by comic-reading Japanese.

La Bodegueta
Rambla de Catalunya, 100 (metro: Diagonal)
Tel: 93 215 4894
L & D *(tapes)* Mon–Sat. D only Sun. €
Spain was once full of bodegas like this one, with massive old fridges, barrels and marble tables where you can

accompany the rough red wine with olives, *tacos de manchego* and a plate of *jamón serrano*. Happily, here you can still do so.

La Gran Bodega
València, 193 (metro: Passeig de Gràcia)
Tel: 93 453 1053
L & D *(tapes)* Tues–Sun. €
A genuine *tapes* bar right down to the authentic aroma of frying food, with a wonderful selection and traditional decor. A corner of Spain in Catalonia.

L'Olive
Balmes, 47 (metro: Passeig de Gràcia)
Tel: 93 452 1990
L & D Mon–Sat. L only Sun.
€€€
L'Olive has long been considered a fashionable place for classic Catalan dishes like *pa amb tomàquet*, *faves* (stewed baby broad beans) and *escalivada* (grilled pepers and aubergines). The slick new premises are not quite as atmospheric as the original ones.

Madrid-Barcelona
Aragó, 282 (metro: Passeig de Gràcia)
Tel: 93 215 7026
L & D Mon–Sat. €€
This is a fun, bustling place in which to lunch on Catalan-Spanish food, well situated just off Passeig de Gràcia.

Mauri
Rambla de Catalunya, 102 (metro: Diagonal)
Tel: 93 215 1020
B, L & T Mon–Sat. B on Sun. €
A classic establishment selling pastries and ready-made dishes for elegant locals who are not inclined to cook, or who meet up with friends for cakes and coffee in the afternoon. Good value set lunch if you feel like mingling with an up-town crowd.

Mex & Cal
Aribau, 50 (metro: Universitat)
Tel: 93 323 4316
L & D daily. €
The best place to eat à la Baja California. Authentic and tasty nachos, burritos, plus cocktails. Attractive, animated atmosphere.

Mora
Avinguda Diagonal, 409 (metro: Diagonal)
B, L & T Mon–Sat. €
Tel: 93 416 0751
If you're on a "shop until you drop" spree in the Eixample, this cafeteria is a good place to drop in for coffee, cakes, *tapes*, a lunch or just a drink. It's versatile and civilised with a personality all its own. Their window displays are always beautiful pieces of design.

Ponsa
Enric Granados, 89 (FGC: Provença)
Tel: 93 453 1037
L & D Mon–Sat. L Sun. €
A highly-polished classic. Old-fashioned good taste and great food, in one of the most attractive streets of the Eixample.

Semproniana
Rosselló, 148 (FGC: Provença)
Tel: 93 453 1820

L & D Mon–Sat. €€
An eclectic style of decoration which makes a change from slick minimalism or traditional marble, and a slightly whimsical menu offering interesting food and a notorious chocolate mousse which goes by the name of Delirium Tremens.

Taktika Berri
València, 169 (metro: Hospital Clínic)
Tel: 93 453 4759
L & D Mon–Sat. €
Basque delights in a *modernista* building that was once a textile workshop.

Tragaluz
Passatge de la Concepció, 5 (metro: Diagonal)
Tel: 93 487 0196
L & D daily. €€
Situated in a lovely little passageway off Passeig de Gràcia, this is a wonderful example of Barcelona design from the early 1990s. The enormous skylight, which lends its name to this fashionable restaurant, gives the impression that you are eating on a light, airy terrace. Modern Mediterranean.

Txapela
Passeig de Gràcia, 8–10 (metro: Catalunya/Passeig de Gràcia)
Tel: 93 412 0289
Tapes daily. €
This place seems to be from a do-it-yourself kit for Basque restaurants, (many of the Irish pubs in Barcelona seem to be similarly standardised), but nevertheless it has a

surprising range of tasty hot and cold *pintxos* (snacks on toothpicks), and it is in a very convenient location.

Xix Kebab
Còrsega, 193 (metro: Hospital Clínic)
Tel: 93 321 8210
L & D Mon–Sat. €
Soothing atmosphere and delicate, very tasty food in this Syrian restaurant.

Bars & Cafés

Pavement cafés are everywhere in this busy district, but Passeig de Gràcia and Rambla de Catalunya are best for people-watching. **La Jijonenca**, Rambla de Catalunya, is where elegant grannies take their families for cool drinks and ice creams in the summer. For a more business-like shot of coffee, **Bracafé**, Casp, is a classic, or the more leisurely **Laie Libreria Café**, Pau Claris, 85, where the abundance of reading matter slows you down. This bookshop also has an attractive dining room with salad buffet. The **Dry Martini**, Aribau 162, is *the* place to be at cocktail hour.

Modernisme

The city's defining architectural style looked to the past for its main influences

Modernisme is Barcelona's great contribution to architecture. Colourful and flamboyant, it was a mix of then-current technology and former styles. It began at the time of the Universal Exhibition in Ciutadella Parc in 1888 and continued up until around 1930, and it corresponded to the Arts and Crafts and Art Nouveau movements in the rest of Europe, with which it shared a preoccupation with sinuous line, organic form and ornament.

Its greatest practitioners were Lluís Domènech i Montaner (1850–1923), a professor of Barcelona University's School of Architecture, and one of his pupils, Josep Puig i Cadafalch (1867–1957). At the Universal Exhibition Domènech designed what is now the Zoological Museum, based on Valencia's red-brick Gothic Stock Exchange, which afterwards became a workshop for ceramics, wrought iron and glass-making. Furnishings and details were an essential ingredient in *modernista* buildings.

Modernisme was a part of the Catalan *Renaixença* (renaissance) and it looked to the past, taking on Catalan Gothic, with its tradition of iron work, as well as acknowledging the styles of Islamic Spain. The 19th century expansion of the city (the Eixample) gave architects the freedom and space to experiment, and this is where most *modernista* buildings are to be found.

ABOVE LEFT: the monumental Hospital de la Santa Creu i de Sant Pau by Domènech i Montaner is still used as a hospital today.
ABOVE: the dining room in the profusely ornamental Casa Lleó Morera (1905), by Domènech i Montaner.

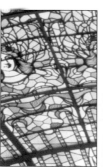

ABOVE: the Palau de La Música Catalana by Lluís Domènech i Montaner is considered one of the most remarkable examples of modernist architecture. Gigantic winged Pegasuses fly from the columns of the upper balcony; the ornate stained-glass ceiling is a masterpiece; and a roll-call of sculptures and ceramics is dedicated to musical muses.

ABOVE LEFT AND RIGHT: elaborate wrought-iron work and stained glass were key decorative features of *modernisme*.
RIGHT: the Illa de la Discórdia (Block of Discord), with Puig i Cadafalch's Casa Amatller on the left and Antoni Gaudí's Casa Batlló on the right.

THE HIGHLIGHTS

Illa de la Discórdia The best starting point to understand *modernisme* is the "block of discord", three neighbouring buildings in Passeig de Gràcia. Within a few metres of each other are Domènech's Casa Lléo Morea, Puig's Casa Amatller and Gaudí's Casa Batlló *(see page 162)*. Gaudí did not regard himself as a *moderniste*, but it is impossible not to compare his work with theirs, and though there are great differences in style, the discord is not obvious.

Palau de la Música Catalana A UNESCO World Heritage Site, this is a sumptuous building, though its facade, crowded with sculptures and dazzling mosaics, is rather cramped down Carrer de Sant Francesc de Paula. There are tours of the building, but it is best if you can attend a concert beneath the stained-glass dome that suffuses the auditorium with a mellow light *(see page 107)*.

Hospital de la Santa Creu i de Sant Pau Domènech's extraordinary hospital was the most advanced in Europe when it was completed in 1901. It is essentially a series of pavilions connected by underground tunnels *(see page 167)*.

CaixaForum The Casaramona textile factory built by Puig i Cadafalch at the foot of Montjuïc is now the CaixaForum cultural centre *(see page 146)*.

Casa Thomas Built by Domènech in Carrer de Mallorca for the engraving business of a relative, this now houses b.d., an upmarket design shop that sells excellent reproductions of *modernista* furniture and fittings.

ANTONI GAUDÍ'S MASTERPIECE

The Sagrada Família, symbol of the city, was dreamed up by a religious patriot with astonishing vision

Antoni Gaudí i Cornet was born in Reus in 1852 and studied in Barcelona's School of Architecture. His principal patron was the industrialist Eusebi Güell i Bacigalupi, for whom he designed a town house, Palau Güell *(see page 85)*, the would-be garden suburb of Park Güell *(see page 175)* and Colonia Güell, a workers' estate outside the city. Casa Milà, his best-known town dwelling, was designed for the textile manufacturer Pere Milà i Camps *(see page 164)*.

Undoubtedly Gaudí's greatest work, however, was the Temple Expiatori de la Sagrada Família (Expiatory Temple of the Holy Family), which he embarked on at the age of 31. His church was to be 60 metres (197 ft) wide with a nave 90 metres (295 ft) long. Deeply religious and a passionate Catalan, Gaudí spent the last 27 years of his life living in a hut on the site. When he was fatally injured by a tram in 1926, the only parts of the church to be completed were the Nativity facade, one tower, the apse and the crypt, where he is buried.

• *Contact details and opening times on page 166.*

LEFT: the Sagrada Família, the much-loved symbol of Barcelona.

ABOVE: Antoni Gaudí (1852–1926) spent most of his career in Barcelona. He is buried in the crypt of the Sagrada Família.
RIGHT: the Pasión (Passion) facade facing the Carrer de Sardenya, with sculptures by Josep Maria Subirachs.
LEFT: two of the mosaic-encrusted spires of the Sagrada Família.

THE HIGHLIGHTS

Passion Facade Visitors enter through a door in the west face of the building where angular figures of Christ's passion have been sculpted by the Catalan artist Josep Maria Subirachs, an avowed atheist.

The Nave Running north–south, the nave has a forest of tree-like pillars. Gaudí eschewed straight lines. His original design for the 1,300 bench seats was to have them so close together that slovenly worshippers would be unable to cross their legs.

The Towers For a view over the church, take a lift (or climb the 400 steps) to the top of one of the spindly towers that rise above the east and west facades, sparkling with Venetian mosaics and tinkling with bells. Four more will rise above the Glory (south) facade. Gaudí also envisaged a giant central tower, much taller than Barcelona Cathedral's, with four further large towers around it, representing the evangelists.

Nativity Facade On the east side of the building, this is the only facade completed by Gaudí, in 1904. Beautifully and ornately carved and dripping with symbolism, its doorways represent Faith, Hope and Charity.

Ambulatory This external cloister will provide a sheltered walkway all the way round the outside of the building.

The Crypt and Museum The crypt is by the original architect, Francesc de Paula Villar i Lozano, who was employed for just one year, and this is where Gaudí is buried and services are held. On the same lower floor are drawings and models of the church, as well as a collection of artefacts, but most of Gaudí's plans were destroyed during the Civil War.

ABOVE: the central figures on the immensely detailed Nacimiento (Nativity) facade, the only facade that Gaudí completed.
LEFT: the temple remains a work in progress.

ABOVE THE DIAGONAL

Avinguda Diagonal effectively cuts the city in two.
In the little explored area north of this divide are
some of the city's most distinctive districts and
worthwhile excursions

Two well-worn clichés about urban Barcelona are that it has traditionally turned its back to the sea, and that people who live above the Diagonal (the arterial road that slices through the city at an angle, from west to east) never come down below it. Neither are now true. The development of the waterfront in the 1990s has succeeded in dispelling the former and, along with the whole urban-renewal programme, has drawn uptown people downtown. Nightlife in the Old Town also boomed in the 1990s – young *pijos* and *pijas* (a snooty set who speak Castilian despite their Catalan roots), whose natural habitat is around **Plaça Francesc Macià**, do now venture down on a Friday night.

The converse seems to be the case for tourists. Many visitors never make it above the Diagonal, and are unaware of this large part of the city.

Gaudí's Parc Güell

There are, of course, isolated pockets above the Diagonal which are star attractions. One is the **Parc Güell ❶** (daily, May–Aug 10am–8pm. Apr and Sept 10am–7pm, Mar and Oct 10am–7pm, Nov–Feb 10am–6pm; free), the second most visited park in Barcelona after the Ciutadella. It owes its attraction to the fact that it was designed by Gaudí. It was origi-

nally planned as a garden city on the estate of the wealthy industrialist Eusebi Güell, who went on to commission Gaudí for several other projects. The estate was to encompass 60 building plots, but only five buildings were completed: the two pavilions flanking the entrance, both designed by Gaudí, and three others inside the park, one of which is today the **Casa-Museu Gaudí** (10am–8pm in summer, 10am–6pm in winter; entrance charge) where the architect lived from 1906 until his death in 1926.

Map
on page
176

LEFT: the serpentine mosaic bench in Gaudí's Parc Güell.
BELOW: detail, Parc Güell.

TIP

Getting to the main sites above the Diagonal is straightforward. For Parc Güell take metro line 3 to Vallcarca, then use the escalators leading up to a side entrance. The Palau Reial de Pedralbes is also reached directly on metro line 3.

Some of his furniture, drawings and projects are housed here.

In creating Parc Güell, Gaudí used shapes which harmonised with the landscape. Always aware of the struggle between man and nature, he built a complex garden of staircases, zoomorphic sculptures, sinuous ramps and viaducts.

The most important single element of the park is a two-tiered plaza 86 by 40 metres (280 by 130 ft). The lower part, made up of a series of columns in the form of a *sala hipóstila*, was designed to be the housing estate's market-place. The upper portion is an open area with grand views over the city, surrounded by an undulating bench of mosaics, whose detailing is largely the work of Josep Maria Jujol. Recently restored, this serpentine seat is quite spectacular and, like the park, should not be missed. Built between 1900 and 1914, it has been declared a monument of world interest by UNESCO.

Upper echelons

A classic example of residential life "above the Diagonal" is the area around **Parc Turó** ❷, pinpointed by the roundabout **Plaça Francesc Macià** (on many bus routes, including the luxurious Tombbus from Plaça de Catalunya), where one begins to leave the 19th-century Eixample and enter the upper reaches of the Diagonal. Modern office blocks, hotels, smart shops and expensive properties are the trademark. In the park, just at the end of **Pau Casals** (a monument to the famous Catalan cellist is at the entrance), it is not uncommon to see immaculate, well-behaved children playing under the watchful eye of a fully uniformed nanny.

Also known as **Jardins Poeta Eduard Marquina**, the park was a project of landscape architect Rubió i Tudurí, and has two distinct areas. One is made up of lawn, hedges and flowerbeds laid out in a

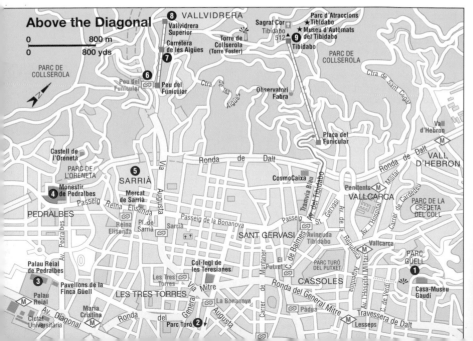

classic geometric pattern, the other contains children's playgrounds, a small lake and an open-air theatre. Sculptures by Clarà and Viladomat, among others, dot the interior of the park.

Palau de Pedralbes

From Plaça Francesc Macià the Diagonal is wider and the traffic faster, revving up for one of the main routes out of town. Walk, or catch a bus, along its tree-lined way as far as the **Palau Reial de Pedralbes** ❸, passing the large shopping centre **La Illa** on the left. The Royal Palace is the result of a 1919 conversion of the antique Can Feliu into a residence for King Alfonso XIII during his visits to Barcelona. It is elegant, and the classical garden peaceful, but has little sense of history.

The main building cannot be visited, apart from the two museums it houses. The **Museu de Ceràmica** (Tues–Sat 10am– 6pm, Sun 10am– 3pm; entrance charge) shows the history of Spanish pottery from the 12th century, and has some interesting 20th-century pieces from Artigas, Miró and Picasso. The **Museu de les Arts Decoratives** (same opening times) shows the development of craft techniques from medieval times to the present day, ending with Spain's only industrial-design collection.

The grounds

The garden, built to a "geometric decorative outline" in the 1920s, also by Rubió i Tudurí, integrated the existing palace garden with land ceded by Count Güell. What remains of his neighbouring estate are the lodge and gates, the **Pavellons de la Finca Güell**, designed by Gaudí, which can be seen by going back down the Diagonal and turning left into **Avinguda Pedralbes**. This avenue sweeps up through ever more exclusive blocks of apartments, with manicured lawns and swimming pools. This is the district of Pedralbes. There is no corner *colmado* or neighbourhood spirit here: each flat is its own exclusive island. A few beautiful *modernista torres* (large, detached houses)

A vase in the Museu de Ceràmica, where there's a fascinating display of Spanish pottery.

BELOW: the Palau de Pedralbes.

Treasure in the monastery, where you can also see the nuns' cells and refectory.

BELOW: view from Tibidabo.

remain, though most have become homes for the elderly, institutions, colleges, or even a consulate (USA). Some have been left to deteriorate to make way for a more profitable building plot.

Monestir de Pedralbes

At the top, by the Creu de Pedralbes, are the welcomingly old stones of the monastery complex, the **Monestir de Pedralbes** ❹ (Tues–Sun 10am–2pm; entrance charge). This is one of the most peaceful corners of the city, the perfect antidote to the crowds of the Old Town and the frenetic Eixample with its roaring traffic.

The monastery was founded in 1326 by Queen Elisenda de Montcada, widow (and fourth wife) of King Jaume II. She herself took the vows of the Order of St Clare, and today some 20 nuns are still in residence. The fine Gothic architecture, most notably the unusual three-tiered cloister, evokes the spiritual side of monastic life, while the rooms that are open to the public provide an insight into the day-to-day life of the monastery's inhabi-tants. There are some remarkable 14th-century murals by the Catalan artist Ferrer Bassa.

The monastery is easily reached by bus or FGC train to **Reina Elisenda** station.

Genteel Sarrià

While up here at the foot of the **Collserola** hills, take the opportunity to visit **Sarrià** ❺ by walking a little further along Passeig Reina Elisenda de Montcada, which leads straight into the **Plaça Sarrià** (also reached in under 10 minutes from Plaça de Catalunya and other central stations on the FGC line). Recognisable as a former village, despite being a sought-after city residence today, it is more charming than Pedralbes, and the wealth more discreet.

This is a real neighbourhood with a soul: it has a market, old ladies in cardigans queuing for lottery tickets, smoky bars and the attractive church of **Sant Vicenç** at the centre of things. The main street leading down from the church, **Major de Sarrià**, has been paved, encouraging strolling. The pastry shop **Foix de Sarrià**, founded in 1886, makes an elegant corner. **Casa Joana**, another old established business and little changed, still serves good home cooking at a reasonable price. Sarrià is reminiscent of a provincial Catalan town: passageways lead off through the backs of pretty houses with gardens bursting with bougainvillea; and in a side street with *modernista* villas you can still find a haberdashery with a bentwood chair at the counter and walls lined with underwear in boxes.

Escape from the city

From Sarrià you can get a taste of the **Parc de Collserola** by taking a walk on the city side of the hill, overlooking the whole of Barcelona. The trip is equally manageable from the centre with the efficient and frequent FGC train service from Plaça de Catalunya. Another overlooked part of Barcelona, the Parc de Collserola is a green belt measuring 17 by 6 km (11 by 4 miles), which is literally on the city's doorstep. Its 8,000 hectares (20,000 acres) of vegetation border the Ronda de Dalt ring road, and spread over the Collserola range of hills to Sant Cugat and beyond.

This easily accessible area is a bonus to city living. It is best known for its highest peak, Tibidabo (512 metres/1,664 ft) and its distinctive skyline, with the Sagrat Cor church, a 20th-century confection, and the Torre de Collserola communications tower *(see page 180)*, forming a dramatic backdrop to Barcelona. But it is a lot more besides. The hill is a venue for all kinds of leisure activities, from horse riding to nature trails, picnic spots, restaurants and *merenderos*, open-air restaurants where you can order a paella cooked on an outdoor wood fire. You can even barbecue your own food, a popular local tradition on Sundays.

Vallvidrera

If you prefer to walk with one eye on the city, the next stop after Sarrià on the FGC train is **Peu del Funicular ❻** ("foot of the funicular") to **Vallvidrera**, a suburban village on the crest of the hill where the desirable homes come with a spectacular view. There are frequent services from this station and, by particular request (at the press of a button), the funicular will stop halfway to Vallvidrera at **Carretera de les Aigües ❼**.

This is an ideal spot for a quick burst of fresh air and exercise, or relative cooling-off in the heat of the summer: the *carretera* is a track cut into the side of the hill, that winds on way beyond Tibidabo. Popular with joggers, cyclists, ramblers, dog-walkers and model-aeroplane clubs, it is perfect for stretching city legs, particularly on bright blue, pollution-free days (worth waiting for) when the views are breathtaking. The whole layout of Barcelona and its geographical context becomes clear.

For an enjoyable round trip,

Map on page 176

Model-aeroplane enthusiasts flock to the Parc de Collserola at weekends.

BELOW LEFT AND RIGHT: the Sagrat Cor church tops Tibidabo, the highest peak of Collserola.

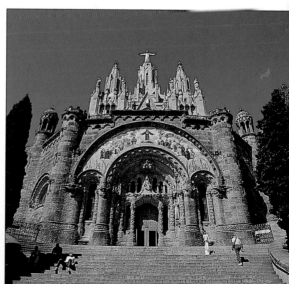

BELOW: hands on in the Science Museum.

walk as far as the point where the track crosses the Tibidabo funicular, where a badly indicated footpath leads down to the Plaça del Funicular. Here catch the tram, or walk to Avinguda Tibidabo FGC station which will return you to the city centre.

Panoramic view

Alternatively, return to the Vallvidrera funicular, taking it as far as **Vallvidrera Superior** ❽, an attractive *modernista* station in this pleasant village, evocative of the days when city dwellers would spend the summer up here for the cooler air. The air still feels a few degrees cooler, even in the height of summer, and definitely cleaner.

The No. 211 bus will take you to the striking communications tower, the **Torre de Collserola**, designed by Norman Foster for the Olympics and sometimes known as the **Torre Foster** (Wed–Sat 11am–2.30pm and 3.30–8pm; entrance charge). Up close it is even more impressive, with giant stays anchoring it to the hill. A lift will take you up to

the observation deck on the tenth floor for a panoramic view 560 metres (1,837 ft) above sea level. On clear days you can see as far as Montserrat and the Pyrenees.

The Collserola park on the other side of the hill is another world, a mere train ride through the tunnel to **Baixador de Vallvidrera** station (just 13 minutes from Plaça de Catalunya). The contrast of the pine-scented cooler air that hits you as soon as the train doors open is quite extraordinary. Walk up a well-landscaped path to the **Centre d'Informació del Parc de Collserola**, the information centre (daily 9.30am–3pm): a helpful base with an exhibition about the wildlife in the natural park, maps, advice and a bar/restaurant.

Close to it is **Villa Joana** (weekends 11am–3pm), an atmospheric 18th-century house. This is where Jacint Verdaguer lived until his death in 1902. It is now a museum dedicated to the much-loved Catalan poet, with some rooms preserved from the year he died. Various footpaths lead off into the woods of pine and cork oak to *fonts*

(natural springs) and picnic spots. After several days in the steamy city, this area is the answer, especially if you have children.

Tibidabo heights

The best-known and visible summit of the Collserola range is **Tibidabo ❾**. Its popularity means moving in large crowds and queuing, but it still has its charms. You can reach the summit from Sarrià, by going along Bonanova, which leads to Avinguda del Tibidabo, becoming Passeig Sant Gervasi at the end. It is a tiring street to walk along since, as an important route along this top part of town, it is always congested. The daily traffic swells even further in the mornings and mid-afternoons when parents deliver and collect their children from the abundance of expensive schools in the area, and ladies of leisure drive to the gym. The bus journey is more pleasant and offers an interesting slice of life.

However, a trip to Tibidabo is more likely to be a day's or half-day's excursion directly from the centre of town. The FGC train goes to Avinguda Tibidabo station. Coming out in **Plaça John Kennedy**, pause a moment to take in the colours of La Rotonda, a *modernista* house opposite, which has been converted into a hospital. At the base of Avinguda Tibidabo is Barcelona's last remaining tram service, the **Tramvia Blau**. This open-sided blue wooden tram has been plying the route to the base of the Tibidabo funicular since 1901.

The Science Museum

Nearby, in Teodor Roviralta, is the excellent new science museum, now known as the **CosmoCaixa** (Tues–Sun 10am–8pm; entrance charge). This is one of the most exciting science museums in Europe, with plenty of hands-on exhibits and interesting temporary exhibitions for all ages. Even 3–6-year-olds are catered for in the "Clik dels Nens", a space to play and learn created by the high-profile designer Javier Mariscal. There is a plethora of other innovative ways to enlighten the general public on the subjects of

 Map on page 176

The Torre de Collserola, otherwise known as the Torre Foster, after its architect Norman Foster.

BELOW: the view from the top of the Torre del Collserola.

Map on page 176

Vintage automatons are on display in the Parc d'Attracions.

BELOW: all the fun of the Parc d'Attracions.

science and technology. Among the highlights is the Flooded Forest, a recreation of part of the Amazon rainforest. The museum is funded by the affluent cultural foundation of La Caixa savings bank, and driven by a dynamic director.

The Tramvia Blau rattles up Avinguda Tibidabo, an avenue of beautiful *modernista* houses that winds up the hill. Its former elegance is now diminished, many of the large houses having been converted into institutions, advertising agencies or flats. Furthermore, it was dissected in the 1990s by the Ronda de Dalt. The tram stops at the **Plaça del Funicular**, where there are attractive bars and **La Venta**, a good restaurant with a pretty terrace.

The Top of Tibidabo

From Plaça del Funicular you can catch the funicular to the summit. This lofty playground has been a popular tradition since the turn of the century. It tends to look more interesting from a distance, but the air is sweet, the views spectacular – and children love it. The church, the

Sagrat Cor, topped by the figure of Christ, has little charm but this doesn't prevent the crowds flocking to it. Floodlit at night, it forms a dramatic part of the Barcelona skyline, particularly when wrapped in swirling mists.

The **Parc d'Attracions** funfair has a wonderful retro air and is not exhaustingly large or terrifying. Some of its attractions date back to 1901, when the funicular first reached the top, and some are from renovations that took place in 1986. There is also a museum of automatons, the **Museu d'Autòmats**, displaying fascinating pieces made between 1901 and 1954.

The Parc d'Attracions is open from Easter to December, but the times change according to daylight hours and peak season (with late-evening opening in summer), so check with tourist information offices locally. The tram and funicular run in conjunction with the opening times. You can buy all-in tickets that permit unlimited access to the rides or cheaper tickets for six rides only. ❏

Gràcia

The district of Gràcia lies "above the Diagonal", but has none of the connotations usually associated with the phrase. On the contrary, it is a neighbourhood with its own history and distinctive personality. Its character is preserved in the narrow streets and squares contained within an invisible boundary, which has managed to keep out large-scale projects and expensive residential developments.

Traditionally a *barri* of artisans, it is now becoming a centre for New Age movements. Generations of families remain loyal to the district, and since the 19th century a strong gypsy community has been well integrated here. There are few newcomers, apart from a small number of young people, students and a sprinkling of foreigners charmed by the district's down-to-earth character.

The *vila* (a cut above "village") of Gràcia was once reached from Barcelona by a track through open fields (today's **Passeig de Gràcia**). Its established buildings imposed the upper limit on the Eixample, Cerdà's 19th-century expansion plan for Barcelona; the streets of **Còrsega** and **Bailèn** were built right up to its sides. The upper boundary is loosely **Travessera de Dalt**, and on the western side **Príncep d'Astúries**, although the official municipal district extends a little further.

The main route into Gràcia is along **Gran de Gràcia**, the continuation of Passeig de Gràcia, but it is also well served by the metro (Fontana and Lesseps L3; Joanic L4; Gràcia FGC line). Gran de Gràcia is a busy but elegant street full of shops and *modernista* apartment blocks. It also has one of the best and most expensive fish restaurants in the city, the Galician **Botafumeiro**.

Walking up the hill, take any of the turnings to the right and zig-zag up through streets bustling with a selection of small businesses, workshops, wonderfully dated groceries and trendy fashion shops. At night, shuttered doors open to reveal an infinity of bars and restaurants, ranging

from typical Catalan to the best Lebanese in town. You need to visit Gràcia both during the day and in the evening to appreciate its charms fully.

The whole area is dotted with attractive *plaças*, one of which is named after John Lennon; watch out for the attractive **Plaça del Sol**, which functions as an unofficial centre for the district. Nearby is the **Verdi** multi-screen cinema in a long street of the same name; this is an essential stop on any filmgoer's itinerary, as it always shows *v.o.* (original version) films, as does the smaller **Casablanca** cinema at Passeig de Gràcia, 115.

There is an early Gaudí house, **Casa Vicens** in **Carolines**, a street on the other side of Gran de Gràcia, just above metro Fontana. It is worth a detour to see the facade of this striking house, which Gaudí built for a tile manufacturer.

If you visit Barcelona in August you may coincide with the Festa Major de Gràcia, the main festival of the district. For at least a week around 15 August, the patron saint's day and a national holiday, the narrow streets are extravagantly decorated, music fills the squares both day and night, and everyone has a wild time. It is well worth going along. ❑

RIGHT: the Plaça del Sol, hub of Gràcia.

RESTAURANTS & BARS

Restaurants

This area covers a lot of ground so it has an equally broad span of restaurants, cafés and bars, from student haunts and ethnic restaurants in the Gràcia neighbourhood to top-notch Michelin-starred restaurants in the smarter zones and rustic outdoor restaurants in Collserola Park.

A Contraluz
Milanesat, 19 (FGC: Les Tres Torres)
Tel: 93 203 0658
L & D daily. €€ (set menu €)
In a quiet street in the smart residential Tres Torres area (en route to the Monestir de Pedralbes), this house and garden is a relaxing place to dine, amid a fashionable set. Makes a refreshing change from the downtown heat, dust and noise. The reasonably priced lunchtime menu is a good option.

Amir de Nit
Plaça del Sol, 2 (metro: Fontana)
Tel: 93 218 5121
L & D daily. €

PRICE CATEGORIES

Prices for three-course dinner per person with a half-bottle of house wine:
€ = under €25
€€ = €25–€40
€€€ = €40–€60
€€€€ = more than €60

There are quite a few Lebanese places in Barcelona now but this has always been a firm favourite. It has a large choice of well-prepared, delicious dishes, and its location in one corner of this popular square in Gràcia is perfect, especially for eating alfresco on a summer evening.

Bilbao
Perill, 33 (metro: Verdaguer)
Tel: 93 458 9624
L & D Mon–Sat. €
An animated atmosphere in this traditional eatery in Gràcia, frequented mainly by journalists, artists and writers. Especially busy at lunchtime.

Botafumeiro
Gran de Gràcia, 81 (metro: Fontana)
Tel: 93 218 4230
L & D daily. €€€€
This smart Galician restaurant, haunt of the rich and famous, has a long-running reputation as the place to eat seafood in Barcelona. Oysters are served at the bar.

59 Can Gaig
Passeig de Maragall, 402 (metro: Horta)
Tel: 93 429 1017
L & D Tues–Sat. L only Sun. €€€€
Chef Carles Gaig is a legendary figure in the Catalan capital's culinary world. His restaurant is a bit of a trek from the centre but an essential visit for gourmets.

Can Juanito
Ramón y Cajal, 3 (metro: Fontana)
Tel: 93 210 2016
L & D Tues–Sat. L only Sun. €€
Often overlooked on the tourist trail, this cosy spot in the heart of Gràcia is one of the best places to try classic Catalan dishes like snail stew or salt cod with prawns and potatoes, and the next best thing to being in a village restaurant.

Can Tomás
Major de Sarrià, 49 (FGC: Sarrià)
Tel: 93 203 1077
L & D Thur–Tues. €
People come to Sarrià from all over town for Tomás's renowned *patatas bravas* (fried potatoes served with spicy sauce and/or mayonnaise), made according to his own secret recipe.

Can Tripas
Sagués, 16 (metro: Hospital Clínic)
Tel: 93 200 7642
L & D Mon–Sat. €
Cheap, cheerful and crowded: a paradox amid the elegant shops of the Diagonal/Plaça Francesc Macià area.

Casa Blava
Avinguda de Montserrat, 26 (FGC: La Floresta)
Tel: 93 674 9351
L & D Thur–Sat. L only Tues and Sun. €
A pretty outdoor restaurant covered in a trailing vine where meat and even paella is cooked outdoors on an open wood fire. In January and February they do *calçots* (seasonal spring onions served with garlicky-nutty-peppery sauce). About 15 minutes' walk from the station, which is only a short ride from Plaça de Catalunya.

Casa Joana
Major de Sarrià, 59 (FGC: Sarrià)
Tel: 93 203 1036
L & D Mon–Sat. €
Very good value for this generally expensive part of town. A cosy, family-run restaurant where it's good to choose traditional dishes like *canelons*.

Casa Trampa
Pl. de Vallvidrera, 3 (FGC: Vallvidrera)
Tel: 93 406 8051
L & D Tues–Sat. L only Sun. €
Traditional, homely Catalan restaurant with food to match, right in the centre of this charming "village" that is part of the city. It is just a funicular ride away and well worth the trip.

Flash-Flash
Granada del Penedès, 25 (FGC: Gràcia)
Tel: 93 237 0990
L & D daily. €
Almost a period piece now, this bar was supertrendy in the 1970s. Its wonderful white

leatherette seating and black-and-white Warhol-type prints on the walls still have style and it's a great place for tortillas, sandwiches and snacks.

Hisop
Passatge Marimon, 9 (metro: Hospital Clínic)
Tel: 93 241 3233
L & D Mon–Fri. D only Sat.
€€€
Two young Catalan chefs practise the latest culinary art of deconstructivism with amazing results in this minimalist restaurant, much sought after by foodies.

Jean-Luc Figueras
Santa Teresa, 10 (metro: Diagonal)
Tel: 93 415 2877
L & D Mon–Fri. D only Sat.
€€€€
Small restaurant with a big reputation for artful Mediterranean cuisine with French overtones, not least from its building, once Balenciaga's workshop.

La Balsa
Infanta Isabel, 4 (FGC: Av. Tibidabo)
Tel: 93 211 5048
L & D Tues–Sat. €€€
Prize-winning restaurant of classy wood and glass with views of surrounding greenery in uptown Barcelona. Terraces for eating alfresco. International cuisine.

La Rosa del Desierto
Plaça Narcís Oller, 7 (metro: Diagonal/FGC: Gràcia)
Tel: 93 237 4590
L & D Tues–Sat. L only Sun.
€€
Pioneers of Moroccan

cooking in Barcelona, this well-established restaurant has had a facelift and put up its prices but remains one of the best places to have couscous, offering a choice of 10.

La Singular
Francisco Giner, 50 (metro: Diagonal)
Tel: 93 237 5098
L & D Mon–Sat. €
A wonderful little Gràcia restaurant with a warm, friendly atmosphere and great cooking, using seasonal local produce.

La Venta
Plaça Doctor Andreu, 1 (FGC: Av. Tibidabo)
Tel: 93 212 6455
L & D Mon–Sat. €€€
One of the prettiest restaurants in the city, at the foot of the funicular to Tibidabo. High-class Mediterranean food – the perfect setting for springtime lunches or summer nights on the leafy terrace,

L'Orangerie
Hotel La Florida
Carretera de Vallvidrera al Tibidabo, 83–93 (FGC: Vallvidrera)
Tel: 93 259 3000
L & D Mon–Sat. €€€€.
Brunch (€€€) and D Sun.
The ultimate indulgence for brunch on a Sunday in the first 5-star Relais-Château to open here, perched on top of Tibidabo. Sip cava while overlooking the most panoramic view of Barcelona.

Merendero El Pantà
Camí Pantà, 46 (FGC: Baixador de Vallvidrera)

Tel: 93 204 9163
L Sat–Sun only. €
A typical Collserola down-to-earth merendero (outdoor bar) where carns a la brasa (meat grilled on an open fire) are almost obligatory, served with lashings of allioli, mayonnaise-type sauce made from olive oil and garlic. You'll appreciate the walk in the woods afterwards.

Neichel
Beltrán i Rózpide, 16 bis (metro: Maria Cristina)
Tel: 93 203 8408
L & D Tues–Sat. €€€€
A prize-winner for its modern, stylish design and two Michelin stars, Nelchel looks onto a garden of lemon trees. The owner describes the food as "avant-garde Mediterranean". There is a special "tastes and aromas" menu.

Ot
Torres, 25 (metro: Diagonal)
Tel: 93 284 7762
L & D Mon–Fri. D only Sat.
€€€€
The colourful, laid-back environment in this tiny restaurant in Gràcia does not prepare you for the highly creative dishes that follow in this adventurous set menu (you get no choice but you are unlikely to be disappointed) by two inspired young Catalan chefs. Essential to book well in advance.

Roig Robí
Sèneca, 20 (metro: Diagonal)
Tel: 93 218 9222
L & D Mon–Fri. D only Sat.

€€€€
Mercè Navarro's famed restaurant is a beautifully subtle, elegant space with a terrace, and food and service to match the high standard of the surroundings. A favourite with locals in the know.

Roure
Riera Sant Miquel, 51 (metro: Diagonal)
Tel: 93 237 7490
L & D Mon–Sat. €
A classic, bustling corner bar, very popular with its regulars, serving tapes all day and meals at lunchtime (paella on Thursday). Good value in every sense.

Bars & Cafés

Gràcia is full of old cafés, new trendy bars and ever-popular terrace cafés, especially in its many squares. Try **Café del Sol** in the Plaça del Sol, or the **Virreina** in the Plaça de la Virreina. **Salambó**, Torrijos, 51, is more sophisticated, and **Sol Soler**, Plaça del Sol, 21, is charming, with delicious, alternative tapes. By contrast, the cafés around Plaça Francesc Macià further up the Diagonal are full of expensively dressed residents. The recently opened **Café Vienés**, Passeig de Gràcia, 132, in the Hotel Casa Fuster, is the top of the range in the magnificently restored Domènech i Montaner building.

AROUND BARCELONA

The Catalonian hinterland and long stretches of coastline on either side of Barcelona provide some exceptional opportunities for excursions from the city, most of which are possible on public transport

Barcelona

Barcelona is a great city to be in, but it is also desirable to take a break from the hectic pace now and again. Luckily, there are beaches, mountains, wine country, religious retreats. and historic provincial cities all within easy reach. Travelling to and from the city is a nightmare during the weekday rush hours, Sunday evening, all weekend in summer, and around Christmas, Easter and in August. But visitors who travel outside these times will enjoy straightforward, stress-free journeys.

One easy trip which can be done in half a day or less is a visit to Santa Coloma de Cervello to see **Colonia Guëll ❶**, a 19th-century textile-industry estate with a much admired church crypt (free admission) designed by Antoni Gaudí (FCG trains leave from Plaça d'Espanya for Sant Coloma de Cervello and take just 20 minutes).

Each of the suggested longer excursions is manageable in a day. Taking extra time over them will allow you to relax more, perhaps climbing higher into the Pyrenees or going a little further south. There are two options for journeys to the south of Barcelona (Sitges and Tarragona), two to the west (Sant Sadurní and Montserrat), two going inland to the north (Montseny and Vic),

two going up into the province of Girona (Figueres and Girona), one to the Maresme coast just north of Barcelona (Caldetes), and one to the Costa Brava (Santa Cristina).

Sitges, Santa Cristina and Caldetes all have fine beaches; Montserrat and Montseny, two mountain-top retreats virtually overlooking Barcelona, are also superb natural attractions; Vic, Tarragona, Figueres and Girona are historic provincial centres; Sant Sadurní d'Anoia is at the heart of the Penedès wine-growing region.

Map on page 190

PRECEDING PAGES: the fishing port in Arenys de Mar.
LEFT: Sitges, a short hop from Barcelona on the train.
BELOW: family fun on the Costa Brava.

The Museu Maricel ("Sea and Sky") in Sitges.

Best beaches

A smooth 40-minute train ride or a quick drive through the Garraf tunnels on the C32 motorway will whisk you south to **Sitges ❷**, the closest clean and uncrowded bit of the Mediterranean coast. While sand and sun can be enjoyed in Castelldefels, 20 minutes from Barcelona, or even on Barcelona's city beaches, the gleaming, whitewashed houses and flower-festooned balconies of Sitges are well worth the extra journey time, making you feel a world away in terms of atmosphere. A day on the beach, with a paella for lunch at one of the many restaurants overlooking the sea, is a good idea at any time of the year. What's more, the weather is reputed always to be better in Sitges, so you could leave Barcelona in cloud and arrive to find glorious sunshine.

An international party atmosphere pervades Sitges in summer, and the town has a full calendar of festivals, including Carnival.

Fringed by palms and populated by an intriguingly diverse range of bathers, including a large gay community, the gently curving **Platja d'Or** (Golden Beach) runs from the

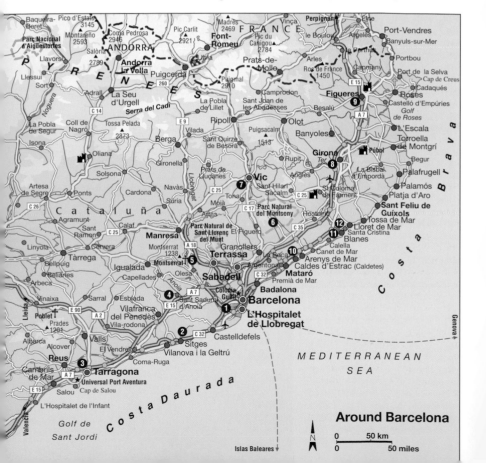

Around Barcelona

0   50 km

0   50 miles

rocky point, La Punta, at the northeast end of Sitges Bay; it starts from the 17th-century Església Sant Bartomeu i Santa Tecla, perched on the headland, and extends 5 km (3 miles) south and west past the Hotel Terramar. The beaches on the other side of the church are also worth exploring. The **Museu Cau Ferrat** (summer, daily 10am–2pm and 5–9pm, winter, Tues–Fri 10am–1.30pm and 3–6.30pm, Sat 10am–7pm, Sun 10am–3pm; entrance charge) is an interesting museum. Once the studio of Picasso's contemporary Santiago Rusiñol, it was a meeting place for artists in the early 20th century. In this 16th-century house built over the rocks are two El Greco paintings, several Picasso drawings, and a unique collection of Catalan wrought iron. The work inside and Mediterranean close by outside are a powerful combination of art and nature. **Museu Maricel** (*mar i cel* means "sea and sky" in Catalan), two buildings connected by a bridge over the street, is notable for the mural paintings by Josep Maria Sert. The **Museu Romàntic** at Sant Gaudenci gives a good insight into 19th-century living conditions and houses the **Lola Anglada** antique-doll collection (opening times for both museums as for Cau Ferrat).

Tarragona

Ninety minutes from Barcelona by train or car, **Tarragona** ❸ still has the feel of a provincial capital of the Roman Empire. Captured by Rome in 218 BC and later the capital of the Spanish province of Tarraconensis under Augustus, the town was the major commercial centre on this part of the Mediterranean coast until Barcelona and Valencia overshadowed it after the Christian Reconquest of Spain in the early 12th century.

Rich in Roman ruins still being unearthed and stunningly beautiful

ancient buildings, Tarragona may be approached from top to bottom, beginning within the walled upper part of the city surrounding the cathedral, continuing on for a tour of the wall itself, the **Passeig Arqueòlogic** or Archaeological Promenade. You can then descend to the next level of the city, featuring the **Rambla**, and conclude with a stroll through the fishing port and lunch on the quay.

Tarragona's **Cathedral**, the centrepiece of the top part of the city, has been described by Catalonia's own travel writer Josep Pla, who had something to say about every town, as "easily and serenely mighty, solid as granite, maternal – a cathedral redolent of Roman virtues projected on to carved stone – a lion in repose, drowsy, unabashedly powerful".

The Passeig Arqueòlogic offers views south over the city, west out to the mountains, north to the hills and trees surrounding the city, and finally east to the coastline and the sea. Below the walls is the middle section of Tarragona, with the wide and stately Rambla ending in the

Pointing out the highlights of historic Tarragona.

BELOW: carvings on Tarragona's cathedral.

Corinthian pillars in the Forum in Tarragona.

Balcó del Mediterrani (Mediterranean Balcony) suspended over the ocean below. The city's luminosity at this point has been much commented on and is indeed remarkable: a crisp elegance and clean air shimmer over the golden sandstone of Roman structures which are nearly 2,000 years old.

The Serrallo section of the port is the main attraction in the lower part of the city, the multicoloured fishing fleet unloading their catch every afternoon, the fish auctioned off within minutes. A lunch at a dockside restaurant – featuring Tarragona wines, fundamental to the Roman Empire, and seafood just out of the nets – makes a delicious end to a visit.

Salou

Just 8 km (5 miles) south of Tarragona is the seaside resort of **Salou**, popular for packages, and its neighbouring theme park **Universal Mediterrania** including **Port Aventura**, the second largest in Europe after Disneyland Resort Paris (Mar–Jan daily 10am–8pm, until midnight in high season; Nov–Dec Fri–Sun only;

entrance charge). People travel for miles to experience the thrills and spills it offers. There are two hotels on the site.

The home of Spanish *cava*

If you feel safer with the more indigenous pleasures of Catalonia, a trip to **Sant Sadurní d'Anoia ❹**, a small town responsible for 80 per cent of *cava* production, is recommended. Sparkling wine made in Catalonia is not champagne; it is *cava*.

A 45-minute train ride from Sants or Plaça de Catalunya stations in Barcelona will drop you in Sant Sadurní, right next to Freixenet, the world's leading producer of *cava*, with vineyards in California and operations in China. Freixenet offers a spectacular tour, including a screening of its famous series of Christmas advertisements, featuring such stars as Liza Minelli, Gene Kelly, Raquel Welch, Plácido Domingo, Penélope Cruz and Paul Newman. A glass of *cava* is presented to guests as a finale. *Cava* has been produced in Sant Sadurní since 1872 by Josep Raventós, founder of the Codorníu empire who carefully studied the winemaking techniques, the *méthode champenoise,* of Dom Perignon and made Catalonia's first bottle of *cava*. It is an important part of life in Catalonia: baptisms, weddings, even routine Sunday lunches are occasions for popping corks. On 20 November 1975, the day Franco died, *cava* was given away free in Barcelona.

Gastronomy and wine

In addition to tours of the Freixenet and beautiful *modernista* Codorníu wine cellars, or any other of the 80 producers in this area, Sant Sadurní offers excellent gastronomical opportunities at local restaurants well-known for fine *cava* and seafood. Between late January and mid-March, the *calçotada* is a traditional feast starring long-stemmed *calçots* (something between a spring onion and a leek), dipped in a *romesco* sauce of oil, peppers, garlic and groundnuts. *Cava* flows freely at these rustic banquets, accompanied by lamb or rabbit grilled, as are the *calçots,* over coals.

Wine making in this region can be traced back to the 5th century BC. About 14 km (8 miles) from Sant Sadurní is **Vilafranca del Penedès**, a centre of still-wine production which is dominated by the world-famous Torres, whose winery and extensive vineyards can be visited.

The town has one of Europe's best wine museums, the **Museu del Vi** (Tues–Sat 10am–2pm and 4–7pm, all day in summer, Sun 10am–2pm; entrance charge). The Penedès region, one of the world's leading wine producers, has over 300 wine- and *cava*-producing companies, most of which can be visited. Information is centralised through the tourist office in Vilafranca (tel: 93 892 0358).

The region is attractive for walking and cycling. The Montserrat massif to the north rises above row after row of vines stretching down to the Mediterranean in the south, with moist sea breezes and 2,500 hours of sunshine a year. Around Sant Sadurní even children have opinions on *bruts*, *secs* and *brut natures*; in the Penedès, Bacchus reigns.

Montserrat

Catalonia's most important religious site is **Montserrat ❺** (daily 8.50am–7.30pm; www.abadiamontserrat.net). Here athletes pledge barefoot pilgrimages if their prayers are answered and vital competitions won. Groups of young people from Barcelona and all over Catalonia make overnight hikes at least once in their lives to watch the sunrise from the heights of Montserrat. "La

Moreneta" (the Black Virgin), said to have been made by St Luke and brought to Barcelona by St Peter, resides in the sanctuary of the Mare de Deu de Montserrat. There is a separate door at the front of the basilica for people wanting to see and touch this statue of Madonna and Child.

Looming 1,236 metres (4,055 ft) over the valley floor, Montserrat, the highest point of the Catalan lowlands, stands central to the most populated part of Catalonia. Forty-eight km (30 miles) west of Barcelona, it can be reached easily and spectacularly by train (plus cable car) from Plaça d'Espanya station. The advantage of going by car, however, is the opportunity of seeing this landmark from different angles. In the words of the Catalan poet Maragall, from varying perspectives Montserrat can look like "a bluish cloud with fantastic carvings, a giant's castle with a hundred towers, thrown towards the sky, its needles veiled by the fog hanging among them like incense … above all an altar, a temple."

The basilica is packed with works of art by prominent painters and

Map on page 190

A tile in the Museu del Vi in Vilafranca shows a medieval reveller.

BELOW: the aptly named Montserrat, a compound of *mont* (mountain) and *serrat* (serrated).

During the 40-year Franco regime, when the Catalan language was officially forbidden, baptisms and weddings were still held in Catalan at Montserrat.

sculptors, including paintings by El Greco in the sanctuary's museum. Catalan poets have dedicated some of their most inspired verse to Montserrat, while maestros such as Nicolau and Millet have composed some of their finest pieces in honour of the sanctuary. Goethe is said to have dreamed of Montserrat, and Parsifal sought the Holy Grail here in Wagner's opera.

Montserrat's famous *escolans*, the oldest boys' choir in Europe, sings twice a day, at 1pm (noon on Sunday) and 7pm.

There are several excursions to be made from the monastery. Via Crucis, the Way of the Cross (behind Plaça de L'Abat Oliba) leads to the hermitage of Sant Miquel. From Plaça de la Cru a cable car runs down to Santa Cova, a chapel in a grotto where the Virgin is said to have been hidden during the Moorish occupation.

BELOW:
Montserrat, home of La Morenta (the Black Virgin) and Catalonia's most important pilgrimage site.

On a clear day it is worth taking the funicular (plus a 20-minute walk) up to Sant Joan, one of the mountain's 13 small *ermitas* inhabited by hermits until Napoleon's troops, having hanged the monks, hunted them

down and killed them. Montserrat's highest point is **Sant Jeroni**, from where Catalonia spreads out before you. On very clear days it is even possible to see Mallorca in the Balearics.

Montseny forest

Montserrat and the Montseny range of mountains in the **Parc Natural de Montseny** ❻ occupy, in some way, polar extremes in Catalonian spiritual life. Whereas Montserrat is vertical, acute and passionate, Montseny is smooth, horizontal, massive and placid. *Seny* in Catalan means sense, patience, restraint, serenity, and is a byword for a description of the national characteristics.

Best explored by car, this monumental mountain forest is presided over by four peaks: Turó de l'Home, Agudes, Matagalls (all around 1,500 metres/5,000 ft) and Calma i Puigdrau, a lower peak at 1,215 metres (4,050 ft). Lesser terrain features and water courses connect and define these four pieces of high ground, tracing out an autonomous geographical entity which always appears hulking and mist-enshrouded on the

horizon, often confused with cloud formations.

The village of **Montseny** can be reached via Palautordera and Sant Esteve de Palautordera. This road continues on to Brull, through the pass at Collformic and over to Tona, near Vic on route C17, traversing the entire Montseny massif. The road up from Sant Celoni, just off the *autovia* towards France, via Campins and Fogars de Montclus, arrives at the **Santa Fe** hermitage, a vantage point which seems little more than a stone's throw from Montseny's highest points. The oaks and poplars are colourful in autumn, an unusual sight in Catalonia, where forests of deciduous trees are uncommon.

Montseny, no more than 40 minutes from Barcelona, is a botanical anthology, including some of the southernmost fir trees in Europe, other specimens from all over the continent, and evergreen oak.

Country towns

An easy hour north by train or car, **Vic ❼** is an elegant market town with interesting buildings, sophisticated shops and good food. It is the meeting place of industry, commerce and agriculture, a mixture of rural and urban life with a strong ecclesiastical and cultural tradition. Especially known for its Romanesque bell tower, Josep Maria Sert's epic murals, and the magnificent Plaça Major with its Saturday market, Vic is an entity distinct from Barcelona. The Vic accent in Catalan is unmistakable and becomes, if anything, more acute in the Catalonian capital as natives of this small city emphasise their separate identity.

Vic's **Cathedral**, a neoclassical structure completed in 1803 and with a graceful 11th-century bell tower, is best known for the series of murals covering the interior walls. Sert left his personal vision in the voluptuous, neo-baroque figures performing colossal deeds. His triptych on the back of the cathedral's western door depicts the injustices in the life of Christ and, by association, in the history of Catalonia. With the cathedral in ruins as his background, Jesus expels the moneylenders from the Temple and is, in turn, condemned

Map on page 190

Josep Maria Sert, having completed the murals in Vic cathedral only to see them destroyed by fire at the beginning of the Civil War, began repainting them in 1936, continuing until he died in 1945.

BELOW LEFT: an inland valley swooping down to the sea.
BELOW: the elegant market town of Vic.

to be crucified while Pilate washes his hands and Barabbas, the thief, is cheered by the crowd. Certain faces (Pilate, Barabbas) are said to be those of Franco's lieutenants, but El Generalísimo himself, during a visit to Sert's work while it was in progress, did not seem to see the resemblance.

The philosopher Jaume Balmes (1810–48), a native of Vic, is buried in the 14th-century cloister, as is Sert. The **Museu Episcopal** has an impressive collection of Romanesque and Gothic pieces, including altarpieces and sculpted figures collected from local chapels and churches. It is well worth visiting, especially now its treasures are re-housed in a new building designed by leading Barcelona architects Correa and Milà. Note especially the Romanesque textiles and *El Davallament de la Creu* (*The Descent from the Cross*), an especially fine 12th-century sculptural work in polychrome wood.

The **Plaça Major**, or central square, surrounded by low arcades, is a metaphor for the sense and feel of this agro-industrial town. Open, unrelieved by the equestrian statue some critics feel it should have, the square stands on its own, as the city itself does, flat and firm on the plain, the Plana de Vic.

Girona province

Girona and Figueres can be combined for a memorable excursion from Barcelona. **Girona** ❽, the capital of the province, is a most attractive city, full of history, tasteful shops and restaurants and only an hour's drive from Barcelona. It is known for its **Ciutat Antiga** (Old Town) and especially for its 13th-century **Jewish Quarter**, which is considered one of the two most important and best preserved in Spain (the other is Toledo's). The River Onyar separates Girona's old section from the modern part of the city, which lies west of the river.

The footbridges over the Onyar provide some of Girona's most unforgettable views into the old city, including reflections of the buildings on the banks of the river as well as taller structures such as the **Sant Feliu** bell tower and the cathedral. The 12th-century **Església de Sant Pere de Galligants** is one of the city's oldest monuments, with a delightful Romanesque cloister built before 1154. From here you can walk around the city walls as far as Plaça de Catalunya.

Girona's old city, built on a hill, is known for its lovely stairways, such as the baroque *escalinata* of 96 steps leading up to the cathedral, or the stairs up to **Església de Sant Martí**. **Santa Maria Cathedral**, described by the ever-present Josep Pla as "literally sensational" in its force and magnitude, was built by architect Guillem Bofill, who succeeded in covering the structure with Europe's largest Gothic vault.

The cathedral's **museum** (summer, Mon–Sat 10am–8pm, Sun

BELOW:
Girona, beside the
River Onyar.

10am–2pm; winter Tues–Sat 10am–2pm and 4–6pm, Sun 10am–2pm; entrance charge) is most notable for its *Tapis de la Creació*, a stunning 12th-century tapestry depicting God surrounded by all the flora and fauna, fish and fowl of Creation. Equally impressive is Beatus' *Llibre de l'Apocalipsi* (Book of the Apocalypse), dated 975. The **Església de Sant Feliu**, the **Arab Baths** and the lofty plane trees of **Devesa Park** are other important landmarks of this ancient city of sunless alleys, graceful stairways, and the Onyar, flowing through as imperceptibly as time.

Dalí's birthplace

Figueres ❾, only another half-hour north on the A7 motorway, is the major city of the **Alt Empordà** (Upper Ampurdán), a fresh, busy country town which, in many ways, could be on either side of the border with France. Like many provincial cities in Spain, Figueres seems to have time on its hands. The **Rambla** is the scene of the traditional *passeig,* the constitutional midday or evening stroll. Also on the Rambla, on the top floor of the Hotel de Paris, is Spain's only toy museum, the **Museu de Joguets** (July–Sept daily 9am–7.45pm, Oct–Jun Mon–Sat 10am–1pm and 4–7pm, Sun 11am–1.30pm and 5–7.30pm). The huge collection of beautifully made, old-fashioned toys enthrall adults as well as children.

However, Figueres is best known as the birthplace of the surrealist artist Salvador Dalí, whose museum is aptly located in the former municipal theatre. The **Teatre-Museu Dalí** July–Sept daily 9am–7.15pm, Oct–June Tues–Sun 10.30am–5.15pm; entrance charge) is one of the most visited museums in Spain and has a wide range of Dalí's work, including the *Poetry of America*, or *Cosmic Athletes*, painted in 1943, a portrait of his wife Gala as *Atomic Leda*, and the huge ceiling fresco dominating the Wind Palace Room on the first floor. Whether you regard him as a genius or not, there is no denying that this museum, with its tricks and illusions, provides an entertaining show.

The day can be happily com-

Map on page 190

Dalí memorabilia is on sale everywhere, from prints to melting watches, but the most memorable souvenir of the painter is his beloved landscape, ever-present in his work and all around you.

BELOW: the ceiling fresco in the Wind Palace Room of the Teatre-Museu Dalí.

Dalí Tourism

Visitors are flooding into the province of Girona to visit the surreal world of Salvador Dalí, which through the endeavours of the Gala-Salvador Dalí Foundation now includes his very surreal private world. Visiting Dalí's home in Port Lligat, Gala's castle in Púbol or the museum itself, it is clear the two worlds were inseparable.

To get a broad view of the art and a vivid idea of the man, the best introduction is the museum in his home town Figueres, the **Teatre-Museu Dalí**. Thirty km (20 miles) away on the coast, near Cadaqués, is the **Casa-Museu Salvador Dalí**, a fascinating glimpse of Dalí's life with his wife and muse Gala, where he ate, slept, entertained and painted. These old fishermen's cottages have limited space, so small groups are admitted every 10 minutes. Book in advance (daily 10.30am–9pm in summer; 10.30am–6pm in winter, closed Mon and Jan–mid-Mar; tel: 97 225 1015).

Bought by Dalí for his wife in 1970, the **Castell Gala Dalí** is very atmospheric, set in a landscaped garden in Púbol, in the stunning Baix Empordà (daily 10.30am–8pm in summer; 10.30am–6pm in winter, closed Mon and Nov–mid-Mar).

TIP

The coast north of Barcelona can easily be explored by rail. A regular service leaves from Plaça de Catalunya.

pleted with a meal in one of Figueres' many good restaurants, or made perfect by dinner in the **Hotel Ampurdán**, which has one of Catalonia's most famous restaurants, on the outskirts of town. The hotel is also a good base for Dalí-tourism in the region: both Dalí's house in **Port Lligat**, near Cadaqués, and the castle he bought for his wife, Gala, in **Púbol**, are open to the public *(see box, page 197)*.

Costa del Maresme

The beaches just north of Barcelona have a much lower profile than Sitges, and are much maligned for the railway line that runs alongside them. As a result, they are often less crowded. In recent years most have been overhauled, with some beaches being widened, promenades landscaped and marinas built. It is worth travelling beyond Badalona, which is more of an industrial suburb of Barcelona. However, if you only have half a day both Masnou and Vilassar de Mar are acceptable. Inland from Mataró, an industrial

town and capital of the region, the quiet village of Argentona makes a pleasant detour.

One of the most attractive resorts is **Caldes d'Estrac** ⑩, also known as **Caldetes**. The slightly longer journey is well rewarded – about 40 minutes from Barcelona by car on the speedy new C32 and about 45 minutes on the train from Plaça de Catalunya. Caldetes is a spa town – several hotels have thermal baths – and the small town has many charms and pretty *modernista* houses. The long, sandy beaches never seem to get too crowded, and the sea is usually clear.

Early evening in Caldetes is a particularly pleasant time, when freshly showered families dress up in casual-smart clothes to promenade and have a drink on the esplanade, centring on a vintage merry-go-round and a bustling bar (with good snacks and meals). You can enjoy all this, have dinner and get back to Barcelona for the night without too much effort.

The beaches of Caldetes merge with those of **Arenys de Mar**,

BELOW: the church of Santa Maria in Arenys de Mar.

known for its attractive fishing port and famous restaurant, the **Hispania**, favoured by King Juan Carlos.

The next town north, **Canet de Mar**, also has a refurbished waterfront and interesting 19th-century architecture, notably the home of Domènech i Montaner, one of the leading *modernista* architects. His studio can be visited at weekends (11am–2pm; entrance charge).

Just beyond Canet de Mar is **Sant Pol**, a pretty, whitewashed village.

The Costa Brava

To get away entirely from Barcelona it is worth going as far as the southernmost beaches of the **Costa Brava**. Officially beginning at **Blanes** ⑪, this stretch of coast is distinguished by its bold, rocky shoreline punctuated by small sandy inlets. The clear, bright water and this rugged coast mark the difference between the beaches of the Maresme and those of the Costa Brava. The further north you go, the more rugged and magical the coast becomes.

During the summer, passenger boats work in and out of the *calas* or coves. You can board a boat at Blanes for **Santa Cristina** ⑫ or be dropped at some remote *cala* which may be at the bottom of a sheer cliff and inaccessible from land.

Santa Cristina, between Blanes and **Lloret de Mar**, is one of the first inlets of the Costa Brava, and is only about an hour from Barcelona. Access to Santa Cristina is easy – you can go by train to Blanes and bus, or by car along the coast, but the proximity to the city of this sandy enclave has made it extremely popular with Barcelonans. Other visitors might do well to stay in town at the weekend and save this trip for a weekday.

With its twin beaches bordered and divided by rocky promontories, Santa Cristina's lovely hermitage stands at the top of the steep paths down to the water. The chapel and house were left to the town of Lloret de Mar by a wealthy 18th-century landowner who moved to Cuba. At that time the shorefront was worth nothing; the valuable property in those days was inland, where there were arable fields.   ❏

Map on page 190

TIP

At Santa Cristina there are several simple restaurants on the beach where paella is prepared in the afternoon. These places are relaxed, outdoor spots where dining in bathing suits is quite normal. They also serve excellent seafood *tapes* of squid, sardines, wild mushrooms, shrimp or prawns.

BELOW: the beach at Sant Pol.

RESTAURANTS & BARS

Restaurants

In rural areas all over Catalonia are well-kept roadside restaurants that are popular for weddings, baptisms and other family occasions, where you can be sure of a good, traditional meal, with *pa amb tomàquet* and pork dishes as staples. There is also an increasing number of restaurants where creative young chefs are practising their art (advance booking essential), as well as village bars, where a wholesome dish of the day, unpretentious and delicious, may have been cooked for local workers. Eating hours tend to be earlier than in the city.

Arenys de Mar

Hispania
Real, 54
Carretera N11
Tel: 93 791 0306
L & D Mon, Wed–Sat. L only
Sun. €€€€
A classic of Catalan cuisine, which has been in the same family for 50 years. The king is said to be a regular. Known for their seasonal dishes using fresh local produce, peas from Llavaneres or fresh clams from the port of Arenys. Their *crema catalana*, the national dessert, is legendary.

Begur

La Pizzeta
Ventura i Sabater, 2
Tel: 97 262 3884
D daily, Jun–Oct. Sat–Sun only, Apr–May. Closed Nov–Mar. €
Much more than pizzas in this creative, trendy restaurant in the garden of an old village house. Charming and cheap so book early.

Caldes d'Estrac

Can Manau
Sant Josep, 11
Tel: 93 791 0459
L & D daily, Jun–Sept. D only Fri–Sat, Oct–May. €
This small *fonda* serves good, simple food in its pretty courtyard, although the creative flair of Xavi Manau, son of the former owner, is now coming to the fore, resulting in delicious dishes like squid tossed with wild mushrooms.

Pizzeria Estrac
Cami Ral, 5
Tel: 93 791 3188
L & D daily, Jun–Sept. D only Fri–Sat, Oct–May. €
Pasta and particularly good home-made pizzas in this attractive restaurant in the heart of this pretty village. Pizzas can also be taken away.

Cambrils

Joan Gatell-Casa Gatell
Passeig Miramar, 26
Cambrils Port
Tel: 97 736 0057
L & D Tues–Sat. €€€

This is the place to come if you are passionate about fish. Famed for choosing the freshest of the catch in this fishing village near Tarragona, and frying, grilling or baking it to perfection. The simpler the better, but if you go for rich sauces don't miss the *bullabesa de la casa* which you may have to order in advance.

Castelldefels

Patricio
Passeig Marítim, 159
Tel: 93 665 1347
L only Thur–Tues. €
A relic from times before the bulldozers moved in to make a new promenade, this is the one place you can still eat paella with your toes in the sand, or try grilled meats with *allioli*, their speciality. Only 20 minutes from Barcelona but there's nothing between your dining table and the vast expanse of beach and blue Mediterranean. Essential to book at weekends.

Figueres

Hotel Empordà
Antigua Carretera de França, s/n
Tel: 97 250 0562
L & D daily. €€€
Its founder, the late Josep Mercadé, has become a legend, much like his fellow citizen Dalí. One of the first

chefs to reinvent Catalan dishes back in the 1950s, his charisma and inspiration remain in this well-established and unpretentious restaurant.

Girona

El Celler de Can Roca
Carretera de Taialà, 40
Tel: 97 222 2157
L & D Tues–Sat. €€€€
One of the most established of the new wave of avant-garde restaurants in Catalonia, this is regarded by many as one of the best. It is run by the three famed Roca brothers: Joan is the chef who conjures up dishes like a carpaccio of pigs' trotters with vinaigrette, Josep advises expertly on wines and Jordi creates exotic desserts.

Maresme

El Cau
Carretera Badalona–Mollet, Km. 6
Sant Fost de Campsentelles
Tel: 93 395 1852
L & D Tues–Sat. L only Mon. €€€€
You can't get much more authentic than this no-frills restaurant up a winding road in the hills behind Badalona, where the traditional Catalan dishes are excellent. The crowds of demanding local clients who brave the bends to get here are proof enough.

Penedès

El Mirador de les Caves
Carretera Sant Sadurní-
Ordal
Subirats
Tel: 93 899 3178
L & D Tues–Sat. L only Sun &
Mon. €€€
When visiting *cava* country this is a good spot to sample the end product and indulge in a good meal while gazing across the vineyards that have produced it.

Roses

El Bullí
Cala Montjoi
Bookings: Fax: 97 215 0717
e-mail: bulli@elbulli.com
Apr–mid-Oct.
The restaurant that needs no introduction, having rapidly become one of the most famous in the world, along with its inspiration, Ferran Adrià, who is regarded by experts as the best chef in the world. If you want to experience his foams, textures, deconstructions or whatever else has been engineered in the laboratory during the winter months, be sure to book months in advance by fax or e-mail. No telephone reservations accepted.

Sant Celoni

El Racó de Can Fabes
Sant Joan, 6
Tel: 93 867 2851
L & D Tues–Sat. L only Sun.
€€€€
Chef Santi Santamaria is another star in Catalo-

nia's culinary constellation and, like Ferran Adrià, his fame has spread abroad so people come from far and wide to enjoy his creations in the attractive setting of this country restaurant. Faced with more competition now, but he still has three Michelin stars. A choice of tasting menus.

Sitges
The temptation to eat a paella overlooking the sea is irresistible and there are several places along the seafront to choose from. In the narrow streets leading up to the centre there are more unusual options.

Al Fresco
Pau Barrabeig, 4
Tel: 93 894 0600
D only Tues–Sun. €€€
Excellent fusion between Mediterranean and the Far East results in unusual, delicious food, served in a pretty court yard shaded by abundant greenery.

La Santa Maria
Passeig de la Ribera, 52
Tel: 93 894 0999
L & D daily. €€
Traditional restaurant where large families meet for Sunday lunch, assured that nothing will have changed for years. A good spot for *paella*, overlooking the main promenade.

Picnic
Passeig Marítim, s/n,
Tel: 93 811 0040
L daily. D Fri–Sat. €€

You will feel privileged eating seafood *tapes* on this sunny terrace, which is as near to the beach as you can get and a suntrap in winter. Indoors, the smarter restaurant serves fish and dishes like rice with small octopus and artichokes, or their own version of *suquet*, a fish stew with monkfish.

Vilanova i la Geltrú

La Fitorra
Hotel César
Isaac Peral, 4–8
Tel: 93 815 1125
L & D Tues–Sat. L only Sun.
€€
Delicious food at a reasonable price with immaculate and friendly service in this delightful hotel with a personal touch. Their lunchtime buffet can be eaten in the shady garden, bursting with hibiscus flowers.

Vic

Ca L'U
Plaça Santa Teresa, 4
Tel: 93 886 3504
L & D Thur–Sat. L only Sun, Tues, Wed. €
Cal L'U is just the kind of place you'd hope to find in this idyllic market town. It has starched white table cloths, no concessions to style nor culinary creativity, but offers excellent local food and a great family atmosphere. It attracts plenty of regular customers, for whom it forms and essential part of their visit to Vic.

PRICE CATEGORIES

Prices for three-course dinner per person with a half-bottle of house wine:
€ = under €25
€€ = €25–€40
€€€ = €40–€60
€€€€ = more than €60

LEFT: out for lunch.

TRANSPORT

GETTING THERE AND GETTING AROUND

GETTING THERE

By Air

Iberia, the national carrier, and other major airlines connect with most parts of the world, sometimes via Madrid. Various companies compete over cheap deals to Barcelona from many European cities, especially off-season, and there are charter flights in summer. Increasingly popular are the companies who sell via the Internet, such as www.easyjet.com and www.bmibaby.com.

RyanAir flies to Girona (tel: 902 361 550) and Reus (tel: 938 804 4451) airports. Both have shuttle-bus connection to Barcelona. Tickets are available at the airports and the journeys take about 1 hour (€11 single, €19 return). Flights to the US are operated by Delta (tel: 901 116 946), KLM (tel: 902 222 747) and Iberia (tel: 902 400 500).

Barcelona airport is 12 km (7 miles) south of the city in El Prat. The distribution of airlines in the three terminals sometimes changes, so confirm on arrival from which terminal your flight will depart. Airport tel: 93 298 3838. A third runway opened in 2004, which will almost double the number of flights per hour. A new terminal is planned so the number of long-haul flights should increase.

Airlines flying out of Barcelona to other parts of Spain include:
Iberia: Diputació, 258. For information and bookings, tel: 902 400 500.
Air Europa: tel: 93 298 3328. For bookings call 902 401 501.
Spanair: tel: 902 131 415.
Air Nostrum: (part of Iberia) tel: 902 400 500.

By Train

An international service, the Talgo, a high-speed, comfortable train, runs daily from Paris, Montpellier, Milan, Zurich and Geneva. All other international connections involve a change at the French border, in Port Bou on entering Spain and Cerbère when leaving. These trains have few facilities, so travel prepared.

The direct trains (Talgo) terminate in the Estació de Sants, Barcelona's central station, in Plaça Països Catalans. Some stop in Plaça de Catalunya. For international train information and reservations, tel: 902 243 402.

National long-distance trains terminate in Estació de Sants and some in Estació de França, Avinguda Marquès de l'Argentera.

For national train information, tel: 902 240 202, www.renfe.es.

By Bus

The international bus companies Julià, Via (Eurolines) and Linebús run a regular service all over Europe, linking up with the national bus companies in each country. Buses arrive and depart from either Estació d'Autobusos Sants (tel: 93 490 4000), or Barcelona Nord (tel: 902 260 606). In the UK, contact Eurolines, tel: 01582 404511.

By Car

Barcelona is 160 km (100 miles) or 1½ hours' drive from La Jonquera on the French border and can be easily reached along the A7 (or E15) motorway

DISTANCES

Distances to other cities in Spain by road from Barcelona:
Tarragona: 98 km (60 miles)
Girona: 100 km (62 miles)
La Jonquera (French border): 149 km (93 miles)
Valencia: 349 km (217 miles)
San Sebastián: 529 km (329 miles)
Bilbao: 620 km (385 miles)
Madrid: 621 km (386 miles)
Salamanca: 778 km (483 miles)
Málaga: 997 km (620 miles)
Sevilla: 1,046 km (650 miles)

(*autopista,* toll payable) and then, nearer Barcelona, the C33. The cost from France into town is approximately €10. Alternatively, the national route N11 is toll-free but tedious.

Be careful when you stop in service stations or lay-bys: professional thieves work this territory. If you stop for a drink or a meal try not to leave the car unattended.

The worst times to travel, particularly between June and September, are Friday 6–10pm, Sunday evening (7–12pm) or the end of a bank holiday, when tailbacks of 16 km (10 miles) are common. Normal weekday rush hours are 7–9am and 6–9pm.

The ring roads (*cinturones*) surrounding the city can be very confusing on arrival. It is worth studying a road map beforehand. The Ronda de Dalt curves around the top part of the city, and the Ronda Litoral follows the sea.

GETTING AROUND

On Arrival

Whether you arrive in the airport, rail or bus station, or in your own car, you will probably stand out as a tourist, so be alert and keep your bags or car attended.

From the airport

Barcelona is only 12 km (7 miles) from El Prat airport and is easily reached by train, bus or taxi.

Trains to Plaça de Catalunya depart every 30 minutes from 6.13am–11.40pm and take about 25 minutes, also stopping at Sants, the main station. The same service to the airport operates from 5.38am–10.11pm. Approximate cost is €2.60. After Plaça de Catalunya this service continues to Arc de Triomf and on to the Maresme coast as far as Mataró.

Aerobús, an efficient bus service, is perhaps the best way to and from the airport. It runs to Plaça de Catalunya from each ter-

ABOVE: the metro is fast and cheap.

minal every 12 minutes, stopping at strategic points en route. It operates 6am–midnight (6.30am–midnight at weekends), and the fare is €3.50 single and €5.90 return (2005 rates).

The night service (106) leaves from Plaça d'Espanya from 10.55pm–3.50am.

To reach most central parts of Barcelona by taxi will cost about €15–20 plus an airport supplement and a token amount for each suitcase. To avoid misunderstandings, ask how much it will cost before getting into the taxi. "*Cuánto vale el recorrido desde el aeropuerto hasta …* (e.g.) *Plaça de Catalunya?*" Get the taxi driver to write down the answer if necessary.
Iberia: tel: 902 400 500.

TAKING TAXIS

All Barcelona taxis are black and yellow, and show a green light when they are available for hire. There are taxi ranks at the airport, Sants station, Plaça de Catalunya and other strategic points, but taxis constantly move around town and can be hailed on any street corner.

Rates are standard and calculated by meter, starting at a set rate and clocking up at a rate governed by the time of day: night-times, weekends and fiestas are more expensive. Travelling by taxi is still extremely affordable here compared to

Airport: tel: 93 298 3838.
RENFE (train services): tel: 902 24 02 02 (national routes), 902 24 34 02 (international routes).

Public Transport

Barcelona is a manageable city to get around, whether on foot or by public transport. The latter is efficient and good value.

Metro

The metro is Barcelona's underground network. It has six colour-coded lines: 1, 2, 3, 4, 5 and 11. Lines 2 and 11 are equipped for wheelchairs and prams, with lifts at every station. Trains are frequent and cheap, with a set price per journey, no matter how far you travel. It is more economical to buy a card that allows 10 journeys (*Targeta* T-10), available at any station, at banks or *estancs* (tobacconists). It can be shared and is valid for FGC trains (*see below*) and town buses. Trains run 5am–midnight Mon–Thur and Sun, 5am–2am Fri and Sat.

FGC

The local train service, Ferrocarrils de la Generalitat de Catalunya (FGC), interconnects with the metro, looks like the metro and functions in the same

other major European cities.

If your journey goes outside the metropolitan area, the rate will increase slightly. The final charge is what shows on the meter, except when supplements are due for luggage, dogs or a journey to or from the airport.

Drivers do not expect a tip though a small one is always appreciated. A sticker inside the rear window details (in English) the rates and conditions.

Taxis equipped for wheelchairs or a group (7 seats) are available, tel: 93 420 8088 or 93 303 3033.

TOURIST BUSES

A convenient way of getting an overall idea of the city is to catch the official city Tourist Bus (Barcelona Bus Turístic), which takes in the most interesting parts of the city. You can select a northern or a southern route, and get on and off freely. It also offers discounts on entrance charges.

The buses operate year round with frequent services, the first leaving Plaça de Catalunya at 9am. The fleet includes buses equipped for wheelchairs and open-air double deckers.

For information and tickets ask at the tourist information office in Plaça de Catalunya or the one in Estació de Sants. Other companies offering bus tours around the city include:
Julia Tours
Ronda Universitat, 5.
Tel: 93 317 6454/6209.
Pullmantur
Gran Via de les Corts Catalanes, 635.
Tel: 93 317 1297.

way but extends beyond the inner city area to towns on the other side of Tibidabo, such as San Cugat, Terrassa and Sabadell (all from Plaça de Catalunya) and to Manresa and Igualada (from Plaça d'Espanya). It is a useful service for reaching the upper parts of Barcelona and for parts of Tibidabo and the Parc de Collserola.

The metro ticket is valid on this line within a limited area, but to travel beyond is more expensive. The FGC lines are shown in a darker blue on the metro map. Within town the timetable is the same as the metro, but beyond it varies according to the line. Check in a station or call 010 for transport information. For FGC, tel: 93 205 15 15.

Bus

The bus service is good for reaching the areas the metro doesn't,

and for seeing more of Barcelona. Single tickets are the same price as metro tickets and can be bought from the driver, or a multiple card (*Targeta* T-10) of 10 journeys can be punched inside the bus. Most buses run 5 or 6am–10pm. There are some night services (the Nit bus), but lines vary so check on the map or at bus stops.

A more exclusive, expensive bus, the Tomb Bus, is convenient for covering the shopping area between Plaça de Catalunya and the top end of Avinguda Diagonal (Plaça Pius XII), which is not well connected by metro. The Tibibus runs from Plaça de Catalunya to Plaça del Tibidabo (on the top of the hill).

Cycling

Barcelona is now a cyclist-friendly city, with bike lanes, parking facilities and many great traffic-free places to cycle, such as the port, marinas, and along the beach front from Barceloneta to Diagonal Mar. Bikes can be taken on trains free of charge (*for bike rental see page 224*).

Barcelona on Foot

Walking is one of the best ways of getting around Barcelona – despite the traffic fumes. It is ideal for seeing the many details of Barcelona that cannot be charted by maps or guide books – *modernista* entrances and doorways, ancient corner shops, hidden roof gardens, balconies, local characters, daily life.

For guided walking tours of the city:
Barcelona Walking Tours
Gothic Quarter: Saturday and Sunday in English at 10am and Spanish at noon. April–September: also on Thursday and Friday at 10am.
Picasso Route: a glimpse of the artist's life in Barcelona ending with a tour of the museum. Saturday and Sunday at 10.30am. Information and booking: Turisme

de Barcelona, Plaça de Catalunya, tel: 807 117 222; from outside Spain tel: +34 93 285 3834.
The Route of Modernism:
A do-it-yourself route using a book available from Centre del Modernisme, Passeig de Gràcia, 41, tel: 93 488 0139. The book can also be found in centres at the Hospital Sant Pau and the Pavellons Güell.
La Ruta del Gòtic: If you are part of a group (minimum 10 people) you have the opportunity to take a 3-hour guided tour of the Gothic Quarter. Information and tickets: Museu d'Història de la Ciutat, Plaça del Rei, tel: 93 319 0222.
Guided Tours of Palau de la Música Catalana: Sant Francesc de Paula, 2, tel: 93 268 1000. There is also a guided tour by bicycle: **Un Cotxe Menys**, Espartaría, 3, tel: 93 268 2105.

Barcelona Addresses

Addresses are indicated by street name, number, storey, door. So Muntaner, 375, 6° 2ª means Muntaner street No. 375, 6th floor, 2nd door. The first floor of a building is *Principal*, often abbreviated to *Pral.* Some buildings have an *entresol* or mezzanine. An *àtic* is a top floor or penthouse, usually with a terrace.

Travelling Outside Barcelona

By train

The following stations currently function as described, but before planning any journey it is advisable to call RENFE (the national train network) for the latest information and ticket deals, tel: 902 240 202. It is wise to purchase tickets in advance (on this number), especially at holiday times. If you pay by credit card, tickets can be collected from machines at Sants and Passeig de Gràcia stations, which avoids the queues.

Estació de Sants, in Plaça Països Catalans, is for long-distance national and international trains. Some of these will also stop in **Passeig de Gràcia** station, which is convenient for central parts of town. Confirm beforehand that your train really does stop there.

Regional trains leave Sants for the coast south and north of Barcelona, including a direct train to Port Aventura theme park and the high-speed Euromed to Alicante, which makes a few stops in between. In Sants station, queues can be long and ticket clerks impatient and not very helpful. **Estació de França**, Avinguda Marquès de l'Argentera: long-distance national trains.
Plaça de Catalunya: apart from the metro and Generalitat railways (FGC), RENFE has a station in Plaça de Catalunya. Trains to Manresa, Lleida, Vic, Puigcerdà, La Tour de Carol, Mataró (Maresme Coast) and Blanes.
Plaça d'Espanya: FGC trains to Montserrat, Igualada and Manresa.

By coach

There are regular long-distance coach lines running all over Spain which leave from the Estació d'Autobusos Barcelona Nord, Alibei, 80, or Sants bus station. For information, tel: 93 265 6508. Bus services to other parts of Catalonia are operated by:
Costa Brava: Sarfa
Tel: 902 302 025.
Costa Maresme: Casas
Tel: 93 798 1100.
Delta del Ebro: Hife
Tel: 93 322 7814.
Montserrat: Julià
Tel: 93 490 4000.
Pyrenees: Alsina Graells
Tel: 93 265 6866.
Catalunya Bus Turístic offers day trips to different parts of Catalonia, such as Figueres and Girona (to the north), including the Dalí Museum; or Sitges (to the south), which includes the Colonia Güell and Codorníu, the *cava* producer. Information available from tourist offices, or tel: 93 285 3832.

By sea

There is a regular passenger and car service between Barcelona and Mallorca, Menorca and Ibiza with the Trasmediterránea company, based at the Estació Marítima, Moll de Barcelona, tel: 902 454 645; www.trasmediterranea.es for information, or book through a travel agent. There is also a Fast Ferry service, which takes four hours as opposed to the usual eight. For information and bookings contact: Fast Ferries, tel: 902 414 242. Another company, Buquebus, has catamaran-type boats which can get you to to Palma de Mallorca in three hours (www.buquebus.com).

Driving in Catalonia

Driving is the most flexible way to see the rest of Catalonia, but cars are better left in a parking place while you are in town. Avoid parking illegally, particularly outside entrances and private garage doors: the police tow offenders away with remarkable alacrity, and the charge for retrieval is heavy. You will know this has happened if you find a document with a triangular symbol stuck on the ground where your car was. This paper will give details of where you can retrieve your vehicle. Street parking, indicated by blue lines on the road and a nearby machine to buy a ticket, is limited. Convenient (but expensive) car parks are in Plaça de Catalunya, Passeig de Gràcia, and Plaça de la Catedral.

Drivers are supposed to stop for pedestrians at zebra crossings and when the green man is illuminated on traffic lights, but often they don't.

SPEED LIMITS

- Urban areas: 50 kph (30 mph)
- Roads outside urban areas: 90–110 kph (55–70 mph)
- Dual carriageways outside urban areas: 120 kph (75 mph)
- Motorways: 120 kph (75 mph)

BREAKDOWNS

In case of breakdown on the road call the general emergency number **112**, which has a foreign language service and can connect you with the relevant service. On motorways and main roads there are SOS phone boxes.

A useful organisation is the RACC (Royal Automobile Club of Catalonia), tel: 902 452 452; emergency number for members: 902 156 156.

Car hire/rental

Hiring a car is a good way to explore the area around Barcelona. It may be cheaper to make arrangements from home before you leave. There are some good deals to be had by booking on the Internet. A few of the car hire companies are:
Avis: Còrsega, 293–295
Tel: 902 180 854 or 93 298 3602 (airport).
Europcar: For information and booking, tel: 902 105 030.
Hertz: Tuset, 10
Tel: 93 217 3248 or 93 298 3638 (airport).
National-Atesa: Muntaner, 45
Tel: 93 323 0701 or 93 298 3433 (airport).
Over: Josep Tarradellas, 42
Tel: 902 410 410. Good-value local company.
Vanguard: Viladomat, 287
Tel: 93 439 3880. Motorbikes also for hire.
www.pepecar.com is a good option if you book in advance on the Internet, but beware of added extras. The office is conveniently located in Plaça de Catalunya.

Licences and insurance

Members of the EU can use the driving licence from their own country of residence. Those from outside the EU must have an international driving licence. You should have a Green Card (international motor insurance), available from your own insurer.

A CCOMMODATION

SOME THINGS TO CONSIDER BEFORE YOU BOOK THE ROOM

Accommodation

Following the surge in tourism in post-Olympic Barcelona, fuelled by budget flights, there was a dearth of hotel rooms, but in the last few years there has been feverish building and renovation work to provide more accommodation in the city. There are now around 400 hotels and guest houses *(pensions)* ranging from basic rooms accommodating 3 or 4 beds to 5-star GL (Gran Luxe) sumptuous hotels.

At the top end of the scale establishments are suitably indulgent in avant-garde or historic buildings, with privileged views and impeccable service at a high price.

In the moderate range there is a wide choice with an equally diverse price range according to the services offered or the location. Further away from the centre, better deals are available and these are a good option considering the city's efficient public transport system which can whisk you to the centre in a matter of minutes.

The inexpensive range is most problematic. The few good hotels and *pensions* in this bracket are sought after, so they get booked up months in advance, especially over busy periods like holidays and half-terms. *Pensions* range

from basic to decent, with just a few notable exceptions where an effort has been made to modernise or give some extra value. There are plenty in the centre, mostly in the Old Town, particularly in the streets leading off La Rambla. Some do not accept bookings in advance so be prepared for dragging suitcases around, but at least that gives you the advantage of checking out the rooms first.

Rates vary dramatically, mostly on a supply and demand basis. Now that there are more rooms available the client has more chance of getting a rate way below the standard price quoted, especially at weekends or off-peak times of the year. However, if there is a trade fair or large congress taking place, Barcelona still seems to be short of rooms. Ironically – and fortunately for the many Northern European and American travellers who take their holidays in mid-summer – July and August are not considered peak times, whereas September and October are high season. Good deals can also be found through internet booking, directly with the hotel or through the many booking services on the web. Special offers are advertised, often with bargains for families. There are several new hotels along the recently

developed waterfront near Diagonal Mar where high standard accommodation can be found at a reasonable price. As they are a taxi or metro ride from the centre they are less popular, but the advantage of sea views and more peaceful nights are well worth considering.

As a reaction to the increased number of tourists, opportunist residents have been quick to see a gap in the market and provide alternative forms of accommodation. Self-catering has become a new phenomenon in the city, with developers renovating whole buildings in the Old Town to offer as tourist lets.

A quick search on the internet comes up with several agencies that have a range of flats on their books like www.flatsbydays.com or www.oh-barcelona.com. At the luxurious end is www.cru2001.com, a building where each flat has an individual design based around a literary theme. As it offers the opportunity to select the area and to buy food from the market, as well as favourable rates, self-catering has become a popular choice.

Bed and Breakfast accommodation is also widely available now, and has the advantage of friendly local advice and a closer insight into Barcelona life. One agency with a wide choice of rooms is www.bcnrooms.com.

TRANSPORT

Hotel Chains

Aside from the recommended hotels listed below you could also contact the central offices of the following hotel chains to see what they have available when you are planning to travel.

Derby Hotels
Tel: 93 414 2970
www.derbyhotels.es/.
Group H 10
Tel: 902 100 906
www.h10.es
Guitart Hotels
Tel: 972 347 000

www.guitarthotels.com.
Hoteles Catalonia
Tel: 93 418 4818
www.hoteles-catalonia.es/.
NH Hotels
Tel: 93 412 2323
www.nh-hoteles.es.

ACCOMMODATION LISTINGS

ACCOMMODATION

LA RAMBLA

Ambassador
Pintor Fortuny, 13
Tel: 93 412 0530
Fax: 93 302 7977 €€€€
Just off La Rambla. Comfortable rooms and a little rooftop garden that makes a pleasant retreat from the bustle.
Catalunya Plaza
Plaça Catalunya, 7
Tel: 93 317 7171
Fax: 93 317 7855 €€€
On the square itself, so just about as central as you can get. Standard hotel comfort behind an attractive façade, with a few of the original 19th-century features remaining.
Citadines Barcelona-Ramblas
La Rambla, 122
Tel: 93 270 1111
Fax: 93 412 7421 €€€
Excellent value for money. Food shopping can be done at the Boquería market or local supermarket. Pleasant breakfast buffet bar and good views from the rooftop.
Comercio
Escudellers, 15
Tel: 93 318 7420
Fax: 93 318 7374 €€
All the necessary services and basic comforts and it's just off La Rambla. All rooms have en suite bathrooms,

and some have 3, 4 or 5 beds available.
Continental
La Rambla, 138
Tel: 93 301 2570 €€
In a prime position near the top of La Rambla, this historic hotel's individual character is a welcome change. Swirling carpets and floral décor can be forgiven when you can sit on a balcony watching the world go by – and at a reasonable price. Ask for a room at the front.
Duques de Bergara
Bergara, 11
Tel: 93 301 5151
Fax: 93 317 3442 €€€
www.hoteles-catalonia.es
The magnificent late 19th-century entrance hall inevitably gives way to modernised bedrooms, but the place still has charm and is well located just off Plaça Catalunya. Surprisingly it has a small pool with peaceful terrace tucked in behind.
Ginebra
Rambla de Catalunya, 1
Tel: 93 317 1063
Fax: 93 317 5565 €€
This is on the simple, basic side; not all rooms have en suite bathrooms. However, it is very clean, staff are friendly and the location

is central, with views of Plaça Catalunya from some rooms. All windows are double-glazed. A good deal.
Kabul
Plaça Reial, 17
Tel: 93 318 5190
Fax: 93 301 4034 €
Long-established youth hostel in a privileged position on this magnificent square just off La Rambla. Rooms extend to dorms for up to 20. Renowned for a party atmosphere.
Mercure Barcelona Rambla
La Rambla, 124
Tel: 93 412 0404
Fax: 93 318 7323 €€€
A mix of old and new. Bedrooms are modernised but down to earth, while there is an upstairs lounge revealing how the hotel looked in former times.
Le Meridien Barcelona
La Rambla, 111
Tel: 93 318 6200
Fax: 93 301 7776 €€€€
www.lemeridien-barcelona.com
A large, plush hotel, well positioned on La Rambla, due to reopen in March 2005 after being made even plusher. The Presidential Suite with a 360º view of the old town, will be a snip at €2,000.

Oriente
La Rambla, 45
Tel: 93 302 2558
Fax: 93 412 3819 €€€
www.husa.es
Once a charismatic old favourite, the Oriente, in the heart of La Rambla, has been through a low period. However, after refurbishment by the Husa chain it has recovered some of its former glory, including the splendid ballroom, but at the expense of some of its personality.
Pension Teruel
Plaça Bonsuccés 6, 3º
Tel: 93 302 6120
Fax: 93 317 6914 €
Spotlessly clean and in

ACTIVITIES

A – Z

PRICE CATEGORIES

Prices are for a standard double room without breakfast or IVA (VAT).
€: under €50
€€: under €100
€€€: under €200
€€€€: over €200

LANGUAGE

an excellent position overlooking a small, tree-filled square, five minutes from Plaça Catalunya and half a minute from La Rambla, which make up for the basic rooms.

Pulitzer
Bergara, 6-10
Tel: 93 481 6767
Fax: 93 481 6464 €€€
The latest in this street of classy hotels is sleek and smooth at a reasonable price considering all it offers and the central location.

Regina
Bergara, 2–3
Tel: 93 301 3232
Fax: 93 318 3236 €€€
www.reginahotel.com
High quality rooms and service and a central location just off Plaça Catalunya.

Rivoli Ramblas
La Rambla, 128
Tel: 93 302 6643
Fax: 93 317 5053 €€€
www.rivolihotels.com
Behind the elegantly cool 1930s façade is a modern hotel with tasteful rooms. The barman

of the Blue Moon cocktail bar downstairs plays great music, which makes a refreshing change from typical hotel background musack.

Roma Reial
Plaça Reial, 11
Tel: 93 302 0366
Fax: 93 301 1839 €€
Set in a corner of a stunning square. The rooms are basic but acceptable, although for the price something better can probably be found if you settle for a less

ostentatious location, such as nearby Carrer Boquería, where there are plenty of cheaper options.

Royal
La Rambla, 117
Tel: 93 301 9400
Fax: 93 317 3179 €€€
www.hroyal.com
Despite the rather mediocre 1970s exterior, the interior is fully refurbished and, considering its position on La Rambla, it is good value for a modern hotel with most mod cons.

BARRI GÒTIC

Albinoni
Portal de l'Àngel, 17
Tel: 93 318 4141
Fax: 93 301 2631 €€€
www.hoteles-catalonia.es
Many vestiges of the Albinoni's former life as the Rocamora palace remain, including the splendid staircase and beautiful tiled floors. Combined with modern details and tasteful décor this is a really good option, and well situated between the Gothic quarter and the Eixample.

Colón
Avinguda Catedral, 7
Tel: 93 301 1404
Fax: 93 317 2915 €€€
www.hotelcolon.es
A classic, in the centre of the Barri Gòtic, facing the cathedral. Bedrooms in their floral style seem more English than Spanish. Request a room with a view of the Cathedral Square

Duc de la Victoria
Duc de la Victoria, 15
Tel: 93 270 3410 €€€
Very reasonably priced for what it offers, this modern hotel in a quiet

location between La Rambla and the cathedral is surprisingly personal and friendly.

Gran Hotel Barcino
Jaume I, 6
Tel: 93 302 2012
Fax: 93 301 4242 €€€
www.gargallo-hoteles.com
The location is the chief factor. A bit expensive for what is on offer but there's no denying the luxury of being a stone's throw from Plaça Sant Jaume, the seat of government and nucleus of all fiestas.

Jardí
Plaça Sant Josep Oriol 1
Plaça del Pi
Tel: 93 301 5900 €€
After months of refurbishment this extremely popular hotel is still quite basic, but it's worth trying to get a room if you can, as it overlooks two of the most attractive squares in the Barri Gòtic.

Levante
Baixada de Sant Miquel, 7
Tel: 93 317 9565
Fax: 93 317 0526 €
www.hostallevante.com

Basic accommodation with friendly atmosphere (and price). Prides itself on the tale that the young Picasso was a frequent visitor in its former life as a house of ill repute. Just off Avinyó, one of the trendiest streets in the area.

Neri
Sant Sever, 5
Tel: 93 304 0655
Fax: 93 304 0337 €€€€
www.hotelneri.com
Barcelona's first boutique hotel is in a 17th-century palace giving on to Sant Felip Neri, one of the most atmospheric squares in the Gothic quarter, near the cathedral. As there are only 22 exclusively designed rooms, early booking is essential.

BELOW: the magnificent Plaça Reial.

Nouvel
Santa Anna, 20
Tel: 93 301 8274
Fax: 93 301 8370 €€€
www.hotelnouvel.com
Located in a pedestrian street just off La Rambla, this attractive old building has a modernised interior and comfortable, spacious rooms.

Racó del Pi
Pi, 7
Tel: 93 342 6190
Fax: 93 342 6191 €€€
www.h10.es
Set in the very heart of the Barri Gòtic, around the corner from the Plaça del Pi, this small hotel has been built within an old palace. There are only 37 rooms

so it tends to get booked up early. At the upper end of this price bracket.
Rialto
Ferrán, 42
Tel: 93 318 5212
Fax: 93 318 5312 €€
Modernised and straightforward, nothing fancy, but located in an interesting street just off Plaça Sant Jaume.

Suizo
Plaça de l'Angel, 12
Tel: 93 310 6108
Fax: 93 310 4081 €€€
Pleasant, homely and comfortable, in a good position in the Barri Gòtic. Request a room on Baixada Llibreteria for an attractive outlook and more peace and quiet.

LA RIBERA

Banys Orientals
Argenteria, 37
Tel: 93 268 8460
Fax: 93 268 8461 €€
www.hotelbanysorientals.com
One of the best options in town with impeccable slick interiors and stylish details, and it's in the hottest spot for shopping, wining and dining. Unbeatable value, so book well in advance.
Park Hotel
Avinguda Marquès de l'Argentera, 11
Tel: 93 319 6000
Fax: 93 319 4519 €€€

A gem of 1950s architecture, quite rare in Barcelona, opposite the Estació de França, and near the Parc de la Ciutadella. It is on the edge of the Born district, which is awash with cafés, restaurants and bars and within walking distance of the beach. The rooms are well designed.
Pensió 2000
Sant Pere Més Alt, 6, 1er
Tel: 93 310 7466
Fax: 93 319 4252 €€
A noble marble staircase leads to this

friendly family guesthouse, which is a cut above the average *pension* and right opposite the Palau de la Música. Excellent value.
Pension Ciudadela
Comercio, 33, 1º, 1ª
Tel: 93 319 6203 €
Opposite the Estació de França this humble guesthouse has decent rooms at a vry reasonable price, and is within staggering distance of the Born nightlife.
Triunfo
Passeig de Picasso, 22
Tel: 93 315 0860

Fax: 93 315 0860 €€
A simple, clean *pension* set between the Born and the Parc de la Ciutadella. A convenient and reasonably priced place to stay. All the buildings along this avenue are elegant.

EL RAVAL

Aneto
Carme, 38
Tel: 93 301 9989
Fax: 93 301 9862 €€
A small hotel with no frills, but clean, with all mod cons and conve-

PRICE CATEGORIES

Prices are for a standard double room without breakfast or IVA (VAT).
€: under €50
€€: under €100
€€€: under €200
€€€€: over €200

niently situated, with the Boqueria market and good restaurants nearby.
España
Sant Pau, 9
Tel: 93 318 1758
Fax: 93 317 1134 €€
E-mail: hotelespanya@tresnet.com
Magnificent Modernist décor on the ground floor by Domènech i Montaner is refreshingly set off by kitsch touches and the 1950s-style bar. Rooms modernised, but fairly basic. Popular with American

intellectuals. At least eat here: the set lunch is good value and the wonderful surroundings are worth every euro.
Gaudí
Nou de la Rambla, 12
Tel: 93 317 9032 €€€
A modern hotel without much personality but the treat is the view: get a room at the front, so you can feast your eyes on Gaudí's Palau Güell opposite. The top floor rooms have small terraces which are worth fighting for.

Hosteria Grau
Ramelleres, 27
Tel: 93 301 8135
Fax: 93 317 6825 €€
Book early for this popular, well-kept *pension*, which is in a good position for shopping and

visiting both the Eixample and Old Town alike. Excellent breakfasts in the adjoining bar.

Inglaterra
Pelai, 14
Tel: 93 505 1100 €€€
A good-looking hotel within an old façade, equally well located for the bohemian Raval or the elegant Eixample. Stands out from the crowd in this modern, medium-priced range.

Mesón de Castilla
Valldonzella, 5
Tel: 93 318 2182
Fax: 93 412 4020 €€€
Furniture is old-fashioned; cupboards and chairs in a kind of rustic style. A bit quirky, but at least gives the feeling of being somewhere different (as opposed to anywhere). Very good location. The owners are friendly and helpful.

Peninsular
Sant Pau, 34
Tel: 93 302 3138
Fax: 93 412 3699 €€
In a former convent, with rooms around an inner courtyard filled with hanging plants. An impressive lobby and dining room, and basic but clean rooms.

Reding
Gravina, 5–7
Tel: 93 412 1097
Fax: 93 268 3482 €€€

In a quiet street just off Pelai. Well equipped, fairly standard, comfortable accommodation.

Sant Agustí
Plaça Sant Agustí, 3
Tel: 93 318 1658
Fax: 93 317 2928 €€€
www.hotelsa.com
This hotel is comfortable and clean, overlooking a quiet square. Worth paying more for one of the luxury rooms on the fourth floor.

THE WATERFRONT

AC Front Marítim
Passeig García Faria, 69–71
Tel: 93 303 4440
Booking: 902 292 295 €€€
One of the hotels on the new stretch of waterfront developed between Vila Olímpica and Diagonal Mar. Being just a taxi ride away from the inner city buzz can be advantageous, especially if you wake up to sea views. Slick and comfortable.

Arts
Passeig de la Marina, 19
Tel: 93 221 1000
Fax: 93 221 1070 €€€€
www.harts.es
The hotel with the highest profile in town, this is one of the two towers that mark the entrance to the Olympic Village, on the sea front. It has a light and airy feel. Rooms with panoramic views.

Barcelona Princess
Avinguda Diagonal, 1
Tel: 93 356 1000
Fax: 93 356 1022 €€€€
www.princess-hotels.com
On the cutting edge in all senses: designed by leading Catalan architect Oscar Tusquets, situated in this brand new

district of Barcelona, the Diagonal Mar, and offering all possible facilities. Prices are subject to radical cuts, too, so it is worth trying to bargain to sleep at this giddy height with views of sea and city.

Duquesa de Cardona
Passeig Colom, 12
Tel: 93 268 9090
Fax: 93 268 2931 €€€
www.hduqesadecardona.com
A classically elegant hotel that has recently emerged in these long-overlooked, handsome buildings giving on to the original waterfront and the old harbour. The pool and terrace on the roof are a hidden treasure in this part of town. Luxurious details at a moderate price.

Grand Marina
World Trade Center
Moll de Barcelona, 1
Tel: 93 603 9000
Fax: 93 603 9090 €€€€
www.grandmarinahotel.com
You feel as if you are aboard the most luxurious cruise ship – it's a heady experience without the seasickness. Some of these comfortable bedrooms, with

hydro-massage baths, jut out into the port, while those at the rear have a panoramic view of Barcelona.

Marina Folch
Mar, 16, pral
Tel: 93 310 3709
Fax: 93 310 5327 €€
Just behind Passeig Joan de Borbó is another world, that of the real Barceloneta, which resembles parts of Naples. Looking at the façade you may get the wrong impression. The interior has been renovated and the rooms are tasteful. There are only 10 rooms, and even company directors like staying here, so booking is essential.

Sea Point Hostel
Plaça del Mar, 4
Tel: 93 224 7075
Fax: 93 246 1552 €
www.seapointhostel.com
An unbeatable position for a youth hostel right on Barceloneta beach. This forward-thinking chain of youth hostels has a branch in La Ribera – Gothic Point – and one in Gràcia – La Ciutat.

BELOW: a hotel near the beach is ideal in summer.

MONTJUÏC

There are not many hotels on Montjuïc, but these two are recommended.

Apsis Milleni
Ronda Sant Pau, 14
Tel: 93 441 4177
Fax: 93 324 8150 €€€
Though officially in the Raval this modernised hotel is within easy access of Montjuïc and the trade fair site. Standards are high at a reasonable price. Good deals for family rooms

Barcelona Plaza
Plaça d'Espanya, 6–8
Tel: 93 426 2600
Fax: 93 426 0400 €€€
www.hoteles-catalonia.es
A modern, functional hotel popular with business clientele due to its proximity to the Fira de Barcelona trade fair site. Situated at the foot of Montjuïc, it is well located and easy to reach from theairport.

THE EIXAMPLE

Actual
Rosselló, 238
Tel: 93 552 0550 €€€
A really welcome newcomer on the hotel scene. It has attractive minimalist décor yet maintains a warm, personal atmosphere. It is already sought after, so try and book early.

América
Provença, 195
Tel: 93 487 6292
Fax: 93 487 2518 €€€
www.new-millenium-hotels.com
On a quiet corner of the Eixample this new hotel prides itself on being different from the average chain hotel. Its modern design does not quite make it in this stylish neighbourhood, but it does offer excellent service and facilities for guests.

Avenida Palace
Gran Via, 605–607
Tel: 93 301 9600
Fax: 93 318 1234 €€€€
www.husa.es
You get classic old-world gilt and chandeliers at new-world prices. Rooms are comfortable and the service is good. Request one of the rooms from the fourth floor upwards, for splendid city views.

Casa Fuster
Passeig de Gràcia, 132
Tel: 93 255 3000
Booking: 902 202 345 €€€€
www.hotelescenter.es
Classified as a 5-star 'Monument' hotel this grand hotel has recently opened in the magnificent Casa Fuster, built by Domènech i Montaner in 1908, with all its *modernista* splendour carefully restored.

Catalonia Berna
Roger de Llúria 60,
Tel: 93 272 0050 €€€
In the heart of the Eixample, this pretty hotel will take you back to the heyday of this 19th-century district. The ornamental façade has been carefully recovered with painted frescos. The interior is conventionally modern.

Claris
Pau Claris, 150
Tel: 93 487 6262
Fax: 93 215 7970 €€€€
www.derbyhotels.es
Well-positioned in the middle of the Eixample, the Claris's strikingly designed interior was built behind the original façade of the Palace of Vedruna and is crammed with valuable art work.

Condes de Barcelona
Passeig de Gràcia, 75
Tel: 93 488 2200
Fax: 93 467 4781 €€€
www.condesdebarcelona.com
Contemporary elegance in two *modernista* buildings facing each other in the Quadrat d'Or of the Eixample. Rooms available with private balcony; there is a roof terrace with mini-pool.

Diplomatic
Pau Claris, 122
Tel: 93 272 3810
Fax: 93 272 3811 €€€
www.ac-hoteles.com
Sleek and crisp in its stylish, faintly 1960s design. The downstairs lounge is spacious and streamlined. Amazing views from the roof terrace, which also has a gym and saunas. Excellent value.

Gallery
Rossello, 249
Tel: 93 415 9911
Fax: 93 415 9184 €€€
Well-situated between Passeig de Gràcia and Rambla de Catalunya. Very pleasant bar on the first floor overlooking the street, and a restaurant that has tables outside in the attractive garden behind.

Gran Hotel Havana
Gran Via Cortes Catalanes, 647
Tel: 93 412 1115
Fax: 93 412 2611 €€€
www.granhotelhavana.com
The rooms here are on the small side but well-thought out and pleasant. Attractive, luminous interior. Well-positioned in the heart of the Eixample with easy connections to the airport.

Gran Via
Gran Vía, 642
Tel: 93 318 1900
Fax: 93 318 9997 €€
E-mail: hgranvia@nnhoteles.es
Faded old-Spain splen-

TRANSPORT

ACCOMMODATION

ACTIVITIES

A – Z

LANGUAGE

dour, which can be a welcome change from the pervading designer modernity of the city. Well-situated near Passeig de Gràcia. Interior rooms are preferable, to avoid Gran Vía traffic. Downstairs there is a large, restful, parquet-floored lounge leading to a spacious terrace.

Hostal Cèntric
Casanova, 13
Tel: 93 426 7573
Fax: 93 425 0347 €€
www.hostalcentric.com
New-generation guest-house, fresh, clean and modern. Excellent value and within walking distance of the Old Town and the Eixample.

Hostal Ciudad Condal
Mallorca, 255
Tel: 93 215 1040 €€
Very clean, respectable little *pension* in the heart of the best part of the Eixample.

Hostal Palacios
Gran Vía, 629 bis
Tel: 93 301 3792 €€
Fulfils the basic requirements, and cheap considering the location. For unfussy customers.

Majestic
Passeig de Gràcia, 70
Tel: 93 488 1717
Fax: 93 488 1880 €€€€

www.hotelmajestic.es
Occupying three buildings on Paseig de Gràcia. Renovation was completed in the late 1990s to transform what was 1970s style into polished sophistication. The eldest daughter of the family that owns it has chosen all the art on display with great skill. Two restaurants, including the famed Drolma, which has only 10 tables where gourmets can sample the exquisite menu by a well-known chef.

Omm
Rosselló 265
Tel: 93 445 4000
Fax: 93 445 4004 €€€€
www.hotelomm.es
Part of the Tragaluz group, this designer hotel is seriously cool and *the* place to be seen. Slick, luminous rooms and a roof-top lap pool with views of the Sagrada Família. Whether you're in the Moo restaurant (run by the star Roca brothers of Girona), or chilling out in the Omm Session club you'll feel you've just dropped in to a fashion shoot.

Paseo de Gràcia
Passeig de Gràcia, 102
Tel: 93 215 5824
Fax: 93 215 3724 €€
Another vestige from the past, with some original fittings. Ask for a room on the 8th floor. Prime location and good value for money in this expensive area.

Prestige
Passeig de Gràcia, 62
Tel: 93 272 4180
Fax: 93 272 4181 €€€€
www.prestigepaseodegracia.com
Low-key elegance in the heart of Passeig de Gràcia in this stylish newcomer. Their claim to individuality is the "Ask Me" service: a team of switched-on young people who can answer your cultural, gastronomic or shopping queries. Experience the typical Eixample inner patio in their small, Oriental-style garden.

Regente
Rambla de Catalunya, 76
Tel: 93 487 5989
Fax: 93 487 3227 €€€
Pleasant hotel in an excellent position. Some attractive original features have survived amid the standard hotel furnishings. Rooftop pool.

Residencia Windsor
Rambla de Catalunya, 84
Tel: 93 215 1198 €€
A gem: intact and impeccably clean, light and airy in contrast to the usual drab, sad *hostales*. Essential to book in advance and to request a room looking on to Rambla de Catalunya. Excellent position near Diagonal.

Ritz
Gran Vía, 668
Tel: 93 318 5200
Fax: 93 318 0148 €€€€
www.ritzcarlton.com
Luxury maybe, but exorbitant even for business accounts. Splendid entrance hall and lobby where tea can be taken. Dalí had a permanent suite here.

Sant Moritz
Diputación, 262
Tel: 93 412 1500
Fax: 93 412 1236 €€€€
www.hcchotels.es
More of interest for its location than its style, despite the splendid classical entrance. However, the San Galen restaurant is recommended in the Michelin Guide. On the ground floor there is a set of rooms for guests with disabilities.

AROUND THE DIAGONAL

Aparthotel Atenea
Joan Güell, 207–211

Tel: 93 490 6640
Fax: 93 490 6420 €€€
Well-designed mini-apartments in a classy part of the city, close to the Plaça Francesc Macià.

Aparthotel Bonanova
Bisbe Sevilla, 7
Tel: 93 253 1563
Fax: 93 418 4497 €€€
Located in a quiet residential area in the

upper part of Barcelona. Reserve a room with a terrace if you can.

Gran Hotel Florida
Carretera Vallvidrera a Tibidabo, 83–89
Tel: 93 259 3000
Fax: 93 259 3001 €€€€
www.hotellaflorida.com
Barcelona's first 5-star Relais Château is the ultimate in luxury,

perched high on Tibidabo hill. Brought back to life from its former glory in the 1940s when the likes of Ernest Hemingway and James Stewart were clients, it has impeccable service and unbeatable views.

Hostal Lesseps
Gran de Gràcia, 239
Tel: 93 218 4434 €
Owned by the same family as the Hostal Ciudad Condal (see page 214) and similar in style, although situated a little further up the city slopes.

Hotel Tres Torres
Calatrava, 32–34
Tel: 93 417 7300 €
The Tres Torres is reasonably priced for this smart residential area. It's a small hotel, and nothing spectacular, but it makes a good alternative in a quiet leafy street in the Tres Torres district near Sarrià. The centre of town is only minutes away on the FGC trains.

Melia Barcelona
Avinguda Sarria, 48–50
Tel: 93 410 6090
Fax: 93 410 6173 €€€€

You could easily forget you're in Barcelona in this hotel and be anywhere in the world, but if sheer comfort is what you're after, then this is an obvious choice.

Rey Juan Carlos I
Avinguda Diagonal, 661–671
Tel: 93 364 4040
Fax: 93 364 4264 €€€€
www.hrjuancarlos.com
A vast construction using plenty of glass and steel. It's at the end of Diagonal and therefore a taxi ride away from everything. It offers maximum comfort and security, which may be why it is favoured by royalty and politicians.

Turó de Vilana
Vilana, 7
Tel: 93 434 0363
Fax. 93 418 8903 €€€
www.turodevilana.com
For anyone who likes to stay well away from the more touristy areas, this small hotel, with only 20 rooms, is ideal. It's not far from the Norman Foster Communications tower and the Parc de Collserola. Modern, compact and pretty.

FURTHER AFIELD

Efficient and frequent suburban train lines (Cercanías) make staying out of town a good option. A 45-minute cool, comfortable train ride will take you from a quiet beach-side hotel to the centre of Barcelona. Rooms are usually easier to book and rates better value. There are several top quality hotels, including Paradors, and an increasing number of self-catering options and rural guesthouses, which range from simple rooms in a traditional farmhouse to more exclusive country houses. An internet search will throw up contacts, but a good start is the Catalan tourist office:
www.gencat.net/probert.

Badalona

Hotel Miramar
Santa Madrona, 60
Tel: 93 384 0311
Fax: 93 389 1627 €

A traditional beachside hotel, last renovated in the 1950s but with all mod cons included. Quirky but fun choice as it's only 10 minutes from Plaça Catalunya by train, or the new tram from Sant Adrià.

Caldes d'Estrac

Kalima
Passeig de les Moreres, 7
Tel: 93 791 48 90 €
Recently opened in a small modernista villa on the promenade overlooking one of the less frequented beaches. The devoted owners take care of every small detail. A gem at a very reasonable price.

Girona

Aiguablava
Platja de Fornells, Begur
Tel: 972 622 058
Fax: 972 622 112 €€€
A stylish, historic, traditional hotel. It overlooks

one of the prettiest beaches on this spectacular coastline.

Ripoll

Mas el Reixac
Sant Joan de les Abadesses
Tel: 972 720 373
www.elreixac.com
Self-catering accommodation in tastefully restored farm buildings just outside an historic village. Walks on the doorstep and skiing 30 minutes away. Log fires and duvets make it cosy in winter.

Sitges

Hotel Subur Marítim
Passeig Marítim s/n
Tel: 93 894 1550
Fax: 93 894 0427 €€€
Right on the seafront, this attractive hotel has personality, plus a lovely pool in the garden. Within walking distance of the centre, but at a peaceful-distance.

Vilanova i la Geltrú

Hotel César
Isaac Peral, 8
Tel: 93 815 1125
Fax: 93 815 6719 €
A delightful hotel run by two sisters, one creative in interior design, the other in the kitchen. Tiny pool in a shady garden a stone's throw from the beach.

Vic

Parador de Vic-Sau
Paraje el Bac de Sau
Tel: 93 812 2323
Fax: 93 812 2368 €
www.parador.es
Traditional parador outside Vic, on the edge of a huge reservoir.

TRANSPORT

ACCOMMODATION

ACTIVITIES

A – Z

LANGUAGE

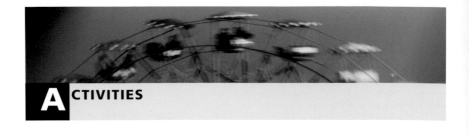

ACTIVITIES

THE ARTS, NIGHTLIFE, FESTIVALS, SHOPPING AND SPECTATOR SPORTS

THE ARTS

Cultural Events

The combination of Catalonia's rich cultural heritage and the dynamism of contemporary movements has made Barcelona one of Europe's cultural capitals. In 2004, a Universal Forum of Cultures was held in and around the city, and across the world by Internet. Apart from its architecture and 46 museums, there is a busy calendar of music and arts festivals, opera, visiting exhibitions and constant activity in design, theatre and the arts in general, to say nothing of daily performances from street artists in the Ramblas and small squares of the Barri Gòtic.

Posters, banners, and the daily and weekly press all herald what's on in Barcelona. The city council has a cultural information centre in the Palau de la Virreina, Rambla, 99 *(see below),* which is very helpful and has leaflets and information on nearly all cultural activities. It also sells tickets. The Generalitat also has a cultural information centre (closed at lunchtime) at the base of the Centre d'Art Santa Mònica *(see below).* The tourist information office in Plaça de Catalunya sells tickets at half-price on the day of a performance. Also two of the savings banks have an efficient system for ticket sales:
Tel-Entrada of the Caixa de Catalunya, tel: 902 101 212.
Servi-caixa of "la Caixa", in most branches of the bank, tel: 902 33 22 11; www.servicaixa.com.

Exhibition Centres

The following centres regularly hold temporary exhibitions of the visual arts. Consult local press for details:
Centre d'Art Santa Mònica
Rambla Santa Mònica, 7
Tel: 93 316 2810
www.cultura.gencat.es.
Caixa Forum, the cultural centre of "la Caixa" Foundation
Avgda Marquès de Comillas, 6–8
Tel: 902 223 040.
Centre de Cultura Contemporània de Barcelona (CCCB)
Montalegre, 5
Tel: 93 306 4100
www.cccb.org.
Seminars and a range of activities as well as installations, exhibitions of contemporary art, and film and music festivals.
Centre Cultural Caixa de Catalunya, La Pedrera, Provença, 261
Tel: 902 400 973
www.caixacatalunya.es/obra social.

Apart from the Gaudí architecture itself, there are free temporary shows in the exhibition space.
Fundació Antoni Tàpies
Aragó, 255
Tel: 93 487 0315
www.fundaciotapies.org.
Permanent collection of work by the artist himself plus very good shows by other internationally acclaimed artists. Beautiful art library upstairs.
Palau de la Virreina
Rambla, 99
Tel: 93 316 1000
www.bcn.es/icub.
Cultural information centre run by the city council: exhibition space, which often features photographic displays.

Art Galleries

Art galleries are usually open Tues–Sat 10.30am–1.30pm and 4.30–8.30pm. They tend to be concentrated into three areas of the city. In approximate order of importance these are as follows:
On Passeig de Gràcia, Rambla de Catalunya and on interconnecting streets (notably Consell de Cent):
Ambit, Consell de Cent, 282.
Carles Taché, Consell de Cent, 290.
Galería Alejandro Sales, Julian Romea, 16.

Galería Senda, Consell de Cent, 292.

Galería Estrany, Passatge Mercader, 18.

Joan Prats, Rambla de Catalunya, 54.

In the old town around Plaça San Josep Oriol (classical), in the Born (contemporary) and in El Raval district, near the MACBA:

Antonio de Barnola, Palau, 4.

Ferran Cano, Plaça dels Angels, 4.

Metrònom, Fusina, 9.

Sala Artur Ramon, Palla, 23.

Sala Pares, Petrixtol, 5.

Trama, Petritxol, 8.

Several in Doctor Dou

In the streets behind Plaça Francesc Macià:

Fernando Alcolea, Plaça Sant Gregori Taumaturg, 7.

Lucia Homs, Avinguda Diagonal, 505.

Music and Dance

Classical music

A busy season of concerts by the Orquestra Simfònica de Barcelona i Nacional de Catalunya (OBC) and visiting orchestras and soloists runs from September to early July. The Festival de Música Antiga (tel: 902 223 040) is held in April and May, and various international music festivals take place outside Barcelona in July and August, including the notable Festival de Peralada, Girona (tel: 93 280 5868).

Barcelona's various arts festivals also include classical music. Among them is one for 20th-century music in October (tel: 93 301 7775), and the Festival de Guitarra de Barcelona in June (tel: 902 101 212/93 232 6167).

The main places to hear classical music are:

Auditori Municipal

Plaça de les Arts.

A huge new music auditorium in the Plaça de les Glories complex.

Caixa Forum (see page 214)

Palau de la Música Catalana

Sant Francesc de Paula, 2

Tel: 93 268 1000.

If you have an opportunity to go to a concert in this extravagant *modernista* concert hall by Domènech i Montaner, then you should go – whatever is on the programme.

Contemporary music

CCCB

Montalegre, 5

Tel: 93 412 0781.

Fundació Miró

Montjuïc

Tel: 93 443 9470.

This gallery hosts a season of 20th-century music, with particular emphasis on Catalan composers.

TRADITIONAL FESTIVALS

Every district *(barri)* of Barcelona has its own annual fiesta, known as the Festa Major, centred on its own patron saint. These usually last several days. The *sardana*, the national dance of Catalonia, can also be seen every Sunday in Plaça Sant Jaume at 7pm (6.30pm in winter), and in the Plaça de la Catedral on Sundays at noon. *Gegants* (giants) and *cap grossos* (comic characters with large heads) parade the streets and usually reunite in the evening at a Grand Ball in one of the public squares. *Castellers* usually perform during fiestas. These acrobatic troupes erect human towers capped with the youngest and smallest. All these things also feature in the traditional fiestas that are celebrated all over Barcelona:

Christmas. During early December the Santa Llúcia Fair of arts and crafts plus Christmas trees is held in the streets around the Cathedral.

Sant Esteve (St Stephen's Day), 26 Dec. Families meet for an even larger meal than on the 25th.

Reis Mags, Epiphany, 6 Jan. Children receive presents from the Three Kings, though modern commerce now indulges them with presents at Christmas as

Jazz

The Terrassa Jazz Festival in the spring and the Barcelona International Jazz Festival in the autumn gather together some leading names. In addition there is a jazz festival in the Old Town, Ciutat Vella, from mid-October to mid-December, and regular jazz and blues sessions in an ever-increasing number of venues. To name a few:

Harlem Jazz Club,

Comtessa de Sobradiel, 8.

Jamboree Jazz and Dance Club, Plaça Reial, 17

Jazz Sí Club, Requesens, 2.

well. In Barcelona the Kings arrive from the Orient by boat.

Carnival (Carnestoltes), Feb or Mar. Wild pre-Lent celebrations close with the "Burial of the Sardine" on Ash Wednesday, a riotous mock funeral. The most extravagant Carnival parades are at Sitges, on the coast.

Sant Jordi, 23 April. A traditional Catalan festival, St George's Day is also now World Book Day, on which men give a rose to their lady, and receive a book in return.

Fira de Sant Ponç, 11 May. Aromatic and medicinal herbs, crystallised fruit and honey are sold in Carrer de l'Hospital.

Sant Joan, 23–4 June. Midsummer's Night, the eve of the Feast of St John, is a big event in Catalonia. It is celebrated with fireworks, *cava* and *coca*, a Catalan cake made with pine nuts and crystallised fruit.

Diada de Catalunya, 11 Sep. Catalonia's national day is less a traditional fiesta than an occasion for political demonstrations and national anthems.

The Feast of La Mercè, 24 Sep. Barcelona's main fiesta is held in honour of the city's patroness. A week of merriment is crowned by the *correfoc*, a nocturnal procession of devils and fire-breathing dragons.

MUSIC HALL AND CABARET

Barcelona has a long and colourful tradition of show business, centred on the Paral·lel area. The shows, the surrounding bars, the characters involved, all provide a sharp contrast to the high design and yuppiedom of the Eixample and upper parts of town. Sadly, with reducing demand, theatres are in decline. The most famous, El Molino, has been forced to shut, although campaigners are striving to re-open it. However, for a global view of Barcelona check in the listings what's on and try a show:
Café Concert Llantiol, Riereta, 7 Tel: 93 329 9009.
City Hall, Rambla de Catalunya, 2 Tel: 93 317 2177.
Teatre Arnau, Avinguda Paral.lel, 60 Tel: 93 441 4881.

Jazzman, Roger de Flor, 238.
La Cova del Drac, Vallmajor, 33.

Rock/pop

Barcelona is on the itinerary of most major international tours. Booking for these is usually through banks and music shops, notably in Carrer de Tallers, just off La Rambla. FNAC in the Triangle shopping centre at Plaça de Catalunya sells tickets for most of the well-known groups performing. On a smaller scale, some interesting offbeat musicians and eternal old timers often pass through. Check the listings. Some key venues:
Bikini, Deu i Mata, 105. People still talk of the Bikini (on another site) where anyone who was anyone went. It reopened here a few years ago and now has a well selected, varied programme of live music – roots, soul and dance music.
La Paloma, Tigre, 27. Wonderful turn-of-the-20th-century dance hall, often used for jazz or world-music concerts.
Luz de Gas, Muntaner, 246. Formerly a music hall. A pretty place for concerts of many descriptions: jazz, ethnic, rock, soul and so on. It turns into a dance place later on but by then you can consider going elsewhere – it's not their forte.
Palau Sant Jordi, Montjuïc.
Razzmatazz, Almogàvers, 122. Important venue. The former Zeleste repackaged and relaunched. Different spaces including a club.
Sala Apolo/Club Nitsa, Nou de la Rambla, 113. Once a music hall, now a trendy club with music from visiting DJs as well as live events.

Salsa

Antilla Barcelona, Aragó, 141–143.
Sabor Cubano, Francisco Giner, 32.
Samba Brasil, Lepant, 297.

Celtic

The city's Irish pubs nearly all have live music sessions. Check the local listings.

Opera and ballet

Gran Teatre del Liceu
Rambla, 51–59
Iel: 93 485 9913/902 332 211 (tickets)
www.liceubarcelona.com.
Barcelona's opera house re-opened in 1999 having been rebuilt after a devastating fire. Despite better technology and more productions, it is still difficult to get tickets.

Contemporary dance

Local companies and visiting groups perform sporadically throughout the year. An important part of the Mercat de les Flors (see Theatre) programme, contemporary dance can also be seen at:
L'Espai
Travessera de Gràcia, 63
Tel: 93 414 3133.

Seasons at the Liceu (above) and the Teatre Nacional (below) and at outdoor locations during festivals.

Theatre

Naturally most theatre productions are in Catalan or Spanish, but for true enthusiasts the theatrical experience should compensate for language problems.
Among the main theatres are:
Artenbrut
Perill, 9–11.
A small-scale, cosy theatre with an interesting programme.
Circol Maldà
Pi, 5, Pral. 2ª
Intimate space in old palace for theatre, music and cabaret.
Lliure
Plaça Margarida Xirgu
Tel: 93 228 9747
www.teatrelliure.com.
Good contemporary productions.
Mercat de les Flors
Lleida, 59
Tel: 902 101 212.
This is the former flower market converted into a theatre complex. It has a very active programme with international groups, unusual productions and alternative music.
Poliorama
Rambla, 115
Tel: 93 317 7599.
Accessible theatre performances, including flamenco spectacles.
Romea
Hospital, 51
Tel: 93 301 5504.
Teatre Nacional de Catalunya
Plaça de les Arts
Tel: 93 306 5700
www.tnc.es.
Ricardo Bofill's neoclassical building is located next to the auditorium near Plaça de les Glòries. It has the space to stage large-scale productions and smaller workshops.
Victoria
Avinguda Paral·lel, 67.
Often stages musicals and ballet performances as well as flamenco spectacles.

Cinema

Barcelona has a great cinema-going tradition. Several cinemas show *versió original* films (VO in listings) – foreign films that have been subtitled rather than dubbed.

Most sessions begin around 4pm. The last and most popular screening will be around 10.30pm, although sometimes at weekends there will be a late-night show, called the *sesión de madrugada*.

Boliche, Avinguda Diagonal, 508. A cinema with four screens.

Casablanca, Passeig de Gràcia, 115.

Filmoteca de la Generalitat de Catalunya, Avinguda Sarrià, 33. A film theatre showing less commercial films and retrospectives.

Icària Yelmo, Salvador Espriu, 61. Fifteen screens.

Méliès Cinemas, Villaroel, 102. Golden oldies.

Renoir-Les Corts, Eugeni d'Ors, 12. Six screens.

Renoir Floridablanca, Floridablanca, 135. Same chain. more conveniently located. Seven screens.

Verdi, Verdi, 32. And, around the corner, **Verdi Park**, Torrijos, 49. Together they have nine screens. Interesting and reliable selection.

Arts Festivals

The Grec Festival, held from late June until early August, is Barcelona's biggest summer cultural event. It brings together a high standard of national and international talent in theatre, music and dance. Performances take place all over the city, but one of the most impressive and appealing venues on a summer night is the Grec Theatre itself, an outdoor amphitheatre on Montjuïc. For information and booking: Palau de la Virreina, Rambla, 99, tel: 93 301 7775 or call the city council information service, tel: 010.

The **Sitges Festival Interna-**cional de Cinema de Catalunya (www.cinemasitges.com) is a well-established annual event every winter.

NIGHTLIFE

Barcelona is internationally known as being the city that never sleeps. Wander down La Rambla after midnight, through the squares of Gràcia or drive across the city and it becomes obvious why. The streets are buzzing, and this is just the beginning: lounge bars are slowly filling and clubs have hardly opened their doors. Most people are still finishing dinner (restaurants tend to open from 9pm) having had a cocktail before, or they are having an after-dinner drink before finding a place to dance. When the clubs close between 3 and 5am there are still the "Afters", bars where the die-hards can continue the *juerga* until 8 or 9am.

This is the usual programme from Thursday to Saturday, though there is still plenty happening on other days of the week. It's easy to understand, especially in summer when 2am is the most cool and comfortable time of day, and the party spirit is infectious. Amazingly, the hard-working Catalans still make it to their offices bright and early the next day.

Bars

The range is infinite, from neon-lit local bars to the designer bars of the 1980s and 1990s, from milk bars to New Age cafés serving juices and infusions, *cocteleries* to *xampanyeries*, from bars with live music to dance halls, chill-out lounges to restaurants which transform into bars when the DJs move in after dinner. The only problem is making the choice, so it's best to follow the crowd who usually lead to the latest, most fashionable place of the week.

Here are some recommendations of old stalwarts mixed with new hot spots.

Pre-dinner bars

Almirall, Joaquim Costa, 33. Dark, enticing old *modernista* bar.

Berimbau, Passeig del Born, 17. Brazilian bar with stunning *caipirinhas* – the Brazilian cocktail you will never forget.

Boadas, Tallers, 1. A classic Barcelona cocktail bar. The cartooned figure of the original owner watches from highly polished walls while his elegant daughter mixes the snappiest Martinis and her waiters attend to your every need. Their *mojito*, Hemingway's Cuban favourite, is highly recommended.

Café del Sol, Plaça del Sol. Terrace on the square. A good start to an evening in the Gràcia district, with its many alternative bars and restaurants.

La Confiteria, Sant Pau, 128. Relaxed atmosphere and good sounds in this pretty bar housed in a former pastry shop.

Dry Martini, Aribau, 162. A large but cosy cocktail bar in which to ensconce yourself; choose between the green room or the red. Serves excellent Martinis.

PUBS

Highly successful among ex-pats and Catalans alike is the new wave of pubs, mostly Irish. Many have large-screen TVs for showing major sporting events.

Flann O'Brien's, Casanova, 264. An Irish pub, of course.

The Clansman, Vigatans, 13. Scottish pub with the malts to prove it.

The Fastnet, Passeig Joan de Borbó, 22. Well-positioned in Barceloneta, with football, Guinness and English pub food.

The Quiet Man, Marquès de Barberà, 11. An Irish pub selling draught Guinness. Good atmosphere and live music.

TRANSPORT

ACCOMMODATION

ACTIVITIES

A – Z

LANGUAGE

CASINOS

The Spanish are avid gamblers, and playing the various lotteries is a favourite pasttime. If you want to do some more serious gambling you have the following waiting for you:

Casino Castell de Perelada
Perelada
Tel: 972 53 8125.
In the province of Girona, 13 miles (20 km) from the French border.

Casino de Lloret de Mar
Girona
Tel: 972 366116.

Gran Casino de Barcelona
Marina, 19–21
Tel: 93 225 7878.

Els Quatre Gats, Montsió, 3. *Modernista* landmark, famous due to the artists, including Picasso, who frequented it at the turn of the 20th century. You can eat in the restaurant or just have drinks at the front.

Gimlet, Rec, 24. Very cool, small cocktail bar in the Born.

Margarita Blue, Josep Anselm Clavé, 6. You can eat Mexican food here both day and night but also come for evening drinks when the place will be buzzing.

Mirablau, Plaça Dr Andreu (at the foot of the Tibidabo funicular). Has a spectacular view over Barcelona day and night.

Pastis, Santa Mònica, 4. More than 40 years old, this small corner of Marseilles at the bottom of La Rambla offering *pastis* to the strains of Brel and Piaf, is a welcome alternative to the high-design and high-tech of bars elsewhere. Tango and live music some nights.

Rita Blue, Plaça Sant Agustí. Even buzzier than its older sister, Margarita Blue, serving Tex-Med food. Music in basement and large, pleasant terrace.

Snooker Club, Roger de Llúria, 42. This is an elegant, modern snooker club which is good for a cool cocktail or an after-dinner drink.

Post-dinner bars

Café Royale, Nou de Zambrano, 3. Cool lounge bar just off Plaça Reial.

El Salero, Rec, 60. *Salero* means salt cellar, and its white interior is one of the most beautiful spaces created in the city in recent years. Open until late.

Gimlet, Santaló, 46. Cocktails and slick, modern design.

London Bar, Nou de la Rambla, 34. Popular both with resident foreigners and a local crowd, this old bar with a marble counter and chandeliers gets more crowded and smokier the deeper you go into it. Regular live music on the tiny stage at the back provides entertainment.

Marsella, Sant Pau, 65. This was probably the last old bar with "No spitting and no singing" signs on the walls. It was popular with local people until some years ago, when it underwent changes. As the old locals expired it has become popular with a young, international crowd. Beware the absinthe.

Nick Havanna, Rosselló, 208. Once famed for its design and for the in-crowd it attracted, this is no longer the most fashionable place in town to go, but it's good value and gives an idea of the Barcelona "design bars" of the 1980s.

Rosebud, Adrià Margarit, 27. If you want a taste of the high life, this sophisticated place has magnificent views and a garden.

Torres de Avila, Poble Espanyol. An extravaganza created by designers Arribas and Mariscal (of Olympic mascot fame), showing Barcelona 90s design at its zenith. No longer as trendy as it once was.

Tres Torres, Via Augusta, 300. What was once a huge private house is now a flashy bar and beautifully lit building. There's no code in this smart drinking hole but you'll find a certain type of wealthy clientele here.

Universal, Marià Cubí, 184. Striking decor on three floors. Dark and loud for dancing downstairs. More refined upstairs where you can dine very well or drink in plush surroundings.

Even later bars & clubs

The "music boxes" of the Port Vell, Maremàgnum and the Olympic Port don't need much explanation. If you are after lots of coloured lights and pumping disco, you can just turn up and choose for yourself, since all are open to the street. Club venues are ever-changing. Check in the local listings for what's current, or better still, ask around.

Club Ommsession, Rosselló, 265. If you can't get to stay in the trendiest hotel in town, at least enjoy its club. Seriously cool.

Discotek, Poble Espanyol. A club with a lot of action in the Spanish Village on Montjuïc.

Dot, Nou de Sant Francesc, 7. Although small, Dot is very popular. In-house and visiting DJs play the best of current styles every night of the week. You can drink, dance and watch movies all at the same time.

KGB, Alegre de Dalt, 55. An old favourite going through a revival, with live music on Friday.

La Boîte, Avinguda Diagonal, 477. A medium-sized, intimate kind of club in the form of an underground box with glittery, 1970s style interior. Live bands (jazz/soul/funk, etc.) from midnight. DJs play very danceable music after they finish.

La Terraza, Avinguda Marquès de Comillas. This is up on Montjuïc, around the back of Poble Espanyol and a great summer venue. Dance to electronic music on the hill until the early hours of the morning, with a fashionable crowd.

Moog, Arc del Teatre, 3. Down an alleyway off La Rambla. This is another small place but very good for techno/electronic. You can dance until 5.30am if you so desire, and even later at weekends.

Otto Zutz, Lincoln, 15. One of the first designer-discos. Best after 2am. Occasional live music.

Salsitas, Nou de la Rambla, 22. One of the latest clubs where you can eat before you dance.
Zentraus, Rambla del Raval, 41. New dance club playing electronic music Tuesday–Saturday.

Tablaos

A *tablao* is a bar/restaurant that has a flamenco show. *Tablaos* are not strictly Catalan, but this import from Andalucía has become popular among Catalans to the point of being trendy. It is advisable to confirm the times of the shows and whether or not dinner is obligatory.
El Patio Andaluz, Aribau, 242. Tel: 93 209 3378.
El Tablao Cordobés, La Rambla, 35. Tel: 93 317 5711.
El Tablao de Carmen, Arcs, 9, Poble Espanyol. Tel: 93 325 6895. A good authentic show and reasonable dinner.
Los Tarantos, Plaça Reial, 17. Tel: 93 318 3067. Stylishly refurbished. One of the most genuine shows.
Sala Rocería Los Almonteños Elkano, 67. Tel: 93 443 2431.

Dance Halls

Cibeles, Còrsega, 363. Becomes the Mond Club from midnight–6am on Friday.
La Paloma, Tigre, 27. Tel: 93 301 6897. A Barcelona classic. Orchestra plays on Thursday to Sunday nights. Sessions from 6–9.30pm and 11.30pm–3.30am. Both these traditional dance halls bring in the DJs after 2am at weekends for the young crowd.

The Gay Scene

If you start off with these places you'll soon get to know where all the rest are.
Arena, Diputació, 233. A lively, easy-going club in the heart of the Gayxample – the name given to this part of the Eixample, full of cool gay bars and clubs.
Bahia, Sèneca, 12. Warm and friendly lesbian bar with good music.
Metro, Sepúlveda 185. A well-known gay club. Best after 1.30am.

SHOPPING

What to Buy

As Europe rapidly becomes one entity and most goods are available in most countries, the bargain that cannot be found back home is a rarity. However, for certain products the choice is much wider, and anything bought abroad is a nice souvenir once the holiday is over.

If you can't face trudging home with virgin olive oil, or fear your holiday budget will disappear if you venture into leather at Loewe, it is still worth seeing the spectacle of the food markets and doing some serious window shopping while in Barcelona.

Shopping Areas

The entire length of Passeig de Gràcia, the Rambla de Catalunya and the interconnecting streets provide enjoyable shopping, ranging from chain stores to top fashion and individual boutiques. The same goes for the Barri Gòtic, now studded with artisanal

SHOPPING HOURS

Most shops open between 9 and 10am and close for lunch between 1 and 2pm, opening again between 4 and 5pm until 8pm. Many clothes and food shops close at 8.30 or 9pm. The large department stores, chain stores and shopping galleries remain open through lunchtime. In the summer smaller shops may close on Saturday afternoon. Only bakeries, pastry shops and a few groceries are open on Sunday (until 3pm).

shops, galleries and trendy souvenirs, and bursting with hip clothes shops, particularly in the Born area. The Avinguda Diagonal, from the top of Rambla de Catalunya up to the roundabout which forms Plaça Francesc Macià, and the streets behind are good for fashion, but they are expensive.

The upper parts of town have their own local district atmosphere and make a refreshing change. Try Muntaner, around the FGC station. One of the best shoe shops in town, Las Maravillas, is at No. 356, and further up is Groc, Toni Miró's shop. If you need a break, good wines by the glass accompany delicate snacks in the Tivoli at No. 361. Gràcia is a relaxed and charming place to shop, with good young designer-fashion and jewellery.

Department Stores and Shopping Malls

The largest department store in Barcelona is **El Corte Inglés**, with a branch in Plaça de Catalunya, another in nearby Portal de l'Angel specialising in leisure, music, books and sports, and others in Avinguda Diagonal. All branches are open Monday–Saturday 10am–10pm. The Plaça de Catalunya and Diagonal (No. 617) branches have excellent supermarkets.

The main shopping centres and malls are:
La Avenida, Rambla de Catalunya, 121.
Barcelona Glòries, Plaça de les Glòries.
Bulevard Rosa (3 locations), Passeig de Gràcia, 55; Diagonal, 474; Diagonal, 609–15. Smaller, more individual shops.
Diagonal Mar, Avinguda Diagonal, 3. A huge complex in a new residential district by the sea, with the usual shops. Large play area for kids.
Galeries Maldà, Portaferrissa, 22.
L'Illa, Avinguda Diagonal, 545. Superior shopping centre for the uptown crowd.

TRANSPORT

ACCOMMODATION

ACTIVITIES

A – Z

LANGUAGE

Maremàgnum, Moll d'Espanya. Shops here are open until 11pm. **El Triangle**. A large development in Plaça de Catalunya including Habitat and FNAC (huge book and music store).

For out-of-hours shopping the best bets are:

7–11, Plaça Urquinaona. Open 7am–3am every day. Good for Sunday shopping.

VIP's, Rambla de Catalunya, 7–9. Open daily 8–2am, until 3am Thursday–Saturday.

Markets

There are covered markets in every district of the city selling fruit, vegetables, meat and fish. A trip to Barcelona would be incomplete without visiting at least one of them. Markets open every day except Sunday from early morning until around 3pm. Avoid Monday; the selection is poor because the central wholesale market does not open.

The largest and most colourful market is the Boqueria on La Rambla, which stays open until 8pm Monday–Saturday. The most exotic and expensive fare is in the entrance; the bargains are to be found in the maze of stalls behind, especially from the local farmers in the adjoining Plaça Sant Galdric.

Book and antique fairs are held with great regularity in Barcelona: look out for posters or announcements in the press.

Other regular markets of interest are:

Coin and stamp market, Plaça Reial. Sunday 9am–2.30pm.

Coin, video games and book market, Mercat Sant Antoni. Sunday 9am–2pm. Attractive market building on the junction of Carrer de Tamarit/Comte d'Urgell.

Els Encants, Plaça de les Glòries. This is a genuine flea market. There are some expensive antiques, some old clothes, and a lot of trash, but among it all bargains can still be found. It gets very hot in the summer, so early morning is better both for bargains and comfort. Open: Monday, Wednesday, Friday and Saturday 8am–7pm (winter) and until 8pm (summer).

Mercat de Concepció, València, between Carrer de Bruc and Carrer de Girona. In this neighbourhood market you can see how Barcelona mixes new design with old.

Mercat Gòtic d'Antiguitats, Avinguda Catedral. Antique market every Thursday. Some interesting collections.

Moll de Drassanes. Weekend bric-a-brac market, by the sea.

Clothes

Leather

It is questionable whether leather garments are still worth buying in Spain, except perhaps at the top end of the market, where design and quality are outstanding. But shoes, handbags and suitcases are worth considering. The best in clothes, bags and accessories is **Loewe**, based in Madrid but with an important and sumptuous branch in Casa Lleó Morera (Passeig de Gràcia, 35).

There are many other shops specialising in leather. **Yanko**, Passeig de Gràcia, 95, is Spanish and specialises in shoes and jackets. Nowhere near as expensive as Loewe, but still pricey.

Cheaper, often good-value leather shops can be found particularly in and around La Rambla and Portal de l'Angel, some of them in strange first-floor surroundings selling at factory prices.

Shoes

These are good value. Look out for Catalan and Spanish designers such as **Yanko** (address above) and **Farrutx** (Rosselló, 218) which trade on sophisticated elegance. **Lotusse** (contemporary classical and very well made) and **Camper** (trendy, comfortable) can be found

---

THE BEST OF BARCELONA DESIGN

Much of Barcelona's stylish image rests upon its reputation for design. To get an idea of how trendy Barcelonans decorate their homes, all you need to do is take a trip around the first floor of **Vinçon**, considered the temple of interior design, at Passeig de Gràcia, 96.

Other design shops in the Eixample include:

Bd Ediciones de Diseño, Mallorca 291. Top designers' work, from Gaudí to Tusquets, in a stunning, *modernista* setting.

Biosca & Botey, Rambla de Catalunya, 129. Noteworthy

among hordes of lighting shops.

Dom, Passeig de Gràcia, 76. Inexpensive fun design.

Dos i Una, Rosselló, 275. Smaller lines include David Valls socks, Mariscal earrings and gimmicks to help solve gift problems.

En Línea Barcelona, Còrsega, 299. Beautiful Spanish and Italian furniture.

Pilma, just around the corner in Avinguda Diagonal, 403.

Among the design shops in the old town are:

Aspectos, Rec, 28. Owner

Camilla Hamm sells tasteful furniture and accessories by both international names and new, innovative designers. Very high prices though.

Ici et Là, Plaça Santa Maria del Mar, 2. More furniture and bits and bobs which are bright, humorous, and which reflect Barcelona's wacky alter ego.

MACBA, Plaça des Angels. The shop of the Contemporary Art Museum is an inspiration.

Matirile, Passeig del Born, 24. One-off lamps made to order, using both new and recycled materials.

at Tascón (branches in Passeig de Gràcia and the Born) or its own shops in Pelai, València, just off Passeig de Gràcia and Elisabets in El Raval. Another local designer, **Muxart** (Rambla de Catalunya, 47, or Rosselló, 230), is wild and wonderful. The best areas for shoes and bags are Portal de l'Angel, Rambla de Catalunya, Passeig de Gràcia, Diagonal and the malls.

Top fashion

Toni Miró is by far the most famous Catalan designer of men's and women's wear, and his clothes are somehow representative of how the middle classes like to dress. They are characterised by their clean lines and subtlety (verging on the inconspicuous or sombre). His shops called **Groc** are at Rambla de Catalunya, 100, and Muntaner, 385. An **Antonio Miró** is at Consell de Cent, 349.

Other designer names are:
Adolfo Dominguez, Passeig de Gràcia, 32.
David Valls, València, 235.
Jean Pierre Bua, Avinguda Diagonal, 469. Good range of international labels for men and women.
José Tomas, Mallorca, 242.
Lydia Delgado, Minerva, 21.
Noténom, Pau Clarís, 159.
On Land, València, 273.
Purificación Garcia, Passeig de Gràcia, 21.
Roser i Francesc, València, 285.

Cheaper fashion

The two biggest fashion stores are **Zara** and **Mango**, with branches all over the city. In the old town, Portaferrissa and Portal de l'Angel are good for young fashion. On and around Carrer Avinyó there are a lot of trendy shops, such as **Loft Avignon**, and El Born is now brimming with boutiques. El Raval is catching up fast: Caníbal, Carmé, 5, has fun, one-off designs, and Riera Baixa is full of second-hand clothes boutiques.

In **El Mercadillo** and **Gralla Hall**, both on Portaferrissa, you can spend some happy hours flitting from shop to shop. The former is cheaper and more

alternative, the latter geared more towards smarter, or club clothing. Both places were old palaces and fun to visit whether you buy or not. When you've had enough, go for a drink or meal on the terrace upstairs at the back of El Mercadillo – such inner patios are scarce and a rare treat.

Food

A taste of Spain back home always extends the holiday. Olives marinated in garlic direct from the market, sausages *(chorizo and sobrasada)*, ham *(jabugo* is the best), cheese (Manchego, Mahon, Idiazabal), nuts, dried fruit and handmade chocolates are all easy to carry. Virgin olive oil, wine, *cava* and *moscatel* are less portable, but still worth the effort. Buy from the markets or *colmados* (grocer's shops, on street corners in every district of the city). Some prime sites for purchasing are:
Casa Gispert, Sombrerers, 23. A lovely old shop selling dried fruits, grains and coffees in sacks, as well as preserves and other delicacies.
Colmado Quilez, Rambla de Catalunya, 63. Another excellent, well-stocked and gorgeous old shop full of delicacies.
El Magnifico, Argenteria, 64. Experts in coffee. They stock a vast range, including the best beans.
Escribà, La Rambla, 83. The family of the late Antoni Escribà, famous chocolate "sculptor" who died in September 2004, continue the tradition in this beautiful shop. They certainly know what they're doing.
Fargas, Boters, 2 (corner of Pi and Cucurulla). For chocolates, sweets and *turrones (see under Planelles Donat below).* Decorative old shop.
La Seu, Dagueria, 16. Seasonal additive-free farmhouse cheeses from all regions of Spain. The Scots owner allows you access to the walk-in fridges; she lets you taste before you buy and provides printed information on

every variety. What you purchase will be packed specially for travel. She also sells the best, most natural olive oils.
Múrria, Roger de Llúria, 85. The shop name should remind you of the street name; or vice versa. This is where you will find the most seriously exquisite selection of foodstuffs in the prettiest of old *modernista* interiors. They have their own *cava* label as well.
Planelles Donat, Portal de l'Angel, 27 (and other branches). Specialists in *turrón* (a sticky nougat-type delicacy traditionally eaten at Christmas). Good ice cream in summer.
Xocoa, Petritxol, 11. Innovative contemporary chocolates, made in Catalonia, with flavours like "five peppers" or "thyme".

Drink

Vila Viniteca, Agullers, 7–9. A magnificent range of fine wines and spirits.
Xampany, València, 200. For serious purchasers of *cava*, with more than 100 types. Also *cava* accessories and memorabilia.

Traditional Crafts

Barcelona has many small shops specialising in traditional crafts.

TRANSPORT ACCOMMODATION ACTIVITIES A–Z LANGUAGE

Whether you are looking for lace, feathers, fans or religious artefacts, there is sure to be someone somewhere making it. Or you may, perhaps, want to commission a guitar, a walking stick or a lightning conductor. The best areas to try are the Barri Gòtic, around the Born or on Carrer de l'Hospital and Carrer del Carme. Many shops are more than 100 years old.

The Generalitat runs the **Centre Català d'Artesania**, Passeig de Gràcia, 55, an exhibition centre with permanent displays, temporary shows, information and a shop.

Shoes

Calçats Solé, Ample, 7. For really original footwear, sturdy leather boots, Mallorcan sandals or rustic shoes from different parts of Spain.

La Manual Alpargatera, Avinyó, 7. A huge variety of *alpargatas*, the classic rope-soled canvas shoes of old Spain. See them being made and choose your preferred design.

Antiques and books

There are many elegant and expensive antique shops in the Eixample and the Barri Gòtic, notably the streets Banys Nous and Palla. Prints and antique books are also a feature of Barcelona, particularly in the labyrinth of pretty streets around the Cathedral.

Librería Violán, just off the Plaça del Rei. Unusual books, prints and striking art deco posters.

Candles

From religious to decorative, candles are quite a speciality of Barcelona. There are several shops near the Cathedral, notably **Cereria Subirá**, Baixada Llibreteria, 7, founded in 1762.

Ceramics

From earthenware cooking pots to elegant dishes or hand-painted tiles, ceramics can be found all over the city, particularly in the Barri Gòtic, at **Molsa** in Plaça Sant Josep Oriol (who also have some antique pots) and **La Caixa de Fang** in Carrer de Freneria. Traditional ironmongers *(ferreterías)* usually have a good collection of the classic brown-earthenware cooking pots at non-tourist prices, as well as wonderful cooking utensils.

Wickerwork

A rustic chair may not be very manageable on a charter flight, but a basket or a mat is easy to carry and will make a good present. Look on the corner of Carrer de Banys Nous and Carrer Ave Maria. Also:

Taller de Cistelleria, Amargós, 16. Even more manageable for transport are these miniature versions of traditional baskets from Catalonia, made by a friendly elderly lady. She also sells normal-sized baskets, but the miniatures are particularly popular.

Lace and fabrics

A dying art, but still popular. Many old shops, with beautiful exteriors, are still dotted around the city.

Casa Oliveres, Dagueria, 11. Full of antique treasures. Specialises in lace and will produce to order.

Coses de Casa, Plaça Sant Josep Oriol, 5. Hand-woven Mallorquín fabrics.

Dona, Provença, 256. Embroidery and embroidery kits.

Rose Mary, Calaf, 4. White linen, bedclothes, tablecloths and towels with elaborate details.

Taller de Lencería, Rosselló, 271. Linen with handmade lace borders.

Glass

Bells i Oficis, Palla, 15. Many choice pieces. They have their own resident designers.

Espai Vidre, Angels, 8. International and Spanish modern glass design plus interesting exhibitions.

Handmade paper

Papirum, Baixada Llibreteria, 2. Handmade paper and notebooks of all sizes. They are not cheap but are beautiful and make great gifts.

Tarlatana, Comtessa de Sobradiel, 2. Marbled papers and bookbinding.

Gloves, shawls and fans

Almacenes del Pilar, Boqueria, 43. Traditional *mantillas* and shawls.

Alonso, Santa Anna, 27. Leather (and other) gloves in the winter; fans in the summer. A beautiful little treasure trove.

Guantes Ramblas, La Rambla, 132. Maybe you'll find those leather gloves *here*; or a wallet or a bag.

BELOW: bric-a-brac for sale at the Thursday market on Avinguda Catedral.

Paraguas, La Rambla, 104. Umbrellas and fans.

Hats

Mil, Fontanella, 20. Supplies of old and new types of headdress.
Sombreria Obach, Call, 2. Hats of many descriptions, mainly traditional (e.g. berets).

Jewellery

For more conventional or very pricey pieces, look on Passeig de Gràcia (e.g. J. Roca, at No. 18), Rambla de Catalunya or many other Eixample streets. In the centre you can find numerous tiny jewellery shops; often they occupy only the entrance of a building, with most of their wares in the window display. For something a bit different, try:
Forum Ferlandina, Ferlandina, 31. Specialises in avant-garde gold and silver jewellery.
Hipòtesi, Rambla de Catalunya, 105. A good, varied range of fine, modern pieces by artists, but not overpriced.
Joaquín Berao, Rosselló, 277. Designer-items with a very individual stamp: smooth and chunky. Only the best materials used.

Knives

Ganiveteria Roca, Plaça del Pi. Impressive window displays, and inside you will find virtually every kind of cutting instrument for domestic use. Or you might like a Spanish-style pen knife for outdoor use.

Toys

A cluster of toy shops can be found leading off either side of Plaça del Pi. The most original of these is **El Ingenio**, at Carrer Rauric, 6–8.

Bookshops

Ancora y Delfin, Diagonal 564.
Altair, Gran Via 616.
BCN Books, Rocaford, 225.
Casa del Llibre, Paseo de Gracia, 62.
Central, Elisabets, 6. Atmospheric bookshop in a former chapel. Small English section, but great for browsing. There's music and a café, too.
Col·legi d'Arquitectes, Plaça Nova, 5. Well-supplied bookshop specialising in architecture and design.
Documenta, Cardenal Casañas, 4. Generally good bookshop.
FNAC, El Triangle, Plaça de Catalunya. Has stocks of English books for adults and children.
Interlibro, Rda del General Mitre, 211.
Kowasa, Mallorca, 235. Photography books only, displayed in a chic space. Wide selection.
Laie Llibreria Cafè, Pau Claris, 85. A good-looking bookshop selling mostly art and media books, and literature. There is a good café/restaurant upstairs. Also has a branch in the CCCB (Contemporary Culture Centre).
Quera, Petritxol, 2. Specialists in maps of Catalonia.
Tartessos, Canuda, 35. Stocks a little bit of everything but a lot of photography. The collection is cosmopolitan, and they also stage small photographic shows at the back.

SWIMMING POOLS

When you just can't face another tourist site and the summer crowds have got too much, a dip in a pool can be the perfect antidote to city fatigue. In and around Barcelona there are plenty to choose from; here is a selection:

Club Natació Atlètic Barceloneta
Plaça del Mar
Tel: 93 221 0010.
Large indoor pool overlooking the sea, and two outdoor pools. Well equipped.

Parc de la Creueta del Coll
Mare de Deu del Coll, 87
Tel: 93 211 3599.
Large outdoor pool/lake, in one of Barcelona's new urban parks, complete with Eduardo Chillida sculpture. Boats can be hired in the winter. Swimming: June to end of August Monday–Friday 10am–4pm, Sunday and holidays 10am–7pm. Ideal for small children.

Piscinas Bernat Picornell
Avinguda de l'Estadi, 30–40
Tel: 93 423 4041.
Olympic pool in a beautiful location on Montjuïc.

Piscina Municipal Can Felipa
Pallars, 277
Tel: 93 308 6047.
Two indoor pools in a stylishly renovated old factory – now a community centre – in Poble Nou. Easy to reach by metro.

Piscina Municipal Montjuïc
Avinguda Miramar, 31
Tel: 93 443 0046.
Two pools with a superb, panoramic view. The Olympic diving events took place here, against the dramatic backdrop of the city.

SPORT

Participant Sports

The city council has been very active in providing sports facilities to the community. Some are the legacy of the Olympic Games.

Bowling

Namco Bowling
Diagonal Mar
Tel: 93 356 2500.
In the new shopping centre.
Open: Sunday–Thursday noon–midnight; Friday–Saturday noon–3am.

Pedralbes Bowling
Avinguda Doctor Marañón, 11
Tel: 93 333 0352.
Open: Sunday–Thursday 10am–2am, and until 4am on Friday–Saturday.

Cycling

Cycling is becoming more popular in Barcelona. The city council issues a guide/map which is available in tourist offices. It

TRANSPORT

ACCOMMODATION

ACTIVITIES

A – Z

LANGUAGE

FOOTBALL

Football is close to a religion in Barcelona. When the favourite local team, Barça is playing, you will know all about it: firstly from the traffic jams to get to the match or to the television; secondly because the town goes silent; and thirdly thanks to the explosion of fireworks, car horns and bugles following a victory.

Fútbol Club Barcelona, Arístides Maillol, tel: 93 496 3600. The stadium, Nou Camp, is one of the largest stadiums in the world, and has a museum that can be visited.

shows suggested routes and bike lanes, and gives advice on taking bicycles on public transport.

Bicycles can be hired at the following places:

Barcelona by Bicycle
Esparteria, 3
Tel: 93 268 2105
www.biketoursbarcelona.com.
Accompanied cycling tours of the old town, with a meal included in the price. Also has bicycles and skates for hire.

Bici-clot
Passeig Marítim. On the beach near the Olympic Village, great for waterfront cycle rides.

Classic Bikes
Tallers, 45
Tel: 93 317 1970
www.barcelonarentbikes.com.
Classic and folding bikes in a central location.

Filicletos
Passeig de Picasso, 40
Tel: 93 319 7885.
Bicycles, tandems and child seats for hire. Open weekends and holidays 10am–dusk. Easy access to Parc de la Ciutadella, the port and the beach.

Icària Sports
Avinguda Icària, 180
Tel: 93 221 1778.

Mike's Bike Tours
Plaça George Orwell
Tel: 93 301 3612.
City tours on US bicycles.

Scenic
Marina, 22
Tel: 93 221 1666.

Golf

There are many courses all over Catalonia (see full list on www.gencat.net/probert). To play, it is essential to prove membership of a recognised club. Weekend fees are usually double the weekday fee. Three courses close to Barcelona are:

El Prat
El Prat de Llobregat
Tel: 93 379 0278.
A premier course, often host to international competitions. Hire of clubs and trolleys.

Sant Cugat
Sant Cugat del Vallès
Tel: 93 674 3908.
Bar, restaurant, swimming pool. Hire of clubs and trolleys. Closed on Monday.

Terramar
Sitges
Tel: 93 894 0580.
Hire of clubs and trolleys. Open all year.

Horse riding

Hípica Sant Cugat
Finca La Palleria, Avinguda Corts Catalanes, Sant Cugat.
Tel: 93 674 8385.
Bus from Sant Cugat to Cerdanyola will drop you off. Excursions from one hour to the whole day in the Collserola hills.

Skiing

During the season cheap weekend excursions are available from Barcelona to the Pyrenean resorts, some of which can be reached by train (check out www.lamolina.com).

Tennis

ClubVall Parc
Carretera de l'Arrabassada, 97
Tel: 93 212 6789.
Courts open: 8am–midnight. Quite expensive.

Water sports

Agencia de Viajes Tuareg
Consell de Cent, 378.

If you fancy a change from sightseeing, hire a deluxe yacht, with or without a captain. Also offers organised boat trips near and far.

Base Nautica de la Mar Bella
Espigó del Ferrocarril
Platja de Bogatell, Avinguda Litoral
Tel. 93 221 0432.
All types of boats for hire by qualified sailors. Sailing courses for the inexperienced. Windsurf hire.

Orsom
Tel: 93 441 0537
www.barcelona-orsam.com.
Hourly and daily sails or charters in this enormous catamaran.

Spectator Sports

Check the weekly entertainment guides or the sports magazines like *El Mundo Deportivo* for a full calendar of events. The daily papers also have good sports coverage.

Most local fiestas have various sporting activities as part of their programme, notably the Barcelona fiesta of La Mercè at the end of September.

American football

The **Barcelona Dragons** play in the Olympic Stadium during the summer season. The ticket booth is in Plaça Universitat, or buy tickets from Servicaixa machines.

SPORTS CENTRE

Can Caralleu sports centre (tel: 93 204 6905) is in an attractive location on the hill of Tibidabo. It has tennis courts, a *frontón* (a wall against which you play the Basque game of *pelota*), volleyball courts and two swimming pools.

Indoor facilities are open to the public Mon–Fri 8–10am and 2–3.30pm, Sun 10am–1pm. Outdoor facilities are open from mid-June to mid-September, 10am–5pm. Tennis courts are available 8am–11pm.

To get there, take bus 94 from Tres Torres/Via Augusta.

Basketball

Basketball is gaining as ardent a following as football. The Barça basketball team is part of the football club and matches are played in the Palau Blaugrana, next to Nou Camp, tel: 93 496 3600.

Motor racing

A new racing track, Catalunya Circuit, was opened in 1991 about 20 km (12 miles) from Barcelona, in Montmeló. For information, tel: 93 571 9700.

Tennis

The Conde de Godó trophy is an annual event at the Real Club de Tenis Barcelona, Bosch i Gimpera, 5, tel: 93 203 7852.

CHILDREN'S ACTIVITIES

Barcelona, like everywhere else in Spain, or Southern Europe for that matter, is very child-friendly, and there will be few places where kids will be excluded. Spanish children are allowed to stay up much later than elsewhere, particularly in the summer months. Eating out is quite easy with children; the variety of local food means that there will always be something to appeal to a child's palate.

However, take care with children when out in Barcelona. Busy roads and inconsiderate drivers call for extra care. You can escape from the traffic in the old town, where there are many pedestrianised streets. The city's beaches are obviously wonderful options for kids, as for anyone else. When you really need to let them run wild take the 10-minute train ride to the Parc de Collserola (see page 178).

Attractions for children

Attractions designed for children include:
L'Aquàrium de Barcelona
Moll d'Espanya, Port Vell

Tel: 93 221 7474.
The biggest crowd-puller in the city.
Parc Zoologic
Tel: 93 221 2506.
Enter via the Parc de la Ciutadella or Carrer Wellington if you're coming from the seafront. Don't miss the dolphin show.
Tibidabo Funfair
Parc d'Atraccions de Tibidabo
Plaça del Tibidabo
Tel: 93 211 79 42.
A good old-fashioned funfair. Take the FGC train, then get the little blue tram (an attraction in itself) and the funicular to the top of the hill.
Parc de la Ciutadella
Apart from open green spaces for riding bikes or just letting off steam, and a play park to keep toddlers amused, boats can be hired on the pond, and rocks studied in the Museu de la Geologia, tel: 93 319 6895.
Skating
Roger de Flor, 168
Tel: 93 245 2800.
A popular ice-skating rink that's equally good for tiring out the kids and cooling off the parents.
Museums may not always

attract children, but those listed below should appeal to a young audience:
Cosmo Caixa
Teodor Roviralta, 55
Tel: 93 212 6050.
The newly renovated science museum is magnificent.
Museu de Cera
Passatge de la Banca, 7
Tel: 93 317 2649.
The waxworks museum is usually a hit with older chilren.
Museu Marítim
Avda de les Drassanes
Tel: 93 318 3245.
Lots of vessels from different ages, as well as a modern Olympic winner.
Places further afield:
Illa de Fantasia
Finca Mas Brassó, Vilassar de Dalt
Tel: 93 751 4553.
An aquatic park 24km (15 miles) from Barcelona in Premià de Mar.
Port Aventura
near Tarragona
108km (67 miles) from Barcelona
Tel: 977 77 9090.
A theme park based on five world locations: the Mediterranean, Mexico, the Wild West, China and Polynesia.

BELOW: Tibidabo funfair on the summit of Collserola.

A - Z

A HANDY SUMMARY OF PRACTICAL INFORMATION, ARRANGED ALPHABETICALLY

A dmission Charges

Most museums have an entry charge ranging from €4 to €7 for the main ones and as little as €2 for the smaller ones. They have the usual reductions for students, pensioners and the unemployed and many are free or reduced one day each month, often the first Sunday of the month. An Articket (€15) allows entry to six key museums: MNAC, Fundació Miró, Fundació Tàpies, CCCB, MACBA, and the Centre Cultural de la Caixa Catalunya/La Pedrera. The tickets are available from tourist offices, from one of the relevant centres or through Tel-Entrada Caixa Catalunya, tel: 902 101 212 (from abroad tel: +34 933 262 946), www.telentrada.com.

Some cultural centres have free entry – the Caixa Forum, Centre d'Art Santa Mònica and the Casa Asia – or only charge for some exhibitions, like the Palau de la Virreina.

People eligible for discounts should carry evidence of their identity.

B udgeting for Your Trip

Gone are the days of cheap holidays in Spain. What you save on budget flights can easily be spent on meals, accommodation, shopping and clubbing. Accommodation is the main culprit, although for budget travellers there are hostels where beds are available in dormitories from €14. Self-catering is

now widely available and is a good solution for families; shopping in the market is an experience and an obvious saving.

Good restaurants are expensive but usually better value and quality than in northern Europe. Bargain hunters should opt for a set menu, available at lunchtime, still excellent value at anything from €6–15.

The dangerous thing about shopping is the temptation to excess, as generally fashion items and some household goods are slightly cheaper than northern Europe, but probably not the USA (see Shopping, page 219).

Cinema tickets cost from €5–8, with discounts on certain days of the week, usually Monday or Wednesday. Check listings in the daily press.

Public transport is good value with a metro/bus T-10 card for 10 journeys at €6, and similar cards available for train travel around Barcelona. Taxis are not prohibitively expensive: a short journey within the centre could be as little as €3, but the fare quickly rises on longer journeys and when stuck in the frequent traffic jams.

One option for serious travellers who intend to cover a lot of ground in a short stay is the Barcelona Card, a ticket valid for anything from one to five days which gives free public transport and entry or discounts on museums, some leisure centres, some restaurants, bars and shops. An adult card for one day is €17 and for five €27.

Low-budget travellers can take comfort from the fact that, Barcelona being a Mediterranean city, life on the streets is free and endlessly entertaining, and no one charges for basking in the sun or swimming at the city's many beaches.

Business Hours

In general, offices are open 9am–2pm and 4–8pm, although some open earlier, close later and have shorter lunch breaks. Most official authorities are open 8am–2pm and close to the public in the afternoon. Companies in the outer industrial zones tend to close at 6pm. From mid-June to mid-September many businesses practise *horas intensivas* from 8am–3pm in order to avoid the hottest part of the day and to get away early on a Friday.

C limate and Clothing

Average temperature: 10°C (54°F) in winter, 25°C (75°F) in summer. December and January have the lowest temperatures, though the cold is often accompanied by bright sunshine.

Rains tend to fall in November

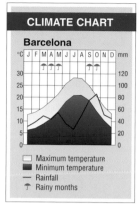

CLIMATE CHART
Barcelona

□ Maximum temperature
■ Minimum temperature
— Rainfall
☂ Rainy months

and February to March. Spring and autumn are pleasant with mild, sunny days. July and August are hot and aggravated by humidity. There are 2,500 hours of sunlight a year.

What to wear

Catalan men and women dress elegantly, though casually. Ties are worn in formal situations and some offices, but not to go out to dinner. In July and August cotton and loose-fitting garments are necessary. Respect local traditions: bathing costumes and bikinis are strictly for the beach. A light jacket is useful any time of the year. In winter, bring a warm jacket which can accommodate various layers, especially in January and February, when the wind blows. Be sure to bring comfortable shoes – Barcelona is a very walkable city.

Consulates

Australia
Gran Via Carles III, 98, 9°
Tel: 93 330 9496
Fax: 93 411 0904.
Canada
Elisenda de Pinós, 10
Tel: 93 204 2700
Fax: 93 204 2701.
Ireland
Gran Via Carles III, 94
Tel: 93 491 5021
Fax: 93 411 2921.

United Kingdom
Avinguda Diagonal, 477, 13°
Tel: 93 366 62 00
Fax: 93 366 62 21.
United States
Passeig Reina Elisenda, 23
Tel: 93 280 2227
Fax: 93 205 5206.

Crime and Safety

Take care, as in any large city. Loosely swinging handbags, ostentatious cameras and even rucksacks are regularly snatched in broad daylight. But do not be alarmed: Barcelona is not a den of iniquity, and with due care and attention, and some common sense, you can avoid dangerous situations.

The old town has a bad reputation for petty crime, so be aware when wandering through it or watching street artists. Wear your handbag across your chest, keep your camera hidden and do not flash your wallet around. Carry enough money for the day, leaving the rest in the safe-deposit box at your hotel.

At airport, railway and bus stations, keep your luggage together and don't leave it unattended. Never leave anything valuable in a car, especially radios, even in a crowded street.

Don't get caught by a few small gangs who perpetrate various tricks to waylay you, like commenting on the dirt on your back and, while "helping" you to remove it, slip the purse from your pocket. Another is a game known as *trila*, a variation of the three-card trick, played by crooks, regulars on La Rambla, in the guise of innocent bystanders. When travelling by car, be careful at traffic lights: a familiar scam is where one person causes a diversion while the other pinches your bag from the back seat, or slashes your tyres.

In the case of a theft, assault or loss, call the general emergency number, 112. You will probably be advised to go to a police station to make a statement

TRANSPORT

ACCOMMODATION

ACTIVITIES

NIA

LANGUAGE

(denuncia). This is vital if you want to claim on an insurance policy or seek further help from the City Police or your consulate.

The main police station is at Nou de la Rambla, 76.

Police

There are three main types of police:

Policia Municipal. Tel: 092. The City Police, known as the Guàrdia Urbana, are responsible for traffic, civilian care and security. They are recognisable by the blue-and-white checked band around their caps and on their vehicles.

Policia Nacional. Tel: 091. The State Police, who wear navy-blue uniforms, are responsible for law and order and civilian security.

Mossos d'Esquadra. Tel: 088. The autonomous police of Catalonia, who, by the end of 2005, will have taken over all responsibilities from the State Police in Catalonia.

Assistance for tourists

The City Police have a special scheme for tourists, at their headquarters (La Rambla, 43, 7am–noon; 7am–2am in summer), offering legal advice, medical assistance, provision of temporary documents in the event of loss or robbery and an international telephone line for the speedy cancellation of credit cards, etc. There is usually someone there who can speak one of the following languages: French, English, German, Italian and Russian.

The general emergency number, 112, can attend to calls in English, French and German.

Customs

Visitors can bring reasonable quantities of cigarettes (300 for EU residents, 200 for the rest of Europe and 400 for non-Europeans), and limited amounts of alcoholic beverages, perfume, coffee and tea. If your camera, computer, etc. is new and you do not have the purchase receipt, it is wise to ask a customs official

to certify that you brought it into the country with you.

Pets may be brought with you if you have a health certificate for the animal, signed by an officially recognised vet from the country of origin and indicating the dates of the last vaccines, most importantly an anti-rabies shot.

Animals are not allowed in restaurants, cafés and food shops.

D isabled Travellers

The city has 158 hotels equipped with facilities for people with disabilities. These can be found at www.bcn.es/turisme or through the tourist office, tel: 93 285 3834. Twenty-eight city museums are wheelchair accessible, as are many public and historic buildings; a complete listing can be found on www.bcn.es/cultura by clicking into the Directories category.

All six of the beaches have suitable access and there are 14 adapted public toilets.

Public transport: some bus and metro lines have disabled facilities; for details click on Transport for Everyone at www.tmb.net.

Car rental: with advance warning Hertz can provide automatic cars.

Taxi service: tel: +34 93 420 8088 for information.

For further information see www.tourspain.co.uk/disabled. For enquiries about services available in Barcelona, contact: Institut Municipal de Persones amb Disminució, Diagonal 233, 08013 Barcelona, tel: 93 413 2775 or sap@mail.bcn.es.

E lectricity

British plugs do not fit Spanish sockets, because wall sockets for shavers, hairdryers, etc. take plugs with two round pins, so British visitors should bring an adaptor, which can be bought at supermarkets, chemists and airports. The voltage is 220v, so US visitors with 110v appliances will need a transformer.

Emergencies

In an emergency go to the "Urgencies" department at one of the main hospitals, or visit an ambulatorio (medical centre). They can be found in every district – ask in any pharmacy for the nearest one.

Hospitals

Hospital Clínic
Carrer de Casanova, 143
Tel: 93 227 5400.
Hospital de la Creu Roja
Carrer de Dos de Maig, 301
Tel: 93 433 1551.
Hospital del Mar
Passeig Marítim, 25–29
Tel: 93 248 30 00.

Emergency numbers

Emergencies (police, fire, ambulance), tel: 112.
Mossos d'Esquadra, tel: 088.
Fire Brigade, tel: 080.
Ambulance service, tel: 061.
Road accidents, tel: 088.
Policia Nacional, tel: 091.
Policia Municipal, tel: 092.

Entry Requirements

Passports are required for people of all nationalities entering Spain. Carry a photocopy of the identification page for everyday use so that the original document can be left for safety in a secure place (such as a hotel safe). If your passport is lost or stolen, you should report the fact immediately to the National Police (Policia Nacional; see left).

Visas are needed by non-EU nationals, unless their country has a reciprocal arrangement with Spain.

Animal quarantine There are no quarantine regulations in Spain but you will need a health certificate before you bring your own animal into the country: the regulations vary according to country of origin. The airline with which you are travelling should be able to provide the information required.

G ay & Lesbian Travellers

The gay scene is thriving and generally very well accepted. Nearby Sitges (just half an hour south of the city on the coast) is a real mecca for gay people, particularly insummer, and is well worth a visit. The drag parade during Carnival in February is renowned.

For advice and information on the latest venues, the lesbian and gay hotline is **Telèfon Rosa**: tel: 900 601 601.

Other useful addresses are:
Casal Lambda
Ample, 5
Tel: 93 319 5550.
From 5pm onwards. A cultural centre.
Coordinadora Gai-Lesbiana
Buenaventura Muñoz, 4
Tel: 93 309 7997.
Col·lectiu Gai de BCN
Paloma, 12
Tel: 93 318 1666.
Sextienda
Rauric, 11
Tel: 93 318 8676.

Guides and Tours

If you want to recruit a professional tourist guide or interpreter, you should contact:
Barcelona Guide Bureau
Tel: 93 268 2422.
City Guides
Tel: 93 412 0674.
Professional Association of Barcelona Tour Guides
Tel: 93 319 8416.

BELOW: joining a bike tour on the Waterfront.

H ealth and Medical Care

Barcelona is a modern European city and there are no special health risks to be aware of, and no inoculations are needed. You should take the usual travel precautions and break yourself into the climate and the food gently. Between June and September you should wear a hat and suncream when out during the day.

Food and drink

In most areas of Barcelona tap water can be drunk without fear, but it is often dosed with purifying salts which make the taste unpleasant. Mineral water is easily available, and Vichy Catalan is soothing for queasy stomachs. Cheap wine can be rough, so take it easy.

Catalan cooking is healthy and nutritious, but a change of diet can affect some digestive systems. Avoid bars and restaurants where oil is used to excess.

Another danger area can be in *tapes*, which in hot weather can be a source of infection if they have been left standing on a counter for too long. Most notorious is anything mayonnaise-based, such as the ubiquitous *ensaladilla rusa* (Russian salad), a potential source of salmonella; in some parts of Spain home-made mayonnaise is banned.

With common sense it is easy to spot the "tired" *tapes* which should be avoided.

Insurance

Residents of EU countries, Iceland and Norway are entitled to receive state medical treatment in Spain if they present a form known as an E111, which must be obtained in their own country. In the UK this can be done through the Post Office. Each member of the family must have his/her own E111. At the end of 2005 the E111 will be replaced by the European Health Insurance Card.

For greater peace of mind, take out private insurance, which is best organised before setting off but can be arrranged on arrival in Barcelona through any travel agency.

If you are insured privately or prepared to pay for private healthcare, Barcelona Centro Médico, Avinguda Diagonal, 612, tel: 93 414 0643 or 24 hours, tel: 639 30 34 64, operates an information service for consultations and appointment bookings.

Buying medicines

Pharmacies *(farmacias)* have a red or green flashing neon cross outside. When closed, *farmacias* post a list of other *farmacias* in the window, indicating the nearest one on duty. Pharmacies stock prescription and non-prescription medications, toiletries, baby food and supplies. Many *farmacias* also stock homeopathic remedies, or will be able to obtain them for you within a day.

The **Allergyshop** (París, 156, tel: 93 322 2668) specialises in treatments for allergies and offers advice.

Dentists

Dentists in Spain are not covered by any of the reciprocal agreements between countries.

The following clinics offer an emergency service:
Amesa
Gran Via, 680
Tel: 93 302 6682.
Open: 9.30am–1pm and 3–6pm.

TRANSPORT

ACCOMMODATION

ACTIVITIES

A–Z

LANGUAGE

ABOVE: forward planning.

Clínica Dental Barcelona
Passeig de Gràcia, 97 pral.
Tel: 93 487 8329.
Emergency service daily from
9am–midnight. English-speaking
dentists.
Clínica Janos
Muntaner 375, 6° 2ª
Tel: 93 200 2333.
Open: Monday–Saturday
9am–1pm and 4–8pm. Sunday
10am–2pm.

L eft Luggage

Left-luggage lockers (consigna) are
available in Sants railway station
4.30am–midnight. There is an
equivalent service at Estació de
França and Passeig de Gràcia stations and at Barcelona Nord bus
station. At the sea terminal on Moll
Barcelona there is a left-luggage
office which is open 8am–1am.

Lost Property

There is a Lost Property Office in
Carrer Ciutat, 9, just off Plaça
Sant Jaume, 9.30am–1pm.
Tel: 906 427 017.

M aps

The Tourist Board issues a good
general map of the city (plano de
la ciudad/plànol de la ciutat). A

transport map is also available
from metro stations. The Guia
Urbana, the taxi drivers' bible, is
the most comprehensive map of
the city on sale at newsstands.

Media

Newspapers

The main daily newspapers are:
El País
Based in Madrid but with a
Barcelona edition, El País is the
most internationally respected
Spanish paper. An English ver-
sion is published by the Interna-
tional Herald Tribune.
La Vanguardia
The traditional (and Conserva-
tive) newspaper of Barcelona has
good coverage of local news and
publishes a "What's On" maga-
zine on Friday.
El Periódico
This is the more popular
Barcelona newspaper, but it is
limited on international news;
published in both Castilian and
Catalan.
Avui
The original Catalan paper.
Catalonia Today
Free daily in English, covering
international, national and local
news in brief. Useful listings and
features on Barcelona.
   International newspapers can
be found on the newsstands
on La Rambla and Passeig de
Gràcia, and also in several inter-
national bookshops, such as
FNAC (Plaça de Catalunya).

Magazines

A wealth of magazines cover
every interest and indulgence.
The main fashion magazines,
such as Vogue, Marie Claire and
Elle publish a Spanish edition.
Most notable of the national magazines are:
Hola: The most famous Spanish
magazine, with illustrated scan-
dal and gossip on the rich and
the royal.
Guia del Ocio: A useful weekly
listings magazine for Barcelona.
Visit their website on:

www.guiadelociobcn.es.
Metropolitan: Barcelona's first
monthly magazine in English is
now well established. Targeted at
residents, it makes interesting
reading and carries useful listings. Distributed free at key
points in the city (and around,
e.g. Sitges) – bookshops, bars
and cinemas. Check out their
website on: www.barcelona-
metropolitan.com.
Barcelona Business: A monthly
newspaper, printed on pink
paper, with incisive comments on
business affairs, unveiling some
of the mysteries of local law and
politics.

Television

The principal channels are TVE1
and TVE2 (state-owned), TV3 and
Canal 33, the autonomous Catalan channels. The local channel
is BTV. Commercial channels
include Antena 3 (general programming), Tele 5 (directed at
housewives at home during the
day) and Canal Plus (mainly films,
for subscribers only). Satellite
programmes are obtainable in
many of the larger hotels.

Money Matters

The monetary unit is the euro (€).
Banknotes are issued in €5, 10,
20, 50, 100, 200 and 500; coins
in demoninations of 1, 2, 5, 10,
20, 50 centimos, and €1 and 2.
Pesetas can be changed at any
branch of the Banco de España.
   Most banks have automatic
tills or cashpoints (ATMs), operating 24 hours a day, where money
can be withdrawn using most
credit and debit cards.
   Keep (separately) a record of
the individual numbers of your
travellers' cheques. If they are
lost or stolen they can be
replaced quickly if you have this
information.

Tax

Tax (IVA) on services and goods is
16 percent, and for restaurants
and hotels, 7 percent. Visitors
from non-European Union coun-

tries are entitled to tax reclaims on their return home at a Global Refund Office. Look out for Tax Free signs in shop windows. When you leave the EU, Barcelona Customs must confirm the purchase and stamp the Tax-Free cheque; you can then take it to the airport branch of Banco Exterior de España and cash the cheque into the currency required.

Banks

Bank opening hours vary, but as a general rule they are open all year Monday–Friday 8.30am–2pm, and also Saturday 8.30am–1pm between 1 October and 31 May. The *Cajas* or *Caixes* (savings banks) offer the same service, but are open on Thursday afternoon instead of Saturday morning between 1 October and 31 May. They also have 24-hour cashpoints.

There are numerous currency-exchange offices in the city centre, including in La Rambla and in the Plaça de Catalunya Information Centre. The larger hotels will also exchange money, although often at a less favourable rate.

Foreign banks in the city:
American Express
La Rambla, 74
Tel: 93 342 7310.
Offers the usual services to clients, including replacing stolen credit cards.
Lloyds Bank
Rambla de Catalunya, 123
Tel: 93 236 3300.
Barclays Bank
Passeig de Gràcia, 45
Tel 93 481 2000.

Credit cards

Major international credit cards, such as Visa, Eurocard and MasterCard can be used, although you will be required to show some form of identity. In the case of loss:
American Express
Tel: 902 375 637.
Diner's
Tel: 901 101 011.
Eurocard, MasterCard, Master-charge, Servired and **Visa**

Tel: 91 519 2100/900 971 231.
Visa International
Tel: 900 991 124.

Tipping

There are no golden rules about this. If you feel the need to leave a tip, make it a token rather than an extravagant one. Some restaurants automatically add a service charge to the total, in which case nothing extra is needed. As a yardstick, in restaurants where a charge is not added, it should be around 5–10 percent and about the same in a taxi. In a bar or café, 80 centimos–€1.50 is enough, depending on the size of the bill.

P ostal Services

Stamps for letters, post cards and small packets can be bought very conveniently in the many *estancs* to be found in every district. These are state-owned establishments licensed to sell stamps, cigarettes and tobacco, and easily recognisable by their orange and brown logo, **Tabacs SA**. Opening hours are loosely 9am–1.30pm and 4.30–8pm. Post boxes are yellow.

The main post office is at the bottom of Via Laietana near the port, in Plaça Antoni López. It has collections every hour and is open Monday–Friday 9am–9pm, Saturday 9am–1pm. Other post offices close at 2pm, apart from the one in Carrer d'Aragó, 282 (near Passeig de Gràcia) which is open until 7pm, but with limited services.

Poste Restante letters can be sent to the main post office addressed to the Lista de Correos, 08080 Barcelona. Be sure to take personal identification with you (preferably your passport) when claiming letters.

Telegrams, telex and fax

These can all be sent from the main post office *(see above)* Monday–Saturday 8.30am–9.30pm or from a small office at Ronda Universitat, 23,

9am–7pm. They can also be sent by telephone, tel: 93 322 2000, or by Internet on www.correos.es. Privately run telephone centres also offer fax services.

Public Holidays

Many bars, restaurants and museums close in the afternoon and evening on public holidays and Sunday. If a holiday falls on a Tuesday or a Thursday it is common to take a *pont* or *puente* (bridge) to link the interim day with the weekend. Roads out of the city are extremely busy on the afternoon/evening before a holiday. August is the annual holiday month and many businesses, including restaurants, close down for three or four weeks.

The following are the public holidays (national and Catalan):
1 January – New Year's Day
6 January – Reis Mags: Epiphany
late March/April – Good Friday (variable)
late March/April – Easter Monday (variable)
1 May – Festa del Treball: Labour Day
late May – Whitsun: Pentecost (variable)
24 June – Sant Joan: Midsummer's Night
15 August – Assumpció: Assumption
11 September – Diada: Catalan national holiday
24 September – La Mercè: the patroness of Barcelona. This is the city's main fiesta
12 October – Hispanitat/Pilar: Spanish national day
1 November – Tots Sants: All Saints' Day
6 December – Día de la Constitució: Constitution Day
8 December – Immaculada Concepció: Immaculate Conception
25–6 December – Christmas

Public Toilets

There is a notorious dearth of public toilets in the city but finally the municipal authorities are planning to remedy the situation:

some kind of public urinals should be installed at strategic points in the city over the next few years. Meanwhile, a few coin-operated cabins exist, although it is usually easier to find a bar. Near the beaches there are 24 facilities (14 adapted for people with disabilities) and others can be found in public centres like the airport, the railway and bus stations, shopping centres and museums.

R eligious Services

Mass is usually said between 7am and 2pm on Sunday and feast days. Evening Mass is held between 7 and 9pm on Saturday, Sunday and feast days.
Catholic Mass
Parroquia Maria Reina
Carretera d'Esplugues, 103
Tel: 93 203 4115.
Sundays 10am (in English).
Anglican
St George's Church
Sant Joan de la Salle, 41
Tel: 93 417 8867.
Sunday 11am (services in English).
Judaism
The Synagogue
Avenir, 24
Tel: 93 200 6148.
Islam
Centro Islàmico
Avinguda Meridiana, 326
Tel: 93 351 4901.
Toarek Ben Ziad
Hospital, 91
Tel: 93 441 9149.

S tudent Travellers

For holders of an international student card (ISIC), or the Euro26 card for any young people under the age of 26, there are many discounts on offer: reduced tickets at museums and other cultural centres, discounts on railways and other public transport, hostels and shops. For details see www.gencat.es/joventut. The card is available in the UK through the National Youth

Agency, tel: 0116 285 3781 or www.euro26.org.

Students may also be interested to know that there is a youth hostel right in the Gothic Quarter, **Gothic Point** at Vigatans, 5; and another, also in the old town, at Carrer Sant Pau, 80 (just off La Rambla). Both offer Internet access and security lockers, and can also arrange bike hire and other activities. There are other youth hostels in the city as well. For more information visit www.youth-hostels-in.com/barcelona.

T elecommunications

Telephone booths are well distributed throughout the city. Providing they are working, they are easy to use and efficient, especially for international calls. Most bars have either a pay-phone or a metered telephone. Public telephones take all euro coins and most accept credit cards. The minimum charge for a local call is 7 céntimos. Telephone cards are available in *estancs* (tobacconists) and post offices. International reverse-charge calls cannot be made from a phone box.

There are also privately run exchanges *(locutoris)*, mainly in the old town, where you talk first and pay afterwards. These are useful for making calls outside Europe and North America, or if you are planning on having a long conversation.

Telephone calls were reduced in price after privatisation of the Spanish telecommunications industry, but they are still higher than in many other countries, particularly the US. Principal walk-in telephone exchanges are situated in Sants railway station (fax service) and Barcelona Nord bus station *(see page 204)*. US access codes: AT&T: 900 99 0011; MCI: 900 99 0014 Sprint: 900 99 0013.

Useful numbers

Operator Services
Information: 1004

Directory Enquiries: 11818
International Directory Enquiries: 11825
International Operator: 11822
Country Codes:
International code: 00
Australia: 61
Canada: 1
Eire: 353
United Kingdom: 44
United States: 1

The Internet

There are plenty of Internet cafés and lounges in the city, and many of the *locutoris (see above)* now offer Internet service. One of the best is:
Easy Internet Café
La Rambla, 31 and Ronda Universitat, 35.
These two branches of the Easy empire are open 24 hours daily all year for cheap Internet access.

Time Zone

Spain is one hour ahead of GMT in winter, two hours in summer (when UK clocks are also advanced by an hour for summer time, so the time difference is still only one hour), and six hours ahead of Eastern Seaboard Time.

Tour Operators and Travel Agents

There are almost 400 travel agents in Barcelona, and in the centre you will find one on nearly every block. El Corte Inglés offers a good service in its Plaça de Catalunya branch. Some leading companies are:
Barceló Viatges
Avinguda Catedral, 5
Tel: 93 317 2570.
Carlson Wagonlit
Via Laietana, 16
Tel: 93 481 2704.
People Express
La Rambla, 95
Tel: 93 412 2337
(for cheap flights).
Viajes Ecuador
Pau Claris, 75
Tel: 93 301 3966.

To find a long list of tour agencies operating from the UK, a helpful website is www.abta.com/destinations/barcelona.

Tourist Information

For general tourist information about the city, call 010. This is the Barcelona city council's efficient service and it can provide a wealth of information, or at least tell you where to find it. It is manned by English-speaking staff.

The "**Red Jackets**" service is available during the summer months. It is run by teams of young people in red-and-white uniforms, who offer help and information to visitors, usually in the Barri Gòtic, La Rambla and the Passeig de Gràcia.

Information offices

Plaça de Catalunya
The main city tourist information centre. Well-equipped and good for hotel and theatre bookings.
Tel: 807 117 222, or from abroad: 93 285 3834.
Open daily 9am–9pm.
El Prat Airport
In Terminals A and B
Tel: 93 478 4704
Open daily: 9am–9pm.

BELOW: pausing for refreshment.

City Hall
Plaça Sant Jaume.
Open: Monday–Friday 9am–8pm, Saturday 10am–8pm, Sunday 10am–2pm.
Sants Station
Open daily: 8am–8pm (summer).
Rest of year: Monday–Friday 8am–8pm, weekends/holidays 8am–2pm.
Tourist Information Centre for Catalonia
Palau Robert
Passeig de Gràcia, 107
Tel: 93 238 4000
www.gencat.es/probert.
Monday–Saturday 10am–7pm, Sunday and public holidays 10am– 2.30pm.
Information on the rest of Catalonia is available in the grandiose Palau Robert, which has comfortable reading rooms with sofas and worktables and Internet connections, as well as a garden and gift shop.

In addition to the above offices, information booths are situated in **La Rambla**, in the **Port** and at the **Sagrada Familia** in summer. They are open daily, 9am–9pm.

Useful addresses

If you would like information about Barcelona before leaving home, contact your nearest Spanish Tourist Office:
Canada
2 Bloor Street West, 34th Floor
Toronto
Ontario M4W 3E2
Tel: 416-961 31 31
Fax: 416-961 19 92.
United Kingdom
79 New Cavendish Street,
London W1W 6XB
Tel: 020-7486 8077 or
09063-640630 (for brochures)
Fax: 020-7486 8034
www.tourspain.co.uk.
Please note that this office is not open to the public except by appointment.
United States
666 Fifth Avenue
New York
NY 10103
Tel: 212-265 8822
Fax: 212-265 8864.

W ebsites

A few useful sites are:
Barcelona on the web:
www.barcelonaturisme.com
www.bcn.es
www.barcelona-metropolitan.com.
Catalonia on the web:
www.gencat.es
Spain on the web:
www.spaintour.com/index.html

Weights and Measures

Spain follows the metric system. To convert kilometres into miles divide by 1.6093; to convert metres into feet divide by 0.3048; to convert kilograms into pounds divide by 0.4536; to convert hectares into acres divide by 0.4047. To convert from imperial to metric multiply by the factor shown.

If this all sounds too complicated, it is simpler to bear in mind that a kilometre is roughly five-eighths of a mile; a metre is roughly three feet/one yard; a kilogram is just over 2lbs, a litre is just under two pints, or a fifth of a gallon, and a hectare is around two-and-a-half acres.

In many of the larger stores and international chains, labels on clothing show European, UK and US sizes.

Women Travellers

Women should have no occasion to feel ill at ease in Barcelona; Spain (and Catalonia in particular) is different in this respect from, for example, Greece or Italy, and women won't encounter harassment when just walking around the city or eating alone. Everyone should be careful, however, when out late at night.

A good source of information on issues of particular interest to women is the Libreria Pròleg, Dagueria, 13. This is the city's specialist bookshop for feminist subjects and women writers. It is also an exhibition space and occasionally holds talks.

TRANSPORT

ACCOMMODATION

ACTIVITIES

N–A

LANGUAGE

LANGUAGE

UNDERSTANDING THE LANGUAGE

Catalan

Castilian (Spanish) and Catalan are both official languages in Catalonia. In the wake of the repression of Catalan under Franco, when its use in public was forbidden, it is undergoing a resurgence, encouraged by the administration, with the aim of fully implementing it in every aspect of daily life. It is often the only language used in public signs, street names, maps, leaflets and cultural information.

Catalan is a Romance language; with a knowledge of French and Spanish you should find it possible to read a little.

In the rural regions outside Barcelona you may come across people who cannot speak Castilian, but in the city even the most ardent Catalanista should respond if you communicate in Castilian, knowing you are a foreigner. Also, many people you meet in bars, restaurants and on public transport will be from other parts of Spain and so will be primarily Castilian speakers.

However, any attempt to speak the simplest phrases in Catalan wil be rewarded with appreciation, particularly of the fact that you are recognising it as the language of their country.

English is widely spoken in most tourist areas, but even if you speak no Spanish or Catalan at all, it is worth trying to master a few simple words and phrases.

Spanish

Spanish is also a Romance language, derived from the Latin spoken by the Romans who conquered the Iberian peninsula more than 2,000 years ago. Following the discovery of America, Spaniards took their language with them to the four corners of the globe. Today, Spanish is spoken by 250 million people in North, South and Central America and parts of Africa.

Spanish is a phonetic language: words are pronounced as they are spelt, which is why it is somewhat harder for Spaniards to learn English than vice versa (although Spanish distinguishes between the two genders, masculine and feminine, and the subjunctive verb form is an endless source of headaches).

As a general rule, the accent falls on the last syllable, unless it is otherwise marked with an accent (´) or the word ends in s, n or a vowel.

Vowels in Spanish are always pronounced the same way. The double ll is pronounced like the y in "yes", the double rr is rolled, as in Scots. The h is silent in Spanish, whereas j (and g when it precedes an e or i) is pronounced like a guttural h (as if you were clearing your throat).

Spanish Words and Phrases

Although it is worth trying to speak Catalan first, if you have a knowledge of Castilian it will be totally acceptable, and better than English. Here are some useful expressions:

Yes *Sí*
No *No*
Please *Por favor*
Thank you (very much) *(muchas) gracias*
You're welcome *de nada*
Excuse me *perdóneme*
OK *bién/vale*
Hello *Hola*
How are you? *¿Cómo está usted?*
How much is it? *¿Cuánto es?*
What is your name? *¿Cómo se llama usted?*
My name is ... *Me llamo ...*
Do you speak English? *¿Habla inglés?*
I am British/American *Soy británico(a)/norteamericano(a) (for women)*

TRANSPORT
ACCOMMODATION
ACTIVITIES
A – Z
LANGUAGE

CATALAN

Good morning Bon dia
Good afternoon/evening Bona tarda
Good night Bona nit
How are you? Com està vostè?
Very well thank you, and you? Molt bé, gràcies i vostè?
Goodbye, see you again Adéu, a reveure
See you later Fins després
See you tomorrow Fins demà
What's your name? Com us diu?
My name is ... Em dic ...
Pleased to meet you Molt de gust
Do you have any rooms? Per favor tenen habitacions lliures?
I'd like an external/internal/double room Voldria una habitació exterior/interior/doble
... for one/two persons ... per a una persona/dues persones
I want a room with a bath Vull una habitació amb bany
I have a room reserved in the name of ... Tinc reservada una habitació a nom de ...
How much is it? Quin és el preu?
It's expensive Es car
Could I see the room? Podria veure l'habitació?
How do you say that in Catalan? Com es diu això en català?
Speak a little more slowly, please Parlou una mica més a poc, si us plau
How do I get to ...? Per a anar a ...?
Is it very far/close? Es lluny/a prop?
Where's the nearest motor mechanic? On és el pròxim taller de reparació?
Can I change this traveller's cheque? Pot canviar-me aquest xec de viatge?

Where can I find a dentist? On puc trobar un dentista?
This tooth is hurting Em fa mal aquesta dent
Don't take it out. If possible give me something for it until I get home No me l'extregui. Si és possible doni'm un remei fins que torni a casa
Please call a doctor Cridi un metge, per favor
Where does it hurt? On li fa mal?
I have a bad cold Estic molt refredat
I want to make a phone call to ... Vull telefonar a ...
It's engaged La línea está ocupada
I am ... I'd like to speak to Mr ... Sóc ... voldria parlar amb el senyor ...
What time will he be back? A quina hora tornarà?
Tell him to call me at this number Digui-li que truqui al número ...
I'll be in town until Saturday Seré a la ciutat fins dissabte

Eating Out

Breakfast/lunch/dinner Esmorzar/dinar/sopar
At what time do you serve ...? A quina hora es pot ...?
Set menu El menu
Menu La carta
We'd like a table for four Una taula per a quatre si us plau
First course Primer plat
May we have some water? Porti'ns aigua mineral
/red wine/white wine? vi negre/vi blanc
The bill, please El compte, si us plau

Some Typical Dishes

Albergínies fregides Fried aubergines
Amanida salad
Amanida catalana Salad with hard-boiled egg and cold meats
Arròs a la marinera Seafood paella
Arròs negre Rice cooked in squid ink
Carxofes Artichokes
Canalons Canneloni
Escalivada Salad of roasted aubergines/peppers
Escudella Thick soup with meat, vegetables and noodles
Espinacs a la catalana Spinach with garlic, pine nuts and raisins
Esqueixada Salt cod salad
Faves a la catalana Broad beans stewed with sausage
Bacallà a la llauna Salt cod baked in the oven
Botifarra amb mongetes Sausage with haricot beans
Estofat de conill Rabbit stew
de vedella veal stew
de xai lamb stew
Fricandó Braised veal
Gambes a la planxa Grilled prawns
Pollastre al ajillo Chicken fried with garlic
Sipia amb mandonguilles Cuttle-fish with meatballs
Suquet de peix Rich fish stew
Postres Desserts
Crema catalana Custard with caramelised topping
Formatge Cheese
Gelat Ice cream
Pastís de poma Apple tart
Postre de músics Mixed nuts and dried fruits

I don't understand No entiendo
Please speak more slowly Hable más despacio, por favor
Can you help me? ¿Me puede ayudar?
I am looking for ... Estoy buscando ...
Where is ...? ¿Dónde está ...?

I'm sorry Lo siento
I don't know No lo sé
No problem No hay problema
Have a good day Que tenga un buen día, or Vaya con Dios
That's it Ese es
Here it is Aquí está
There it is Allí está
Let's go Vámonos

See you tomorrow Hasta mañana
See you soon Hasta pronto
goodbye adiós
Show me the word in the book Muéstreme la palabra en el libro
At what time? ¿A qué hora?
When? ¿Cuándo?
What time is it? ¿Qué hora es?

FURTHER READING

Good Companions

English translations of Catalan works of literature are few, and are difficult to find in Barcelona.
Barcelona, Robert Hughes, Harvill Press, 2001. Describes the city's development in relation to the rest of Catalonia, Spain and Europe. Good on Gaudí and modernism.
Barcelona: A Guide to Recent Architecture, Suzanna Strum, Ellipsis London Ltd, 2001. A look at some of the city's stunning buildings.
Barcelonas, Manuel Vázquez Montalbán, Verso, 1990. Chatty book covering culture, design, history and some of the city's personalities.
Catalan Cuisine, Colman Andrews, Grub Street, 1997. Describes the unique aspects of Catalan cooking.
Eating Out in Barcelona and Catalunya, Craig Allen and Robert Budwig, Rosendale Press, 1994. History of Catalan food and Barcelona restaurant guide.
Forbidden Territory, Juan Goytisolo, Quartet Books, 1989. Autobiography by one of Spain's most important writers.
Homage to Barcelona, Colm Toíbín, Simon & Schuster, 1990.
Homage to Catalonia, George Orwell. Penguin, 1989. Famous account of the author's experiences in the Spanish Civil War.
The City of Marvels (La Ciudad de los Prodigios), Eduardo Mendoza Seix Barral (Spanish), 1999, Collins (English). A novel set in Barcelona.
Teach Yourself Catalan, Anna Poch and Alan Yates, Hodder Arnold, 2004. An update of this classic series of language learning books.

Other Insight Guides

The 190-title Insight Guides series includes eight books on Spain and its islands, all combining the exciting pictures and incisive text associated with this series.

FEEDBACK

We do our best to ensure the information in our books is as accurate and up to date as possible. The books are updated on a regular basis, using local contacts, who painstakingly add, amend and correct as required. However, some mistakes and omissions are inevitable, and we are ultimately reliant on our readers to put us in the picture.
We would welcome your feedback on any details related to your experiences using the book "on the road". Maybe we recommended a hotel that you liked (or another that you did not), as well as interesting new attractions, or facts and figures you have found out about the country itself. The more details you can give us (particularly with regard to addresses, e-mails and telephone numbers), the better. We will acknowledge all contributions, and we'll offer an Insight Guide to the best letters received.

Please write to us at:
Insight Guides
PO Box 7910
London SE1 1WE
United Kingdom
Or send e-mail to:
insight@apaguide.co.uk

Insight Guides

Insight Guide: Spain is an award-winning title in the series, with top photography and complete background reading. *Insight Guide: Northern Spain* provides comprehensive coverage of this alluring region, from the bright lights of Bilbao to the breathtaking Picos de Europa.

Insight City Guides

Like this guide, *Insight City Guide: Madrid* is written by locally-based writers, who show you how to make the most of this dynamic city. Includes detailed listings and a free Restaurant Guide Map to locate the city's favourite restaurants.

Insight Pocket Guides

Madrid and *Barcelona* are both covered in the complementary Insight Pocket Guide series. These books provide a series of timed itineraries for short-stay visitors. Other titles in this series include *Bilbao and Northwest Spain*, *Costa Brava*, *Costa Blanca* and *Costa del Sol*.

Insight Compact Guides

Compact Guide: Barcelona, one of the titles in Apa Publications' third series of books, is the ultimate "portable encyclopedia" to the city. Up to date and packed with facts and photographs, it is the ideal easy-reference book.

BARCELONA STREET ATLAS

The key map shows the area of Barcelona covered by the atlas section. An index of street names and places of interest shown on the maps can be found on the following pages. For each entry there is a page number and grid reference.

Map Legend

═══╬═══	Autopista with Junction
─ ─ ─	Autopista (under construction)
═══	Dual Carriageway
═══	Main Road
═══	Secondary Road
───	Minor road
───	Track
━ ━ ━	International Boundary
─ ─ ● ─	Province Boundary
─ ■ ─	National Park/Reserve
✈ ✈	Airport
✝ ✝	Church (ruins)
✝	Monastery
🏰 🏚	Castle (ruins)
∴	Archaeological Site
∩	Cave
★	Place of Interest
🏠	Mansion/Stately Home
※	Viewpoint
◤	Beach
═══	Autopista
═══	Dual Carriageway
═══	Main Roads
───	Minor Roads
───	Footpath
─■─	Railway
▭	Pedestrian Area
▬	Important Building
▭	Park
Ⓜ	Metro
🚌	Bus Station
ⓘ	Tourist Information
✉	Post Office
✝	Cathedral/Church
☪	Mosque
✡	Synagogue
⚲	Statue/Monument
∏	Tower

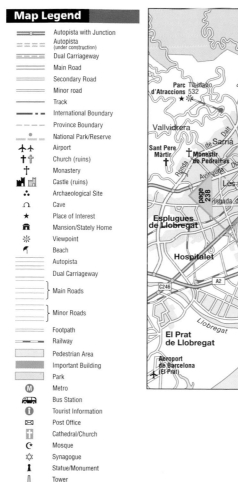

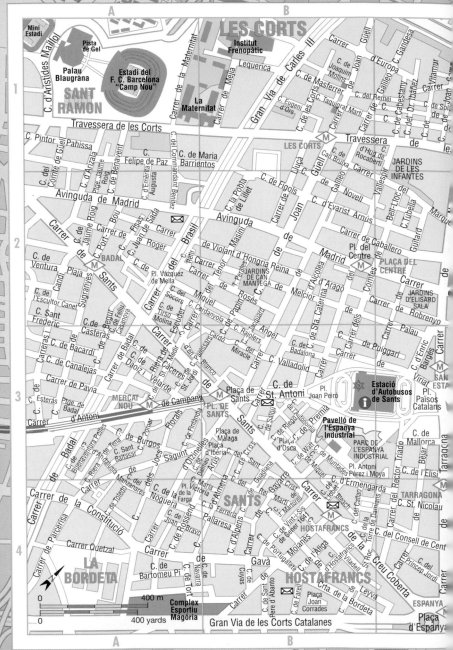

LES CORTS

Mini Estadi
Pista de Gel
Palau Blaugrana
SANT RAMON
Estadi del F. C. Barcelona "Camp Nou"
Institut Frenopàtic
La Maternitat

C. d'Arístides Maillol
C. d'Aristides Maillol
Travessera de les Corts
C. Pintor de Güel
Pahissa
C. del Comte de Güel
C. d'Arzala
Pje. Jaume Roig
C. de Benavent
C. Felipe de Paz
C. d'Emèrita Augusta
C. del Commandant Benítez
C. de Maria Barrientos
Avinguda de Madrid
Lequerica
C. de Melía
C. de la Maternitat
Gran Via de Carles III
C. de Masferrer
C. de Joaquim Molins
C. de Joan
C. del Remei
C. Eugeni d'Ors
C. Taquígraf Martí
C. de les Corts
C. de Güell
C. de Cabestany
C. Galileo
C. de Sòler
C. de Cabestany
Dr. Ibàñez
C. de C.
d'Europa
Güell
Gandesa
Wifrau

LES CORTS
Travessera de
les Corts
C. d'Huà de Rocabertí
C. de Can Bruixa
Carrer
JARDINS DE LES INFANTES
Carrer de Vallespir
Betlloc
del
Marquesat

Carrer de
BADAL
C. de Jaume Roig
Port
C. de Bou
C. de Fisas
C. Juan de Sardà
C. de Roger
Carrer de Brasil
C. de Violant d'Hongria Reina
Avinguda
C. de Tenor Masini
C. de la Pobla de Lillet
C. de Figols
C. de Joan
de Madrid
Pl. del Centre
Carrer de Caballero
C. d'Evarist Arnús
C. d'Evarist Arnús
C. de Novell
PLAÇA DEL CENTRE
Carrer
JARDINS D'ELISARD SALA
Gultard

C. de Ventura
Candi
Plaja
Sugranyes
C. de Badal
Pl. Vázquez de Mella
C. del Tenor
C. de Miquel
JARDINS DE CAN MANTEGA
C. de Rosés
C. d'Alcolea
Carrer de Robrenyo
Palau
C. de l'Escultor Canet
C. de Sant Frederic
C. de Casterás
C. de Begur
C. de Felíu
C. Casanova
C. del Socors
C. de Tirso Molina
C. Cerdanyola
C. Escuder
C. de Papiru
de
Melcior
Carrer de Sta. Caterina
Carrer dels
C. de Puiggarí
Carrer
C. d'Enric Barges
Viriat
SANT ESTA

C. de Bacardí
C. de Canalejas
Carrer de Pavia
C. de Pavia
Carrer de Badal
C. de Daoiz i Velarde
Riera de Caceres
C. de Medir
Carrer de
Jan Pamisanasi
C. blanco
Cardó
C. del Miracle
C. de Rajolers
C. Valladolid
Angel
Jacquard
de
C. de Badalona
de
Palau
SANT ESTA

C. Esterás
Ptge. de Badal
d'Antoni
MERCAT NOU
MERCAT NOU
de Campny
PL. DE SANTS
Plaça de Sants
C. de St. Antoni
C. de Sants
Pl. Joan Peiró
Estació d'Autobusos de Sants
PLAÇA PAÏSOS CATALANS
Pl. Països Catalans

Carrer de Badal
C. de Bonaventura Pollés
C. de Bijenerativa
C. de Burgos
C. Riera d'Andalusia
C. Sant Baltasar
C. de Burgos
C. de Tena
Manzanares
C. del Pratge
C. Florats
C. de Jocs
C. Sagunt
C. d'Olzinelles
C. de Finlàndia
C. Damia
C. Maria de la Farga
C. Aldís
Plaça de Málaga
Pl. Ibèria
Plaça d'Osca
Sants
de Sants
C. de Salou
C. d'Autonomía
C. de Riego
C. de Vallespir
C. de Watt
C. de Sant
C. de Muntades
C. de Miquel
Pavelló de l'Espanya Industrial
PARC DE L'ESPANYA INDUSTRIAL
Pl. Antoni Pérez i Moya
C. de Mallorca
C. de l'Elisi
TARRAGONA
C. St. Nicolau
C. del Consell de Cent
Carrer de
Rector Triado

Carrer de la Constitució
C. de Toledo
C. del Noguera
Pl. Victòria
C. de Rossend Arús
C. de Juan de Bravo
C. Pallaresa
SANTS
C. de Sant
C. de la Ferreria
C. d'Alpens
C. Guadiana
C. de Gavarre
Marti
C. de Matorell
C. de Vint-i-Sis de Gener
C. de l'Aliga
C. de Gavá
C. d'Olzinelles
C. de Portugalete
C. de Premià
C. de Cros
Cristi de
C. Almería
C. de l'Ermengarda
C. de
C. de
C. de
Galileu
C. de Brach
C. Llobet
HOSTAFRANCS
C. de Toras i Bages
C. de la Creu Coberta
Vilardell
C. de Damians
C. del Princep Jordi

LA BORDETA
Carrer de Parcerisa
Carrer Quetzal
C. de Bartomeu Pi
Carrer
C. de Navarra
C. de Tort
C. Cuyas
C. de Sant Pere d'Abanto
Pl. Joan Corrades
HOSTAFRANCS
Crta. de la Bordeta
C. del Farell
C. de Portugalete
C. de Hostafranc
Moianes
C. de Leyva
C. de la Creu Coberta
ESPANYA
Plaça d'Espanya

0   400 m
0   400 yards

Complex Esportiu Magòria
Gran Via de les Corts Catalanes

A   B

D · E

LES CORTS

L'Illa

Avinguda Diagonal
d'Anglesola
C. d'Augustina Saragossa
C. de Balasch
Piscines i Esports
Plaça Sant Gregori Taumaturg
C. de Johann Seb. Bach
MUNTANER
Via Augusta
del Rector Ubach
C. d'Amigo
C. de Tavern

C. de Borì
C. de Ganduxer
i Fonesta
C. de Josep Bertrand
C. Francesc Pérez Cabrera
C. Joseph Beethoven
JARDINS D'EDUARD MARGUINA
C. de Ferran Agulló
Calvet
Carrer de Calaf
C. de Santaló
C. dels Madrazo
JARDINS DE MORAGAS
d'Aribau

de és Deu
Taquígraf
Corts
JARDINS JOAQUIM RUYRA
Plaça de Wagner
Plaça de Joan Llongueras
Av. de Pau Casals
C. del Mestre
Nicolau
C. de / Tenor Viñas
Carrer
de
Carrer
Saguès
la
Forja
Cubí
l'Avenir
Carrer
d'Aribau

Mata
Garriga
Plaça Doctor Ignacio Barraguer
Loreto
Plaça de Francesc Macià
Travessera de Gràcia
Ptce. Marmont

C. del Pergueda
C. de Ecuador
Montnegre
Pep
Plaça Carme
C. Morales
Rita Bonnat
C. de
Borrell
Sarrià
Carrer
de Buenos Aires
Museu Colet
Ptge. de Lluís Pellicer
Avinguda
Diagonal
d'Aribau

Nicragua
C. de Taquígraf Serra
C. Breda
C. de Gelabert
Tarradellas
Carrer
Calàbria
Viladomat
Comte
de
d'Urgell
Villarroel
C. de Casanova
Londres
Muntaner
París

Berlín
Sentmenat
Josep
Rocafort
Carrer
de
Córsega
Carrer
de
Carrer
de
Carrer
de
Córsega
Carrer

Carrer
de
d'Entença
de
JARDINS MONTSERRAT
del
Rosselló
Escola d'Enginyers Tècnics i Industrials
HOSPITAL CLÍNIC
Ptge. Eatlió
Hospital Clínic
Pl. del Dr Ferrer Cajigal
Carrer del Rosselló

Presó Model
Carrer
ENTENÇA
Carrer
del
de
Comte
Provença
Bombers
Carrer

Avinguda
Carrer
Carrer
de
Carrer
Mallorca
de
Muntaner
d'Aribau

Carrer
Carrer
de
de
de
València

ESQUERRA DE L'EIXAMPLE
Roma
Plaça Gall
C. de Casanova

er d'Aragó
Carrer d'Aragó
Rocafort
d'Entença
Carrer
de
Calàbria
de
Carrer de Viladomat
del
Carrer del Comte Borrell
Ptge. d'Aragó
del
Consell
de
Cent
Carrer d'Aragó
de
Carrer

RC AN RÓ
C. de Vilamarí
Carrer
Carrer
de
EIXAMPLE
Diputació
Universitat Central

er
de Toros
Arenes
C. de
ROCAFORT
Carrer
URGELL
la
Carrer
Gran Via de les Corts Catalanes
Gran Via de les Corts Catalanes

D · E

A   B

Gran Via de les Corts Catalanes

C. de la Química
C. de la Mineria
C. de Traia
C. de Mandon
Carrer
Carrer de la
C. d'Indíbil
Sant
C. de Sant Pauli de Nola
C. de Santa Dorotea
C. de Germà
C. de Sant Ferriol
Plaça d'Espanya

SANTS-
del
MONTJUÏC

1. C. de Crisantem
2. C. del Lotus
3. C. Begònia
4. C. del Nord
5. C. Valls

Font Florida
Fde la Guatlla
Fructuós
Carrer de Mèxic
Palau de la Metal-lurgia
Cristina

LA MAGÒRIA

Fira d Barcelo

Carrer
Pl. de Llorca
Estadi Joan Serrahima
Plaça de Sant Jordi

Avinguda del Marquès de
Passeig S. Bertran
C. de Rabi Rubèn
C. Amposta
C. de Morados
C. dels Gimbernat

Caixa Forum
Plaça de l'Univers
Palau de Congressos
Av. de Rius i Ta

Estadi Julià Camonany

Camp de Rugby de la Fuxarda

Av. dels Montanyans

Poble Espanyol

Pavelló Mies van der Rohe

Plaça de Carles Buigas
Comillas
Avinguda de la Reina Maria
Guàrdia Urbana
Plaça Marquès de Foronda
Font Màgica
Palau d'Alfons XIII

Cantera del Borinot

Avinguda

Pista Hipica «La Fuxarda»

Palau de Victòria Eugènia

Institut i Jardí Botànic

Passeig de

Plaça de les Cascades

les Cascades

Pala Munic d'Esp

INEFC-Universitat de l'Esport
Pl. Hidràulica

Mirador del Palau Nacional

Palau Nacional

Mercat les Fl

2

CAN CLOS

Camp de Beisbol

Plaça d'Europa

Piscines Bernat Picornell

Museu Nacional d'Art de Catalunya (MNAC)

Museu Etnològic
M d'Arqueol

Grup de Vivendes de Can Clos
Plaça Alta Can Clos

Torre de Calatrava

JARDINS JOAN MARAGALL

Paulet Albéniz

C. de Pedrera del Mussol

Palau Sant Jordi

ANELLA OLÍMPICA

Passeig Olímpic

l'Estadi

Plaça del Sol
Pl Ne

Pg. Migdia

Muntanya de

Estadi Olímpic

Carrer dels Tres Pins

3

Circuito de Marcha

Passeig Olímpic

Dr Font i Quer

MONTJUÏC

Montjuïc

Zona d'Atletisme i Hoquei

PARC DE MONTJUIC

JARDÍ BOTÀNIC

Camí de la Serp

Carrer dels Tres Pins

Pl. Gran Capità

CEMENTIRI DEL

Pg.   Migdia

Carrer de la Cartoixa

Castell de Montjuïc

SUD-OEST

Camí de la Serp

4

400 m
0
400 yards
0

Ronda del Litoral

Museu M

A   B

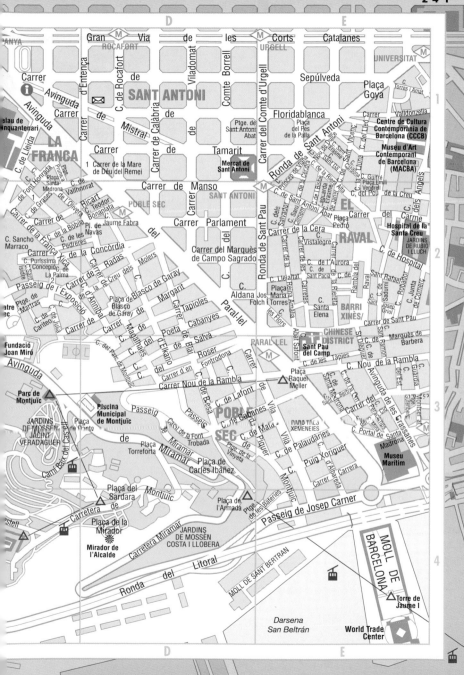

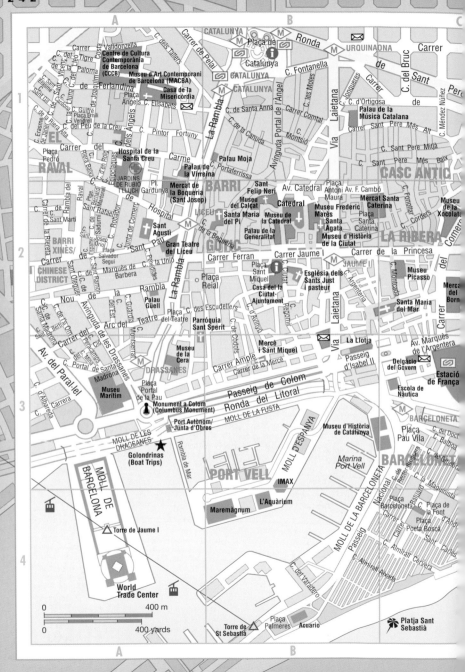

CATALUNYA
Plaça de Catalunya
Ronda
URQUINAONA
Carrer
de
del Bruc
Carrer
CATALUNYA
C. Fontanella
Joaquires
C. d'Ortigosa
Palau de la
Música Catalana
Centre de Cultura
Contemporània
de Barcelona
(CCCB)
Museu d'Art Contemporani
de Barcelona (MACBA)
Casa de la
Misericòrdia
Plaça
Àngels
C. Elisabets
C. de Santa Anna
Carrer Comtal
Carrer Sant Pere Més Alt

EL
RAVAL
Plaça
Pedró
Carrer del
Hospital de la
Santa Creu
Pintor Fortuny
Carme
Palau Moja
Palau de
la Virreina
Av. Catedral
Sant Pere Més Baix
CASC ANTIC

JARDINS
DE RUBIÓ
I LLUCH
Mercat de
la Boqueria
(Sant Josep)
BARRI
Sant
Felip Neri
Plaça
Antoni Av. F. Cambó
Maura
Mercat Santa
Caterina
Museu
de la
Xocolata

BARRI
XINÈS/
CHINESE
DISTRICT
Sant
Agustí
Gran Teatre
del Liceu
LICEU
Museu
del Calçat
Santa Maria
del Pi
Catedral
Museu de
la Catedral
Palau de la
Generalitat
Museu Frederic
Marès
Santa
Àgata
Museu d'Història
de la Ciutat
Plaça
Santa
Caterina
LA RIBERA

Carrer
CHINESE
Palau
Güell
Rambla
Plaça
Reial
Carrer Ferran
GÒTIC
Carrer Jaume I
Carrer de la Princesa
Museu
Picasso
Mercat
del
Born

Palau
Güell
Plaça
del Teatre
Parròquia
Sant Sperit
Plaça
Sant
Miquel
Casa de la
Ciutat-
Ajuntament
Església dels
Sants Just
i pasteur
JAUME I
Santa Maria
del Mar

DRASSANES
Museu de
la Cera
Mercè
i Sant Miquel
Carrer Ample
Carrer de la Mercè
La Llotja
Passeig
d'Isabel II
Delgació
del Govern
Estació
de França

Museu
Marítim
Plaça
Portal
de la Pau
Monument a Colom
(Columbus Monument)
Passeig de Colom
Ronda del Litoral
MOLL DE LA FUSTA
Escola de
Nàutica
BARCELONETA

Port Autònom/
Junta d'Obres
Museu d'Història
de Catalunya
Plaça
Pau Vila
C. del Dock
C. Balboa

MOLL DE LES
DRASSANES
Golondrinas
(Boat Trips)
MOLL D'ESPANYA
Marina
Port Vell
BARCELONETA

MOLL DE
BARCELONA
PORT VELL
IMAX
L'Aquàrium
Maremàgnum
MOLL DE LA BARCELONETA
Plaça
Barceloneta
Plaça de
la Font
Plaça
Poeta Boscà

Torre de Jaume I
Torre de
St Sebastià
Plaça
Pàlmeres
Acuario
Platja Sant
Sebastià

World
Trade Center

0   400 m
0   400 yards

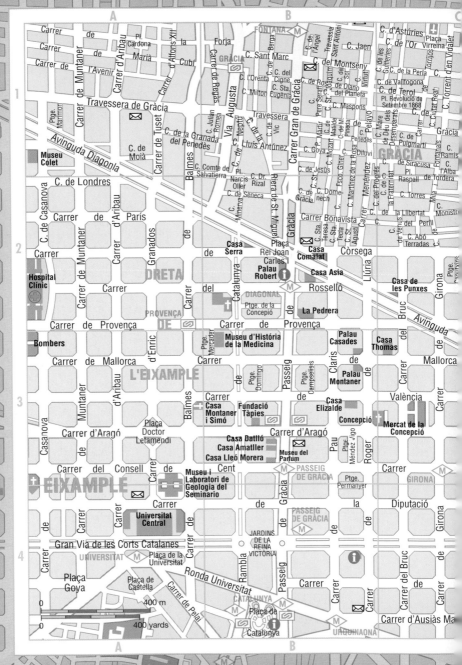

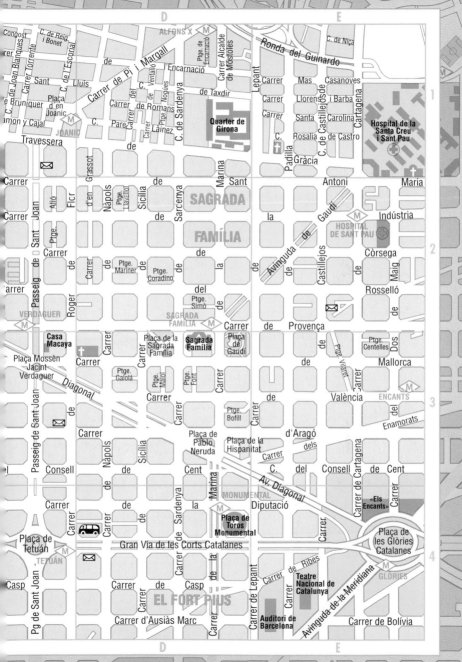

STREET INDEX

ART & PHOTO CREDITS

AGE Fotostock 26, 27, 31 41, 52
AR/Gau 3B, 162T
J.D. Dallet 51, 81
Andrew Eames 16
Annabel Elston 6TR, 35, 54L, 60, 82T, 98T, 101, 109T, 110T, 112T, 113, 125T, 147, 148T, 151T, 152T, 154, 160T, 178T, 182T
Wolfgang Fritz 46, 54R
Jaume Gaul 22, 30, 81T
Andrew Holt 174
José Martin 19, 21, 23, 25
Mike Merchant 34, 80T, 179T
Mike Merchant/Apa 58
Ingrid Morató 4T, 5BR, 18, 19, 134T
Don Murray 55, 106
Museu de Ceramica 177T
Naturpress/Walter Kvaternik 132T.
Kim Naylor 12/13,
Richard Nowitz 98R
Prisma Archivo Fotográfico 8TL, 8TR, 20, 47, 97T, 105, 186/187, 190T, 191T, 191, 192T, 192, 193, 225.
Mark Read 50, 96L
Jeroen Snijders 193T, 195L
Topham Picturepoint 150
Bill Wassman 4BR, 8RR, 14, 18, 45, 77, 79T, 79, 80, 102R, 123,
145, 146T, 166T, 194, 196, 197, 210.
Roger Williams 24, 48
George Wright 38, 93
Gregory Wrona 2/3, 4CL, 6L, 6BR, 7TR, 7R, 8LB, 9L, 9R, 10/11, 32/33. 36, 37, 39, 40, 44, 49, 56, 57, 59, 61, 62, 63, 64, 65, 66, 67, 68/69, 70/71, 74, 75, 80, 83T, 83, 84T, 84, 85T, 85, 86T, 86, 87, 88T, 88, 89T, 89, 91, 92, 94T, 95, 96R, 97, 98L, 99T, 100, 102, 103, 107, 109, 110, 111T, 111, 112, 114T, 114, 115T, 115L & R, 116T, 117, 118, 120, 121, 122T, 122, 123T, 124, 125, 127, 128, 129, 130T, 131T, 132, 133T, 133, 134, 135, 136T, 136, 137, 138, 139, 140, 142, 143, 146, 147, 148, 149T, 149, 151, 152, 153T, 153, 158, 159, 161, 163, 164T, 164L&R, 165T, 165, 166, 167, 175, 177, 178, 179L&R, 180, 181T, 181, 182, 183, 188, 189, 195R, 198, 199, 200, 203, 208, 222.

PICTURE SPREADS

Furious Fiestas – Pages 42/43:
Top row from left to right: Ingrid
Morató, Gregory Wrona.
Bottom row from left to right:
Ingrid Morató, Gregory Wrona,
Gregory Wrona, Prisma.
The Home of Catalan Art – Pages 156/157: Top row from left to right: MNAC, Topham Picture Source, MNAC
Bottom row from left to right: José Martin, MNAC, Museu d'Art Modern.
Modernisme – Pages 170/171:
Top row from left to right: Art Archives, Corbis.
Bottom row from left to right: Don Murray, Bill Wassman, Corbis, Bill Wassman.
Sagrada Família – Pages 172/173: Top row from left to right: Corbis, AISA, Gregory Wrona, Corbis.
Bottom row from left to right: both by Gregory Wrona

Map Production: James Macdonald, Maria Randell, Laura Morris and Stephen Ramsay

©2005 Apa Publications GmbH & Co. Verlag KG, Singapore Branch

Production: Linton Donaldson

GENERAL INDEX

Barcelona Metro

M

a Sant Cu
a Sabade
a Rubi
a Terrassa

Les Planes

Baixador de
Vallvidrera

Vallvidrera
Superior

Túnel de
Vallvidrera

Peu
del Funicular

Ronda de Dalt

Major de Sarrià

Reina
Elisenda

Pg. Bonanova

Consell
Comarcal

T3

Walden

A-2 (Lleida-Tarragona)

Ctra. Esplugues

Pg. Reina Elisenda
de Montcada

Sarrià

Bon
Viatge

T1

Centre Miquel
Martí i Pol

Rambla de
Sant Just

Ctra. Esplugues

Les Tres Torr

La Fontsanta

T2

Sant Martí de l'Erm

L3

Zona
Universitària

Zona
Universitària

La Bonan

Fontsanta
Fatjó

Cornellà

Ignasi
Iglésias

El
Pedró

Pont
d'Esplugues

Can
Clota

Ronda de Dalt

Av de Xile

Palau Reial

Pius XII

Muntar

Av. Pedralbes

Pg. Sant Joan Bosco

Les Aigües

L5

Montesa

La Sardana

Ca
n'Oliveras

St. Ramon

Maria
Cristina

Numància

L'Illa

St Gervas

a Manresa i
Igualada

Can Rigal

Av. Diagonal

Francesc
Macià

Cornellà - Riera

Gavarra

Sant
Ildefons

Can
Boixeres

Can
Vidalet

Pubilla
Cases

Collblanc

Gran Via Carles III

Les
Corts

Trav. de
les Corts

T1 T2 T3

Gra

de l'Hospitalet

Almeda

Can Serra

Rbla.
Just
Oliveras

Florida

Badal

Av. Madrid

Plaça del
Centre

Paris

Prove

J. Tarradellas

L'Hospitalet -
Av. Carrilet

Av. Carrilet

Torrassa

Santa Eulàlia

Plaça de
Sants

Entença

Hospital Clínic

St. Josep

Mercat
Nou

Sants Estació

Mallorca

Bellvitge

Gornal

Hostafrancs

Tarragona

Muntaner

Ronda del Mig

Bordeta

Rocafort

Urgell

Univer

Hospital de
Belluitge

L1

Autovia de Castelldefels

Ildefons
Cerdà

Magòria
La
Campana

Gran via

Espanya

Rocafort

Sant
Anton

Cata

Riu Llobregat

Creu Coberta

Poble
Sec

Av. Paral·lel

Ronda Litoral

Pg. Zona Franca

Parc de
Montjuïc

Paral·

Castell
de Montjuïc

Mirador

L2

D